Skills for the Future

Managing Creativity and Innovation

by

Robert Dilts

with

Gino Bonissone

Meta Publications
P.O. Box 565
Cupertino, California 95014

Library of Congress Card Number 93-084504
I.S.B.N. 0-916990-27-3

Contents

Part Three: Managing Group Creativity

Dedication

We dedicate this book
with deepest affection
and respect to
Gianfranco Gambigliani,
whose vision and friendship created
the foundation for this endeavor.
His commitment to innovation,
his leadership skill and his wisdom
have been a constant inspiration.

Robert Dilts
Gino Bonissone

Acknowledgments

We would like to express our deepest gratitude to **Ivana Gasperini,** our co-scientist in the projects that have served as the practical basis for this book, and our comrade in the mission to 'bring systemic NLP into social systems.' Her insight and encouragement has been invaluable.

We would also like to gratefully acknowledge the efforts of **Giovanni Testa** whose belief in us and in NLP, and whose willingness to take a risk opened the doorway for this project and provided the focus that made the dream become a reality.

Other thanks go to **Todd Epstein**, the co-creator of the S.C.O.R.E. Model, co-author of *Tools for Dreamers* (the companion to this book) and a constant source of co-creativity; and to **Eli Rota** for providing the all important interface between languages that allowed these ideas to take root.

Introduction

Skills for the Future are those skills which will allow us to effectively and ecologically define, move toward, and manage the future amid the challenges of uncertainty and change. The two basic goals for developing skills for the future are to improve performance, and manage change.

Reaching these objectives involves competence in such areas as learning, leadership and, perhaps most importantly, creativity. The focus of this book is on how the cognitive and behavioral technologies of Neuro Linguistic Programming may be used to develop and apply personal and organizational learning strategies together with communication and leadership skills to manage the processes of creativity and innovation.

The overall purpose of this book is to provide models and tools for defining and managing the creative process on both a micro and macro level. The *micro* aspects of creativity relate to the inner thoughts and subjective experiences that are at the basis of an individual's own personal creative activities. The *macro* aspects of creativity deal with (a) how to enhance the creative interaction between two people or a group of people, and (b) the implications of the creative process in the context of an organization and organizational problem-solving.

The book is composed of three basic Parts:

Part One: Personal Creativity

The first Part focuses on the personal or individual aspects of creativity and innovation. It's purpose is to address questions such as, "What are some of your own personal creative strategies?" "How could you define and enhance some of your own creative abilities?" **Part One** shows how some basic NLP models and distinctions may be used to develop more mastery over your internal state and improve your own creative thinking strategies by coordinating your inner *dreamer, realist* and *critic*.

Part Two: Co-Creativity

The second Part explores the processes relating to co-creativity. It addresses the questions, "How how can we enhance creative interactions?" "In what ways might we be able to coach the process of creativity in others or stimulate others to be more creative?" **Part Two** emphasizes skills related to helping others to be more creative and to tap into unconscious creative processes through mental mapping and lateral thinking strategies.

Part Three: Managing Group Creativity

The third Part explores how NLP principles and tools may be used to stimulate and manage creativity in groups of people in organizations; in particular in terms of interfunctional interactions. It addresses questions such as, "How can the creative processes of different people be coordinated?" "In what ways can we define and integrate the different kinds of creative processes necessary to promote a successful team or organization?" **Part Three** focuses on skills related to the identification and direction of different thinking styles and the development of effective communication strategies and creative leadership abilities.

Preface

A considerable amount of thought and effort has gone into the design of this book. As you will notice, the structure of the book has a number of unique features (which seems only fitting since it is a book on creativity and innovation). The reason for these innovations stems from the fact that learning to manage the process of creativity and innovation poses some unique challenges.

First of all, the processes of creativity and innovation demand the acceptance and encouragement of diversity, insight, spontaneity (and other dynamics associated with unconscious mental processing). At the same time, the expansion of creative potential also brings with it an increased need for discretion and systemic awareness.

A second challenge in the design of this book is that, even though creativity is considered mainly a cognitive process, the acquisition of skills for managing the creative process requires an emphasis on interactive and experiential learning. In fact, the material in this book was originally put together for an experiential training course on managing creativity and innovation for top managers at Fiat in Italy.

Another source of innovation is that the design of this book is based on the principles and technology of Neuro-Linguistic Programming, which is also highly interactive, individualized and experiential in nature.

Basic Assumptions About Learning

In order to effectively address these challenges, the design of the book has been based on several important basic assumptions:

1. In order to effectively cover a particular area of skill to be

learned, a wider scope of coverage must be provided for by the instructional materials. This wider range is required in order to account for variations of readers' needs, working contexts and learning styles.

2. The learning of higher level skills (such as creativity and the management of the creative process) involves an increased involvement on the part of the learner. Thus, this book has been designed to encourage and promote self motivated and self managed learning.

3. Multiple representations of a particular content creates a richer learning experience and is more likely to reach a variety of learning styles.

In the model of NLP, it is assumed that learning takes place through the establishment of 'neuro-linguistic' programs. A learner forms internal cognitive maps, through the influence of language and other representations, which become linked to external observations and behavioral responses.

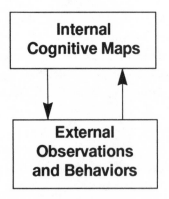

General Structure of the Book

Within the view of NLP, the essential act of learning is envisaged as (a) the formation of an internal cognitive map and (b) the connection of that map to the appropriate reference experiences which give that map practical meaning in terms of external observations and behavioral results. The general structure of the book revolves around these two basic components:

a. *Cognitive Packages*—which define a particular perceptual space to be established or opened. A specific *cognitive package* is a verbal or visual embodiment or manifestation of a particular cognitive or perceptual space.

b. *Learning Activities*—which define the reference experiences needed to give the cognitive package practical meaning. The verbal labels and examples, and the visual symbols which make up cognitive packages acquire practical meaning for a reader only through their connection to personal reference experiences. A *reference experience* is (a) a personal memory, (b) an ongoing observable behavioral demonstration or (c) a constructed (imagined, fantasized) experience, on the part of the reader. The purpose of such experiences is to activate either existing unconscious competence or other already existing perceptions or abilities.

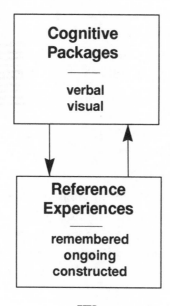

Thus, the various materials in this book serve one of four purposes:

1. Deliver Cognitive Packages
2. Help Widen the Reader's Perceptual Maps
3. Activate Reference Experiences for Cognitive Packages
4. Connect Reference Experiences to Cognitive Maps

Accomplishing these objectives involves helping readers to expand their perceptual maps of the material being covered by stimulating associations between cognitive material and the reader's general or professional reality. Thus, readers are continually engaged in a cycle moving from thinking to doing; from map to territory.

In general, we have attempted to employ a format for each Chapter based on a basic *cycle of cognitive development*, consisting of:

1. *Seeding* distinctions, perceptions and maps in the initial cognitive packages for each chapter.
2. *Unveiling* unconscious competence and reference experiences related to the distinctions, perceptions and maps via learning activities and exercises.
3. *Coding* and categorizing experiences arising during the activities in terms of the relevant principles, distinctions and models.

Basic Meta Methodology for Skill Acquisition

The underlying meta methodology of practical skill development involves the setting of learning goals, the establishment of evidences relating to the achievement of those learning goals, and the definition of the kinds of operations required to reach the learning goals. In general, skill is developed by breaking general goals, or 'macro objectives,' into successively more specific goals, or 'micro objectives.'

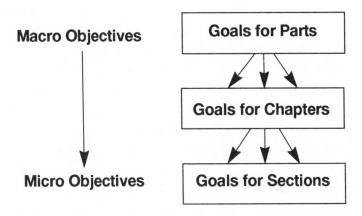

Goals at a *Part* level are related to the development of the general capability of managing creativity. These goals are expressed as learning *themes*. Themes for the Parts are defined in relation to the global capability of creativity or managing creativity.

Goals at a *Chapter* level are expressed in the form of learning *topics* related to the development of specific skills or mixes of skills (conceptual, analytical, observational, procedural, interactive and relational).

Goals at a *Section* level are related to the specific cognitive packages or reference experiences to be dealt with in the Section. These goals are expressed initially as micro objectives for the reader for each section and are summarized at the end of each Section in the form of *key points*.

Evidences and Evidence Procedures for Learning

Unconscious competence or latent competence comes from the establishment of reference experiences. *Conscious competence* comes from the ability to code one's experiences. Coding is the establishment of a connection between a map, abstraction or label and personal reference experiences.

The basic evidence for conscious competence is whether the reader can (1) connect specific reference experiences to the relevant cognitive maps, and (2) connect the elements of the cognitive map to other reference experiences.

As skill increases, the coverage and robustness of the connection is determined by:

1. At how many levels the connection can be made: i.e., what, how and why connections are made between specific cognitive packages and reference experiences;
2. The types of reference experiences that can be connected: remembered, ongoing, constructed;
3. The range of sensory modalities through which the connection can be represented: seeing, verbalizing, feeling.

Micro Structure of the Book

The micro structure of the book has been designed to support the assumptions, principles and methods of learning we have described. In essence, each Part of the book is composed of:

An overview of the Part, which includes:

The titles and general objectives for
the Chapters which make up the Part

The set of assumptions on which the Part is based.

An overview of each Chapter, which includes:

The general objectives of the Chapter

The titles and goals for the sections which
make up the Chapter

Sections for each Chapter, made up of:

The Basic Conceptual Material and/or Learning
Activity for that Section (Macro Package)

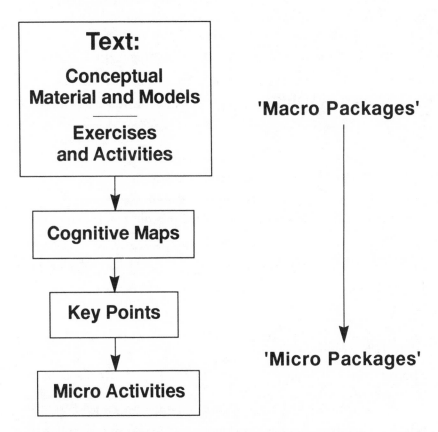

"Cognitive Maps"
Key Points (Micro Packages)
Micro Activities

Text:

Conceptual
Material and Models

Exercises
and Activities

'Macro Packages'

Cognitive Maps

Key Points

Micro Activities

'Micro Packages'

Conceptual Material—Macro Packages

The basic conceptual material for each section is in the form of verbal representations of the principles, models or distinctions (or the relationships between them) that are relevant for that section. These 'macro packages' are primarily in the form of text edited from transcripts of Robert drawn from the creativity seminars delivered at Fiat. In general, this conceptual material follows the pattern of deriving more 'micro level' structures and distinctions from more 'macro level' models and structures. Typically, models are expressions of deeper principles. Distinctions, whether observational or analytical, are more specific information 'chunks' which are derived from and given meaning by the larger model of which they are a part.

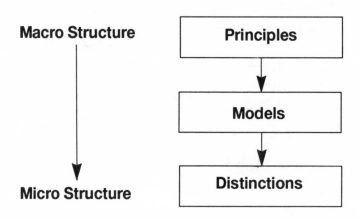

Types of Exercises and Learning Activities

The purpose of the exercises and learning activities is to illustrate key principles and bring the conceptual models and distinctions 'to life.' Usually, a person considers reading a book to be a relatively passive process. In order to get the maximum benefit from this book, however, it is critical that you engage in the activities. In fact you may want to consider this book a kind of 'workbook' and try to find a partner or study group with which to try the exercises and compare your experiences.

There are several different types of exercises which are determined by (a) the class of learning activity, (b) the experiential focus of the learning activity, (c) the type of instructional instrument employed by the activity and (d) the number and types of roles involved in the learning activity.

In general learning activities can be divided into *two basic classes*:

1. *Discovery activities* in which readers engage in an activity with minimally defined formal objectives, for the purpose of establishing behavioral reference experiences which are to serve as the intuitive basis for cognitive packages to come a later time in the book. Discovery exercises allow the reader to have spontaneous experiences untainted and uncontaminated by conscious expectations about what is *supposed* to happen. Discovery exercises promote the development of unconscious competence.

2. *Application activities* in which readers engage in activities with specifically defined objectives, evidence procedures and explicit process instructions for operations. Application activities promote the development of conscious competence with the skills defined by mixes of cognitive packages and other reference experiences.

xxi

The *experiential focus* of a particular learning activity or exercise may be on (1) the remembered experiences of the reader, (2) an external ongoing experience which is unfolding in real time, or (3) on an *as if* experience that is constructed or imagined by the reader.

The kinds of *instructional instruments* that may be used during an exercise include:

    Scenarios and Case Studies

    Questionnaires

    Behavioral Applications

    Role Plays

The type of instructional instrument employed during a learning activity draws out and focuses the learner on different dimensions of a particular reference experience. The type of instrument chosen for a particular exercise relates to the type of skill to be activated or developed (i.e., conceptual, analytical, observational, procedural, interactive). For instance, scenarios and case studies help to develop conceptual skills; questionnaires help promote analytical skill; behavioral applications lead to the development of procedural skills; and role plays help to enhance observational and interactive skills.

In addition to the general type of learning instrument being employed for an activity, *micro tools* are provided for some for exercises. Micro tools may be applied prior to, during or after the learning activity and could include guidelines, checklists worksheets, forms, etc. Such micro tools could be used as a way to (a) plan or prepare for the activity, (b) plot or record progress during the activity, or (c) organizing or verifying the results of the activity.

The number and types of *roles* involved in a particular learning activity or exercise generally depend on the type of learning activity and instrument being employed. The range of roles in the exercises presented in this book includes:

Individual Introspective Role

Pair of Co-Coaches

Trio of Explorer, Guide and Observer

Group of Actors in a "Fish Bowl" of Observers

People familiar with NLP will be used to doing interactive exercises, as that is often the core of learning in NLP. For those who are not so familiar with the NLP approach, it may be helpful to have some guidelines relating to the typical roles found in NLP exercises (and presupposed in some of the exercises described in this book).

Guidelines for Roles During Exercises and Activities

Explorer

- Access experiences and perform activities based on the guide's instructions—so long as they are appropriate and ecological.

- Associate into experiences, including remembered or imagined experiences, acting 'as if' they were occurring in the here and now.

- Be aware of personal subjective experiences and behaviors to varying degrees.

- Disassociate from reference experiences and talk about what was experienced, as if an observer.

- Provide feedback to the guide about (1) personal subjective state or experiences, (2) subjective perception of the progress being made in relation to the defined task, (3) subjective experience of the effects of the guide's actions on changes in explorer's behavior or internal state.

Guide

- Establish and maintain rapport with the explorer throughout the exercise or activity.
- Elicit experiences and responses from the explorer through verbal and non-verbal interactions.
- Assist the explorer to associate into or disassociate from reference experiences.
- Observe and calibrate the explorer's verbal and non-verbal cues.
- Engage in 'active listening' by paraphrasing the explorer's ongoing verbal descriptions in order to get feedback and verify personal perceptions of the explorer's subjective experience.
- 'Backtrack' events that have occurred during the exercise or activity by reviewing key elements of the explorer's behavior and verbal reports that have occurred within the time frame of the entire exercise.

Observer

- Watch and listen to the explorer's non-verbal and verbal cues during the exercise or activity.
- Backtrack key observations of the explorer's behavior and reports at defined points during the activity or exercise.
- Compare personal observations with the guide's observations to create a 'double description.'
- At times, record observations in written form (i.e., notes, checklists, charts, etc.).

Coach ("Meta Person")

- In addition to the tasks of the observer, watch and listen to the verbal and non-verbal behavior of the guide.

- Keep track of the progress of the task over time or activity and provide feedback and information to both the guide and the explorer personal perceptions of what has influenced the direction of events.

- Be available to the guide or explorer during the activity or exercise to provide assistance, observations or feedback as requested by the guide or explorer.

- Provide feedback about personal perceptions of the guides abilities and responsibilities as defined above.

<table>
<tr><td colspan="3">**Roles in NLP exercises**
The 3-role case: explorer, guide, coach</td></tr>
<tr>
<td>**Explorer (A):**
• accesses the experience based on the Guide's (B) instructions
• Is not responsible for writing
• provides feedback to B on the experience at the end of exercise
• 'lives' even recollected or imagined experience 'as if' it were here and now</td>
<td>**Guide (B):**
• elicits Explorer's (A) experience through exercise questions
• observes A's verbal/non-verbal clues
• does 'active listening' during elicitation to 're-phrase' what 'A' is saying
• 'recapitulates what A said to interconnect the phases of A's experience
• maintains rapport</td>
<td>**Coach (C):**
• supports/advises B when appropriate
• observes Explorer's non-verbal/verbal clues
• checks whether rapport is maintained between A and B
• checks the 'quality' and pattern of B's elicitation
• provides feedback to B at the end of the exercise</td>
</tr>
</table>

Cognitive Maps

A *'Cognitive Map'* is combination of a flow chart, block diagram and 'mind map.' Cognitive maps capture key concepts and key words and express them visually in terms of their relationships, implications and aims. The maps in this preface of the 'Exercise Contexts' and the 'Roles in NLP' exercises are a couple of examples of such cognitive maps. Oftentimes, visual cognitive maps are able to bring out and express relationships that are not easily represented or obvious in a verbal representation. The cognitive maps in this book were made by Gino to map the flow of the creativity seminars. In addition to his participation in the overall instructional design, the cognitive maps are Gino's contribution to this work.

Key Points

Key Points are an attempt to capture the essential ideas and concepts expressed in each section. They summarize and encapsulate the micro level learning objectives for each section in as simple and direct a form as possible. Simply reading the learning goals for each section and skimming the maps and key points can provide you with a quick but comprehensive overview of each section.

Micro Activities

The purpose of the *Micro Activities* is to provide the opportunity for self managed learning on the part of the reader and to bring more depth to the conceptual material in the book. Micro Activities essentially involve using memory, imagination or the on-going environment to enrich the reader's experience of either:

a. The global capability or skill being explored.
b. The connection between the global capability being taught and an exercise or learning activity.
c. The connection between the global capability being taught and the reader's reality.
d. The connection between a learning activity and the reader's reality.

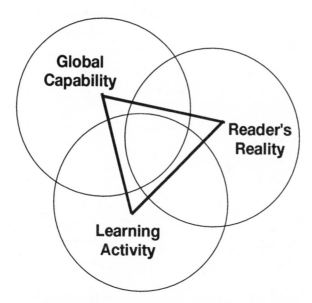

Relationships Covered by Micro Activities

Taking the time to read through and try the various micro activities can greatly enhance your understanding and mastery of the concepts and skills presented in this book. In addition to enriching your experience of the material, the micro activities can provide an excellent opportunity for readers to self assess their own comprehension of the principles and distinctions presented in the book.

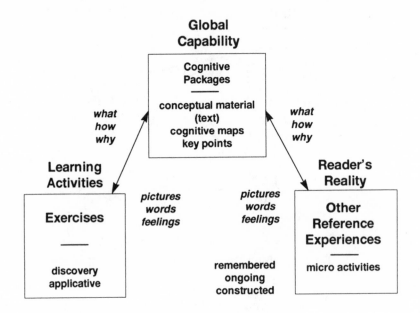

Micro Structure of the Book

This book is the culmination of quite a journey and adventure for us. We hope that it is just the beginning of a new and exciting adventure for you.

Robert Dilts
Santa Cruz, California

Gino Bonissone
Milan, Italy

June, 1993

part one

Personal Creativity

Defining the Scope of Creativity

Structure of the Creative Process

Physiology and Creativity

Implementing Personal Creativity

Overview of Part One
Personal Creativity

The purpose of Part One is to:

1. Provide a foundation for understanding the creative process in general.
2. Assist readers in applying some specific principles and methods for increasing creativity to themselves as individuals.

Part One is made up four chapters:

Chapter 1   Defining the Scope of Creativity

Sets the overall principles, distinctions and frames for defining and exploring the creative process.

Chapter 2   The Structure of the Creative Process

Introduces a set of models and distinctions for identifying various levels of cognitive structure in one's own creative process and the creative strategies of other individuals.

Chapter 3   Physiology and Creativity

Presents exercises to help (1) experientially develop introspective awareness of one's behavioral patterns related to creativity and (2) to elicit and observe these processes in other individuals.

Chapter 4   Implementing Personal Creativity

Provides a number of strategies and methods to enhance and enrich personal creativity based on the creative process of Walt Disney.

Overview of Part One
Personal Creativity

The material to be covered in Part One is based on a set of *assumptions* about creativity.

Assumptions

Creativity in human beings is a natural, ongoing process that has structure. This structure is defined by the interaction of cognitive maps and behavioral patterns.

Cognitive maps have different levels of structure which have some elements that may only be perceived through the introspection of personal subjective experience, and others that may be tracked by the observation of external cues.

Subjective cognitive processes are accompanied by micro behavioral patterns which serve to support those cognitive processes and to provide external cues relating to those processes.

There is no one right way to be creative. There is a diversity of strategies which may produce creative responses and results depending on the characteristics of particular individuals and contexts.

Personal creativity is essentially a process of enriching the cognitive maps one has of a particular situation and of enhancing the behavioral flexibility one has in relationship to supporting one's own thinking processes and responding to environmental constraints.

Understanding the structure of and relationships between cognitive maps and micro behavioral patterns make it possible to model and develop techniques and methods that can pragmatically enhance personal creativity in the accomplishment of practical tasks.

Chapter 1

Defining the Scope of Creativity

Overview of Chapter 1

General Objectives for Chapter 1

1. Establish the basic theoretical and operational frameworks for the book.
2. Connect the basic idea of creativity and innovation to relevant goals and objectives within the reader's reality.
3. Create a concrete, personal reference experience for the process of creativity.
4. Introduce some basic practical distinctions and cognitive models related to creativity that readers can relate to their personal experience.

Sections and goals for each Section

Section 1.1 General Frames of Creativity
Introduce basic frames and assumptions about creativity and the creative process. Set the general goals and objectives for the book.

Section 1.2 Definition of Neuro-Linguistic Programming
Introduce and define the basic distinctions and principles of Neuro-Linguistic Programming as the working framework for the book.

Section 1.3 Presuppositions of NLP
Explain the underlying assumptions and presuppositions behind the Neuro-Linguistic Programming model and their implications for creativity and innovation.

Section 1.4 Exploring Personal Creativity
Provide a specific activity in which readers can experience and explore the cognitive and behavioral patterns in themselves that lead to a concrete creative expression.

**Section 1.5 Macro Structure of Experience
            and Creativity (The T.O.T.E. Model)**
Introduce the T.O.T.E. Model as the general operational structure underlying goal oriented behavior and creativity and relate it to the reader's reference experiences.

**Section 1.6 Influence of Different Levels
            of Experience on Creativity**
Introduce the concept of different levels of experience and their influence on the processes of creativity and innovation, and relate them to the reader's reference experiences.

Section 1.1
General Frames of Creativity

The Problem Space of Creativity
(From *Tools For Dreamers*, pp. xiii - xv)

Imagination is more important than knowledge.
—Albert Einstein

Every animal leaves traces of what it was;
man alone leaves traces of what he created.
—J. Bronowski, *The Ascent of Man*

Look around you and chances are that most of what you see will in some way be the product of human creativity: books, buildings, computers, furniture, roads, televisions, telephones, light bulbs, airplanes, music... The list could go on forever. All of these things were at one time just a dream in someone's mind. Now they are a reality. That is something truly magical. What makes it possible? How does it happen? This book is about some of the tools that turn dreams into reality.

As Einstein's comment above implies, knowledge without imagination is useless. Imagination is what brings knowledge to life. Imagination and creativity are the driving force behind change, adaptation and evolution. Human creativity is the source of new possibilities and hope; of dreams, action and accomplishment. It is also the source of uncertainty and insecurity. Imagination and creativity can cause as many problems as they solve if they are not managed appropriately. On a very practical level, managing the process of creativity is one of the most important elements for success and survival, as individuals and organizations strive to adapt to the accelerating changes that are occurring in technology and society on a global level.

Thomas Edison is widely quoted as having said that the process of invention is, "1% inspiration and 99% perspiration." The implication of this statement is that most creative activity is in fact an incremental process that has a structure and requires organization and constant effort to maintain. In many ways, however, creativity has remained elusive—a seemingly mysterious *gift* that you either have or don't have—rather than a set of skills that can be transferred and managed systematically and explicitly.

Certainly, the development and management of the creative process has its own unique problems and issues. Creativity tends to be an individual thing. It is something we tend to learn on our own, in our own way and, in most cases, we are not quite sure how we do what we do when we *are* being creative. Creative people are largely unaware of the strategies they use to create. It is a well-known fact that the things we do best we do unconsciously. We are not aware of all of the sophisticated computations and programs we go through to drive a car, choose what to eat from a menu, or even keep our balance as we walk down the street. We know that we have learned something well when we no longer have to consciously think about it while we are doing it.

For example, as you are reading this you are making meaning out of the words on this page but are probably unaware of exactly how you are doing it. As we speak and write, we make up sentences of our own that follow sophisticated syntactic rules with no consciousness of the process we are going through. Similarly, most of us are not conscious of the rules and strategies which influence our ability to think creatively. The consequence of this limitation of consciousness has been that our creative ability has been a function of such things as our level of inspiration, mood, the number of hours we slept the previous night, etc., rather than being available to us at will. As a result, the explicit management of creativity has been hampered in the following areas:

1. There is a lack of vocabulary about our internal creative processes, making it difficult to discuss creativity with others, even peers;

2. It is difficult to explicitly teach others what we have learned about creativity and how to apply it to their own problems;

3. In some situations we can find ourselves "stuck," without a clue as to what to do about it;

4. It is difficult to identify others who have the potential and/or the ability to contribute what is needed for a particular task.

The purpose of this book is to examine the structure and principles of creativity in order to enhance and supplement the creativity and productivity of individuals, teams and organizations. Using the behavioral technology provided by Neuro-Linguistic Programming we can make the strategies and steps involved in the creative process more explicit on a number of different levels. The specific objectives are to:

1. To define the creative process on an individual, group and organizational level.

2. To create a vocabulary that will support and enhance the creative process.

3. To provide specific ways people can more effectively support, enhance and direct creativity in individuals and teams.

4. To determine ways to identify different types of creative people.

On a personal level, the principles, models and skills to be covered in this book can be applied to:

1. Help people to enrich their maps of the world.

2. Help people uncover some of the assumptions and presuppositions behind their current maps of reality; especially those that may be limiting to creativity.

3. Help people to develop ways to increase their own flexibility and the flexibility of others.

On a professional level tasks requiring creativity are focused toward both solving problems and achieving goals. Some common kinds of organizational tasks in which creativity plays a key role include:

1. Problem search and definition
2. Goal exploration and goal setting
3. Opportunity analysis
4. Task allocation
5. Environmental forecasting and scenarios

The relational dimension of creativity ranges from:

1. Personal creativity in which the individual acts alone, to
2. Co-Creativity where two individuals work together intensively as partners, to
3. Creativity within a group or a team in which creativity is a function of the coordination of different roles and functions.

Professionally, the principles, models and skills covered in this book can also be applied to:

1. Stimulating personal creativity: Enhancing day-to-day creativity and flexibility on a personal level.
2. Managing group creativity: Stimulating innovation within the dynamic patterns of groups and teams.
3. Promoting beliefs, attitudes and skills that enhance organizational creativity.

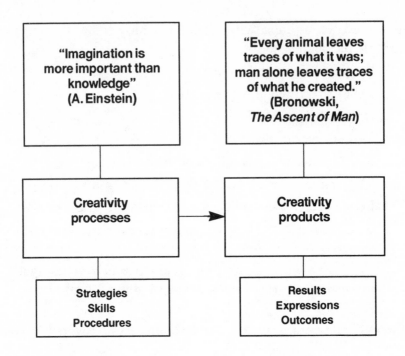

SECTION 1.1 / MAP A

Key Points
There is a distinction between the process and products of
creativity.

Activities
Identify several objects in your environment and imagine or
reconstruct the processes which were necessary to produce
them (i.e., basic research, conception, applied research, design,
engineering, manufacturing, assembly, marketing, distribution,
placement and arrangement).

Think of three examples of creative processes and the products
produced by those processes, e.g. Composition —> Symphony

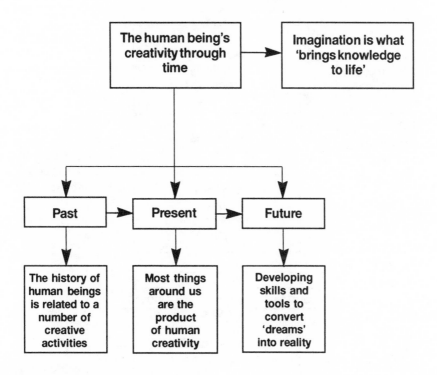

SECTION 1.1 / MAP **B**

Key Points
Creativity is a natural ongoing process that has been a core
part of human survival and success throughout history.
Activities
What are some well known/acknowledged examples/instances
of creativity in history? In your organization?

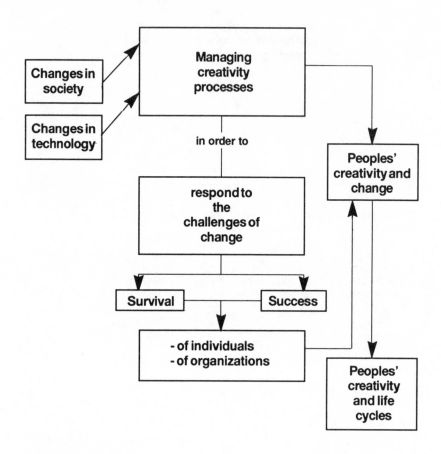

SECTION 1.1 MAP C

Key Points
Creativity is fundamentally about managing the challenges of change. Creativity is both triggered by change and brings about change.
Activities
Identify something creative you do as an individual.
Identify something creative you do with a group or team.

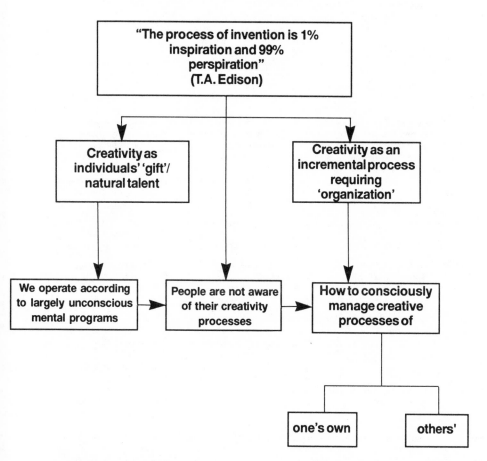

SECTION 1.1 / MAP D

Key Points

Creativity is a result of unconscious processes which lead to insight and inspiration and conscious processes which require incremental steps and effort.

There are creative processes which take place within an individual and creative processes which are the result of the interaction between individuals in groups, teams and organizations.

Activities

Remember an example of a sudden creative insight you have had personally.

Think of a creative result you consciously worked to produce over time.

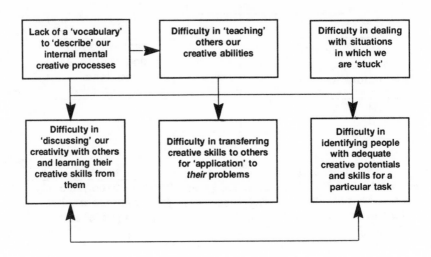

SECTION 1.1 / MAP E

Key Points

The explicit management of individual and group creativity is possible and necessary but poses difficulties due to the need for more explicit vocabulary and workable models relating to the process and structure of creativity.

The products of creativity are easier to describe than the internal processes that produce them.

Activities

How would you describe your own creative process to someone else?

Recall a time you tried to help someone else think more creatively or innovatively about a problem or idea. Where did you encounter difficulties?

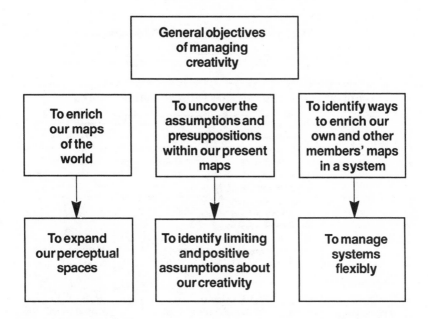

SECTION 1.1 / MAP **F**

Key Points

Creativity is a function of our perceptions of the world.
Creativity is a result of expanding and enriching (1) our
perceptions, (2) our assumptions about what our perceptions
mean, and (3) the flexibility we have in relationship to those
perceptions and assumptions.

Activities

Think of a time you changed your perception about something
in such a way that you were able to be more creative.
Think of a time you helped someone else shift or enrich their
perception of something.
Remember a time you realized you were making an assumption
about something that was unnecessarily limiting you and
changed it.
Recall an instance in which you helped someone else identify
and change an assumption that was limiting them.
In what areas do you think that you/your system have the most
flexibility?
Where would you like to have more flexibility for yourself/your
system?

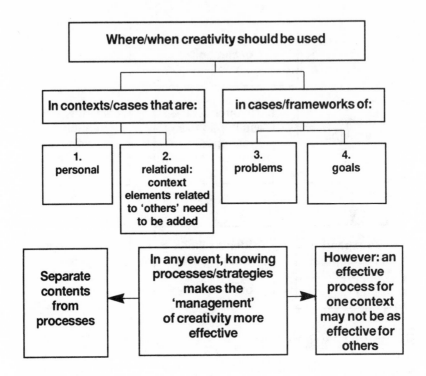

SECTION 1.1 / MAP G

Key Points

There are a number of contexts in which creativity is required
and enacted in organizations which involve varying mixes of
relationship and task elements.

The relational dimension of creativity ranges from (1) personal
creativity in which the individual acts alone, to (2) co-creativity
where two individuals work together intensively as partners, to
(3) creativity within a group or a team in which creativity is a
function of the coordination of different roles and functions.

Tasks requiring creativity are focused toward both solving
problems and achieving goals. Some common kinds of
organizational tasks in which creativity plays a key role
include:

(1) problem search and definition

(2) goal exploration and goal setting

(3) opportunity analysis

(4) task allocation

(5) environmental forecasting and scenarios

When the processes of creativity are separated from the content, the same creative strategies may be applied in different contexts; although a strategy that is effective for producing one kind of goal may not be as effective for others.

Activities

Identify something innovative you have done on your own as an individual.

Think of something you co-created with another person.

Think of a time you worked together with a group or a team to create something or to creatively handle a problem.

In what ways do these different relational contexts affect the process of creativity? In what ways is the creative process similar in these different relational contexts?

With which kinds of tasks do you feel you have been able to be most creative in the past?

(1) problem search and definition

(2) goal exploration and goal setting

(3) opportunity analysis

(4) task allocation

(5) environmental forecasting and scenarios

What kinds of ongoing tasks that you have require the most creative or innovative thinking from you?

What are some future tasks or situations in which you anticipate needing to apply creativity?

Review one of the situations you identified earlier in which you were able to be effectively creative. Which parts of the creative process that you employed in that context do you think you could most easily transfer to another context? Which parts would be most difficult?

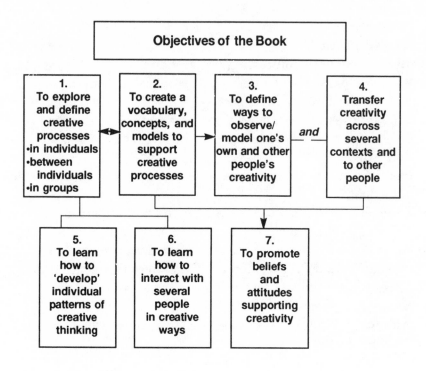

SECTION 1.1 / MAP **H**

Key Points
The specific objectives of the book are to:

a. explore and define the creative process (1) in individuals, (2) between individuals and 3) in groups.

b. develop (1) vocabulary, (2) concepts and (3) models to support and manage creative processes.

c. define ways to observe and model creative thinking strategies in oneself and others.

d. define ways to transfer creative abilities across different contexts and to other people.

e. learn how to enrich individual patterns of creative thinking.

f. learn how to interact more creatively with other people.

g. identify and promote beliefs and attitudes that support creativity.

Activities

Identify the specific personal and interactive contexts in which you would like to apply what you learn from this book. List them on a piece of paper.

What parts of your own creative process are the most difficult to describe or explain? How would having an explicit way to talk about creative process make your job easier?

Which parts of the creative process are the most difficult for you to support?

Which parts of the activities requiring creativity that you are personally involved in are the most difficult for you to manage?

What are the things that you think are the most important to be able to observe for during creativity?

What specifically would you like to know more about your own creative thinking strategies?

Which part of the creative process, within yourself or others, would you most like to model?

In terms of your own working reality, what specific creative abilities do you think would be the most important to be able to transfer across contexts? Which contexts specifically?

Which creative abilities would be most important to transfer to other people? Which people specifically?

What parts of your own creative thinking ability would you enrich if you could?

What patterns of creative thinking in groups or teams you work with would you like see more enriched?

Think of some specific interactions in which you would like to be more creative.

What are some beliefs and attitudes that you think are most supportive of creativity? What kinds of beliefs and attitudes interfere with creativity?

What are some of your specific beliefs and attitudes about creativity?

Section 1.2
Neuro-Linguistic Programming

The model of creativity we will be exploring is based upon the principles and distinctions of Neuro-Linguistic Programming which was developed in California in the early 1970's. This model is based upon research relating to some very basic aspects of human experience. NLP was founded by two people, John Grinder, a linguist, and Richard Bandler who had formal training in mathematics, but also practiced Gestalt therapy.

The name "Neuro-Linguistic Programming" implies the integration of three different scientific fields.

The *neuro* part of Neuro-Linguistics is about the nervous system. A large part of NLP has to do with understanding and using principles and patterns of the nervous system. According to NLP, thinking, creating, vision-making, and all other cognitive processes, are a result of programs executed within the human nervous system. Human experience is a combination or synthesis of the information that we receive and process through our nervous system. Experientially this has to do with sensing the world—seeing, feeling, hearing, smelling, tasting.

Neuro-Linguistic Programming also draws from the field of *linguistics*. In the NLP view, language is in some ways a product of the nervous system, but language also stimulates and shapes the activity within our nervous systems. Certainly, as a manager, language is one of the primary ways a person has of activating or stimulating the nervous systems of other people. So, in this view, creativity is associated with what occurs within our nervous systems. Creativity also has to do with language and how we use language to instruct, to stimulate, and to verbalize the kinds of concepts, goals and issues related to the creative process.

This leads us to the notion of *programming*. Neuro-Linguistic Programming is based upon the idea that the processes of human learning, of memory, of creativity, are a function of programs—neurolinguistic programs that function more or less effectively to accomplish particular objectives or outcomes. That is, that as human beings we interact with our world through our inner programs. We respond to problems based upon these inner programs. We approach new ideas according to the kind of programs that we have established—and not all programs are equal. Different people use different programs to approach problem-solving. Also, some programs are more effective for accomplishing certain kinds of activities than others.

The field of Neuro-Linguistic Programming has developed out of the modeling of human thinking skills. The NLP modeling process involves finding out about how the brain (*Neuro*) is operating by analyzing language patterns (*Linguistic*) and non-verbal communication. The results of this analysis are then put into step-by-step strategies or programs (*Programming*) that may be used transfer the skill to other people and areas of application.

NLP provides a way to look past the behavioral content of what people do to the more invisible forces behind those behaviors; to the structures of thought that allow people to perform effectively. NLP provides a structure and a language that allows one to model the relevant mental strategies used by creative and innovative people so that those inner processes can be communicated about, stimulated and managed in a systematic way.

Most of the techniques and tools of NLP have been derived through a process called "modeling." The primary approach of NLP has been to model effective behaviors and the cognitive processes behind them. NLP initially grew out of modeling exceptional psychotherapists; people who were particularly effective at helping other people change. Many of its contributions to management have been in the areas of communication skills, personal development and coaching skills.

In relation to creativity, we can apply principles and distinctions of NLP to explore the principles of the nervous system, of language and of our programs and the programs of others. NLP allows us to:

1. enrich our own personal creativity;
2. be able to capture ways in which we are creative in certain areas;
3. transfer those to other areas, and
4. be able to stimulate and encourage creativity in other people.

There are overlaps between NLP and other systems of psychology because NLP draws from the neurological, linguistic and cognitive sciences. It also draws from principles of computer programming and systemic theory. Its purpose is to synthesize together a number of different kinds of scientific theories and models. One value of NLP is that it brings together different kinds of theories into a single process. Further, the focus of NLP has been on modeling effective strategies in a way that they may be transferred and adapted to new contexts. The belief system of NLP is that while we all have physical differences, and differences in our backgrounds of experiences, we also share a lot of common features at the process level. At this level we could actually learn to think like Albert Einstein. He might have taken a lifetime of experience to develop the programs that he used to formulate the theory of relativity, but once that program is developed, we can understand its structure and don't need the same lifetime of experience.

So, on the one hand, while NLP is about identifying and appreciating individual differences, and individual styles of creativity, it also asserts that you can learn from other people's experiences because of the basic similarities of our nervous systems.

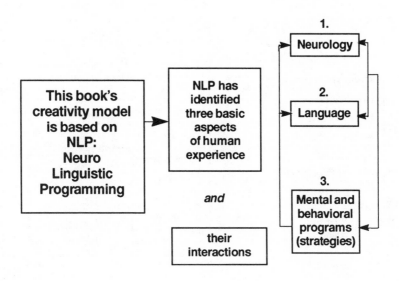

SECTION 1.2 / MAP A

Key Points

The name Neuro-Linguistic Programming relates to three fundamental components of human experience: neurology, language and mental and behavioral programming.

Activities

In what ways are you most aware of your nervous system right now?

Look at something in your environment and be aware of the difference between what you are looking at and the process by which you are seeing it with your eyes. Imagine you can follow the path via which your nervous system receives visual information through your eyes and transmits it to your brain. Repeat this same exercise with your other senses.

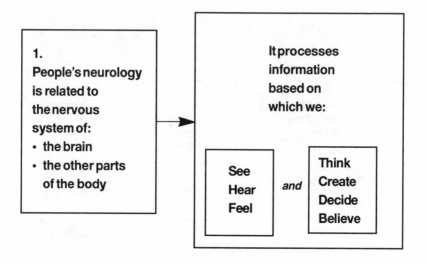

SECTION 1.2 / MAP **B**

Key Points
Neurology refers to the nervous system which includes the brain and the senses.
Activities
How aware are you of your own thought process?
Are you aware of forming images in your mind as you think?
Are you aware of hearing internal sounds?
Are you aware of your feelings?

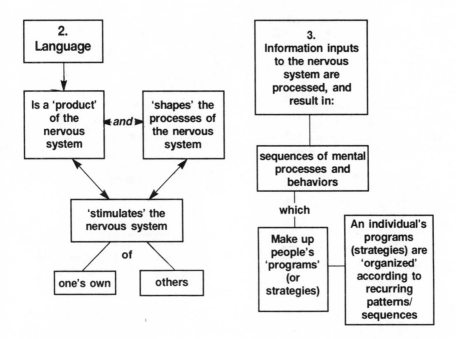

SECTION 1.2 / MAP C

Key Points

Language relates to both communicating and thinking. It is both a product and shaper of the nervous system.

Programs are established sequences and patterns of the interaction between neurology and language which produce our cognitive maps and our behaviors.

Some programs are conscious, others operate below conscious awareness.

Activities

In what way do you use language when you are thinking?

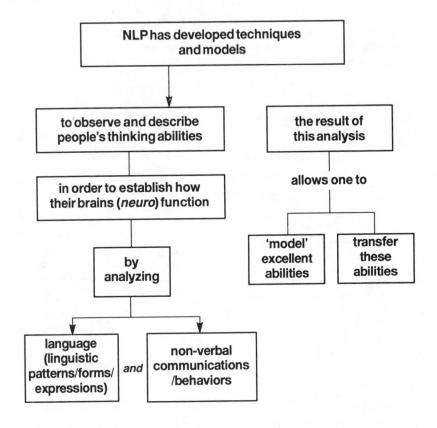

Key Points

NLP has developed techniques and models based on the skills of observing patterns of verbal and non-verbal communication. The basic objectives of NLP processes are to (1) model effective abilities and (2) transfer these abilities to others.

Activities

What kind of non-verbal communication do you notice the most?

What kinds of creative abilities would you most like to model?

What kinds of creative abilities would you most like to be able to transfer to or stimulate in others?

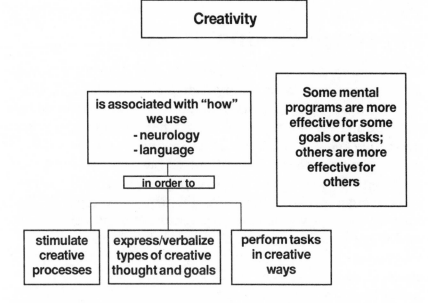

SECTION 1.2 / MAP E

Key Points

In the model of NLP, managing creativity is a function of 'how' we use language and neurological or cognitive process to (1) represent and enrich our maps of a problem or goal, (2) express or verbalize processes which stimulate creative thinking, and (3) improve individual performance and manage change.

Activities

What kind of personal performance would you be able to improve by being more creative or innovative?

Where are the areas of most change for you/your system?

Section 1.3
Presuppositions of NLP

NLP is based upon a set of very fundamental presuppositions about people and about reality that have important implications for managing creativity. NLP starts from the assumption that the map is not the territory. As human beings, we can never fully know reality, in the sense that we have to experience reality through our senses and our senses are limited. A bee perceives a very different reality than we do because the whole sensory organization of the bee is different. We can only make maps of the reality around us through the information that we receive through our senses and through how we connect that information to our own personal memories and other experiences. Therefore, we don't tend to respond to reality itself, but rather to our own maps of reality.

We all have our own world view and that world view is based upon the inner neurolinguistic maps that we have formed. It's these neurolinguistic maps that will determine how we interpret and react to the world around us and give meaning to our behaviors and our experiences, more so than reality itself. Thus, it's generally not external reality that limits us, constrains us or empowers us, but it's rather our map of that reality.

The basic idea of NLP in relation to creativity is that if you can enrich or widen your map, you will perceive more choices available to you given the same reality. So some of the tools we're going to be exploring are tools to help to widen, enrich and add to your maps. The basic presupposition of NLP is that the more rich your map of the world is, the more possibilities that you have of dealing with whatever challenges come up in reality.

When you make a map, it allows you to do things—but it also starts to restrict your way of perceiving it. On one hand, making maps allows us to be more efficient. On the other hand, existing maps can begin to limit your ability to perceive new choices.

Familiarity with something can be a limitation as well as a resource.

If you want to be creative in particle physics, for example, there is a certain amount of background knowledge and information that is required before you can actually start to be creative in that field. But the paradox is that acquiring that knowledge might begin to shape your thinking about the subject and actually inhibit creativity. It's a well known phenomenon that often the people who are most creative in a particular industry or field are people who were not trained in that industry or field. They were able to be creative because they had a fresh perspective.

A second presupposition of NLP is that life and mind are systemic processes. That is, we are a system of interactions and we are also systems within a larger system. The interactions that happen within a human being and between human beings and their environment are systemic and are organized according to certain systemic principles. Our bodies, our interpersonal relationships and our societies form a kind of ecology of systems and subsystems, all of which are mutually influencing each other. Creativity comes naturally out of this process of systemic interaction and interactions between systems. On one level, it's not possible to ever completely isolate any one part of a system from another. Obviously people in a company are influenced by many aspects of the system around them. Part of the process of stimulating and encouraging creativity is taking into account not only the processes that are hapenning within the individual, but also the influences on that person from the system around him or her. For instance, you could put a creative person in a particular kind of system and the system might either enhance that creativity or inhibit it. We need to consider the the total system of interaction that is stimulating, encouraging and releasing the creative process.

The Law of Requisite Variety

In systems theory there is a principle called the law of requisite variety (Ashby, 1956). This principle is very important with respect to the process of managing creativity. Most managers will recognize that, on the one hand, the process of creativity and innovation is necessary and essential for companies to grow, new technologies to develop and for people in organizations to be able to adapt to our changing world. On the other hand, creativity and innovation can also create a lot of problems if it gets out of hand. It is possible to be too creative or too innovative. Creativity can produce disruption. This balance has to be somehow assessed and achieved in the context of the whole system.

The implication of the law of requisite variety is that we need to be constantly exploring variations in the operations and the processes that we use to get results. Even processes that have been effective in the past might not continue to be effective if the environment or the system around it changes. In other words, one of the traps or limits to creativity is past success. It's easy to believe that because something was successful before, it will continue to be successful. But if there are changes in the system around it, those things which used to work will no longer continue to function.

The implication here is that creativity is a necessary ongoing process. Specifically, the law of requisite variety states that "in order to successfully adapt and survive, a member of a system needs a certain minimum amount of flexibility, and that flexibility has to be proportional to the potential variation or the uncertainty in the rest of the system." In other words, if someone is committed to accomplishing a certain goal, that person needs to have a number of possible ways to get it. The number of different ways needed to get the goal depends on the amount of change that is possible within the system in which one is attempting to achieve the goal. As a simple example, let's say someone has a goal to move a chair across a room. When there's not much variation in the environment, he doesn't need much flexibility to accomplish that goal. He picks up the chair and carries it directly across the room. If he were in California, however, and there was an earthquake, he would have to have more potential variability to reach that goal because of changes being introduced in the environment. He might have to dodge a piece of the falling ceiling. Flexibility is needed to adapt and survive.

The point is that creativity is the process of assessing relationships of members of a system to the system itself. And, in fact, under times and contexts of change, the process of innovation and creativity becomes more essential.

Another implication of the law of requisite variety is that the member of a system that has the most flexibility also tends to be the catalytic member of that system—like the queen in a game of chess. This is a significant principle for leadership. The ability to be flexible and sensitive to variation is important in terms of managing the system itself.

A key issue in the management of creativity is how to balance willingness to change with values such as 'consistence' and 'congruence' in behavior. The answer has to do with where we put the flexibility. If one is consistent with respect to his goal, he will have to have flexibility in how he reaches the goal. The issue has to do with at which levels are we flexible. In one sense, where you need to be flexible is determined by where you are determined to be inflexible. If somebody is determined to be competent at, say, leading or motivating people, and that is what they're holding constant. Where they need the flexibility is being able to adapt to different motivations of people, and different environments.

As an analogy, let's say a musician wants to be consistent in producing a certain kind of sound with a certain kind of quality. This person has to be able to adapt to the acoustical variation of different concert halls, different musical instruments, etc. If somebody really is competent, they have to have flexibility in certain areas and inflexibility in others. And so the notion of creativity has to be viewed with respect to the total system.

Competence involves consistency. But as soon as you are consistent in one area, you need to have flexibility in another area to be able to accomodate to the part of the system that is not changing.

As another concrete example, in California they have big skyscrapers that they want to stay fixed. But in order to make sure that the big skyscraper stays fixed in an earthquake, they have to build a foundation that is able to tolerate movements of 16 feet side to side. One of the real secrets of managing creativity effectively is where to put the point of flexibility. It becomes a matter of ecology.

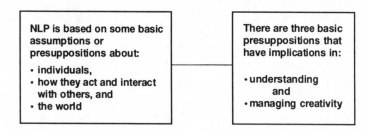

SECTION 1-3 / MAP A

Key Points

The tools, models and techniques of NLP are based on some basic presuppositions about individuals, how they interact with others and the world.

Activities

Think of the relationship between a road map you have followed and the 'territory' it represented.

Think of some other types of maps and how you use them.

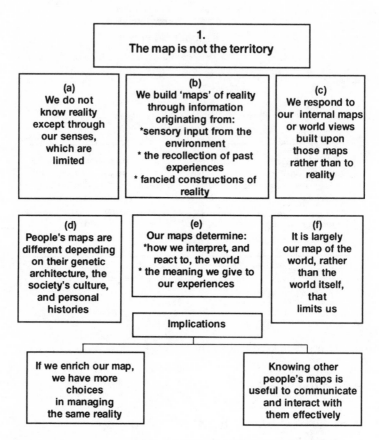

1.
The map is not the territory

(a)
We do not know reality except through our senses, which are limited

(b)
We build 'maps' of reality through information originating from:
*sensory input from the environment
* the recollection of past experiences
* fancied constructions of reality

(c)
We respond to our internal maps or world views built upon those maps rather than to reality

(d)
People's maps are different depending on their genetic architecture, the society's culture, and personal histories

(e)
Our maps determine:
*how we interpret, and react to, the world
* the meaning we give to our experiences

(f)
It is largely our map of the world, rather than the world itself, that limits us

Implications

If we enrich our map, we have more choices in managing the same reality

Knowing other people's maps is useful to communicate and interact with them effectively

SECTION 1-3 / MAP B

Key Points

A fundamental presupposition of NLP is that the map is not the territory; that we construct cognitive maps of the world which are useful but do not necessarily correspond precisely to the world around us.

Our internal maps determine how we respond to the world, especially situations which involve the future.

Activities

Remember an example when your internal model of the world did not in fact match with the world around you.

Recall a time that you changed or enriched you internal world view and it made you more effective or flexible.

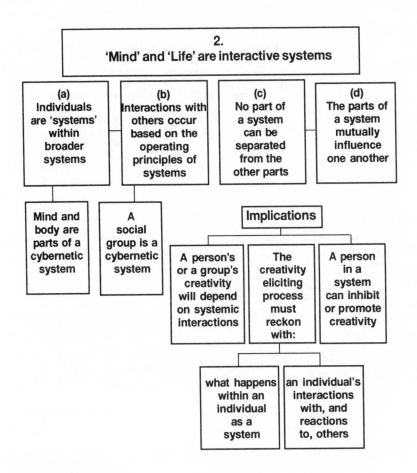

SECTION 1-3 / MAP C

Key Points

Another core presupposition of NLP is that 'life' and 'mind' are systemic processes. Creative processes and organizations are made up of mutually interacting and interdependent elements.

Activities

Think of some examples of mutually interactive systems where changing one part creates changes in the others, (e.g. a mobile, an automobile engine, etc.).

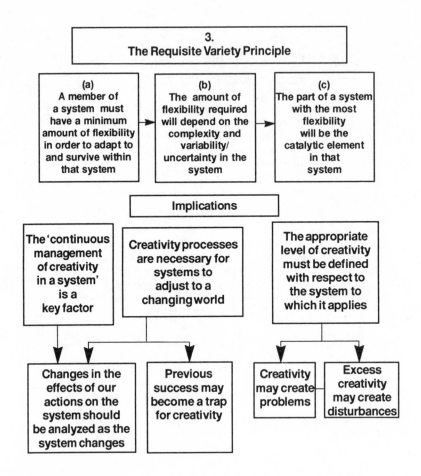

SECTION 1-3 / MAP **D**

Key Points

A member of a system must have a certain minimum amount of flexibility to survive and adapt to changes in the system. The amount of flexibility is proportional to the variability in the system.

Activities

Remember a time you had to do something different in order to accomplish a goal you had already successfully achieved in a particular way before, but had to vary what you did to accomplish it because the system around you was changing.

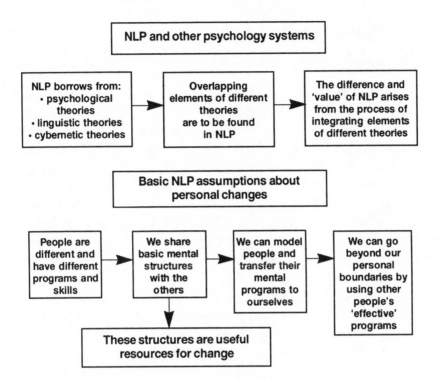

SECTION 1-3 / MAP E

Key Points

People are different and have different programs, assumptions
and skills yet share basic mental and linguistic structures
which make it possible to model and transfer effective cognitive
programs from others.

Activities

Think of something you learned how to do effectively from
someone else. In what ways were you able to do it in exactly
the same way as the other person? In what ways did you have
to adapt it in order to account for your individual differences?
Think of a person who is very different from you in many ways
but that you get along with.

What is the same and different about the two of you?

Which parts of the NLP model seem the most intuitively
obvious to you?

Which parts of the NLP model are you most skeptical about?
Why?

Section 1.4
Exploring Personal Creativity

The richness of our imagination comes from our ability to make maps in our minds. We build our mental maps out of information from the five senses or *representational systems*: *sight, sound, feeling, taste,* and *smell*. Our senses constitute the form or structure of thinking as opposed to its content. Every thought that you have, regardless of its content, is going to be a function of pictures, sound, feelings, smells or tastes, and how those representations relate to one another. We are constantly linking together sensory representations to build and update our maps of reality. We make these maps based on feedback from our sensory experience.

The purpose of this first exercise is to experientially explore how the distinctions and principles I have outlined thus far relate to the personal experience of creativity. Keep in mind that, in the area of creativity, oftentimes the kinds of mental processes that produce creativity are not always directly related to what you're doing. Many times creative ideas come when you are thinking of something else. While this exercise might not initially seem immediately relevant to creativity with respect to your working reality, its purpose is to bring out some principles of creativity and to enlighten you about some of your own personal strategies of creativity through a simple and concrete activity.

All acts of creation involve the mobilization of your nervous system in order to interact with or change your environment. In the belief system of NLP, creativity is creativity regardless of where it's applied. The creative process that somebody uses to prepare a meal might have very deep relevance to creative processes relating to organizing a team or developing a new product. For instance, Mozart's ability to compose music involved a kind of organizational creativity that could be very relevant for somebody who organizes groups of people on the process level. In fact, in the study of leadership I participated in at Fiat, I was fascinated to discover that one of the former top leaders in the company (Ghidella) had had two hobbies that seemed quite interesting in relation to the lateral effects of the creative process. One of his hobbies was classical music. His other hobby was neurophysiology. And in a very interesting way, on a process level, the structure of music and the nervous system have very interesting implications for the structuring of an organization. It might even be essential to have other areas of creativity to draw upon in order for managers to solve company problems.

Exercise: Exploring Personal Creativity

Utilizing whatever you have or can find around you, take 5 to 10 minutes and create something concrete. Make something physical with whatever you can find available. Your question is, "What can I physically make or create with what's available to me within the time limit of 5 to 10 minutes?"

While you are creating, see if you can begin to develop a 'meta cognition' (an introspective awareness) of your own thinking processes and strategies—especially in terms of how you use language and your senses. Try to experience the impact of language and the sensory modalities on your own behavior. In the back of your mind, start paying attention to what sort of thought processes you're going through as you are creating. How do you start, how do you develop it, how do you know that you're finished?

Instructions for Elicitation Process

When you have finished, explore what kind of strategies, patterns, principles and mental processes you used to generate your creation by considering the following questions.

The first one is, "How did you decide what to make?" Was it just a random process, or did you think about it?

Question 2 is, "How did you know that you were finished?" In other words, what satisfied you that you were finished? Do you think the thing that you made was very creative or not? Why?

You might have been pleased with what you made. If so, why? Or why not? This has to do with your evidence for creativity.

The third question is, "What specifically did you do to create?" What were your cognitive operations? Did you just start changing something or did you have a clear idea of what you wanted to do before you started? How did you go about making your creation?

These are the three basic questions:

1. How did you decide what to do?

2. How did you know that you were finished? And were you happy with it?

3. What did you do to create? What was your cognitive creative process?

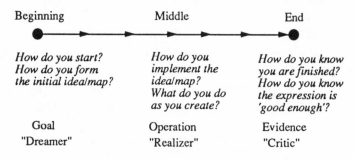

Beginning	Middle	End
How do you start? *How do you form the initial idea/map?*	*How do you implement the idea/map?* *What do you do as you create?*	*How do you know you are finished?* *How do you know the expression is 'good enough'?*
Goal	Operation	Evidence
"Dreamer"	"Realizer"	"Critic"

Figure 1.1

Remember, this is a general exploration; a discovery exercise. Its purpose is to discover some things about your personal creative process and to begin to create reference experiences for key concepts we'll be using later on. The attitude to take towards this kind of exercise is that of being open to discover or explore; of being curious about learning something about your own process. That's how you'll get the most out of it. Try it now.

After the Exercise

Think about how were you using your senses. What kind of thinking style were you employing? According to NLP, you can approach problems visually. Maybe you were aware of making images in your mind. Maybe you had no mental images at all. You were just looking out at something and changing it.

You might have been doing something that was more tactile or physical. You might have had an inner conversation with yourself. You might have asked questions to yourself such as, "Should I make something useful or should I make something that would be interesting to show somebody else?"

You might have used a more visual process, or verbal or logical process. You may have incorporated emotional reactions—having a feeling about something. For example, a lot of artistic creativity is an attempt to express some kind of an emotion.

Of course, it is also possible to combine senses. Think how you used your senses to decide what to make, to determine whether it was finished and whether you liked it.

The purpose of this part of the exercise is to recognize that cognitive strategies have a structure by experiencing the structure in your own creative thinking process. You should also recognize that there are differences in mental processes and strategies depending on the types of products or results produced.

It is important to realize that different people are creative in different ways, even for a simple task. You can relate these differences to the kind of product that is created. A more physical strategy might create something different than a more verbal or visual process. Any strategy can be either an enhancement of creativity or a potential limitation. For example, verbal strategies might be very good at producing certain kinds of results. But, for instance, Albert Einstein talked about how he very rarely used words at all or mathematics while he was coming up with the theory of relativity. Einstein's claim was that he used primarily visual strategy. In fact, he said his the theory of relativity was born out of a kind of adolescent fantasy. He wondered, "What would reality look like if I was riding on a light beam?" And he tried to form a clear picture of this imaginary trip. Einstein's claim was that it was that kind of thinking that was responsible for his discoveries. Of course, his parents probably thought it was completely unproductive, but that's what started the seed of the theory of relativity.

There is also a distinction between conscious and unconscious processes in relationship to 'process' *versus* 'product.' It was probably much easier to be aware of what you were making than how you were making it. You may have also begun to recognize that there are different stages of creativity, even in a very simple creative act and that there are combinations of thinking styles in mental processes.

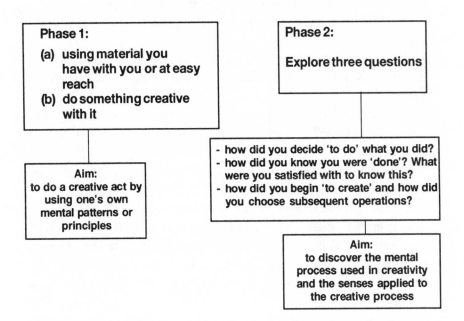

Exercise

Phase 1:

(a) using material you have with you or at easy reach
(b) do something creative with it

Aim:
to do a creative act by using one's own mental patterns or principles

Phase 2:

Explore three questions

- how did you decide 'to do' what you did?
- how did you know you were 'done'? What were you satisfied with to know this?
- how did you begin 'to create' and how did you choose subsequent operations?

Aim:
to discover the mental process used in creativity and the senses applied to the creative process

SECTION 1.4 / MAP A
Key Points

The objectives of the 'discovery' exercise are to:

* Physically create something simple but concrete in ongoing reality and trace the mental and behavioral processes you employed to produce it.
* Recognize that cognitive strategies have a structure by experiencing the structure in your own creative thinking process.
* Notice that there are patterns and consistencies of micro behavior even when one is only thinking.
* Begin to become aware of your own internal creative strategies.

Activities

What stands out to you the most about this experience? What was the most surprising to you? Was it easy or difficult?

How would you label the kind of creative thinking you employed during this activity. Was it a good example of your own creativity?

Did you encounter any interferences to your own creativity during this activity? If so, did they come from outside or within yourself?

If you ran into internal resistances or interferences, were they about *what* to do? *how* to do it? *wanting* to do it? getting a *chance to* do it?

What kinds of beliefs, values and attitudes seemed to come out during this experience? Which ones helped you be more innovative? Which one's got in your way?

Was it easy or difficult for you to be aware of your own internal processes? Which aspects of your own thinking are the easiest for you to be conscious of?

Were you able to sense the intuitive structure of your own thinking strategy?

In what ways does the way you approached this exercise typify your creative process?

Were you aware of going through any distinct stages during your process of creation?

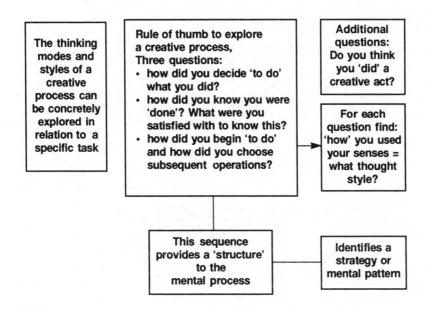

The thinking modes and styles of a creative process can be concretely explored in relation to a specific task

Rule of thumb to explore a creative process,
Three questions:
- how did you decide 'to do' what you did?
- how did you know you were 'done'? What were you satisfied with to know this?
- how did you begin 'to do' and how did you choose subsequent operations?

Additional questions:
Do you think you 'did' a creative act?

For each question find:
'how' you used your senses = what thought style?

This sequence provides a 'structure' to the mental process

Identifies a strategy or mental pattern

Section 1.4 / Map B

Key Points
There are different stages of creativity even in a very simple creative act.
There are combinations of thinking styles in mental processes.
Activities
Make a note of what you learned about the structure of your own creative thinking process.

Events eliciting creativity are sometimes not directly linked to the task to be done	Sometimes creativity originates from thinking of something else	The mental process used to have creativity in one area can help solving problems in other areas	Mental processes should be distinguished from contents. The same mental process can apply to different environments and contexts

Any creative act/ operation 'triggers' the nervous system by using our senses = sensory modalities	According to NLP, a problem can be approached by using 'different' modalities/senses For example: • Internal communications with oneself (telling oneself something) • Visual modalities inside oneself (visualizing something)	People use different styles and processes of thinking: • visual • auditory • verbal • tactile/physical • emotional and their combinations and sequences/ connections	An example of combination: art creations to express emotions

SECTION 1.4 / MAP C

Key Points

There are differences in mental processes and strategies depending on the types of products or results produced. Different people are creative in different ways, even for a simple task.

Activities

Ask another person to do this exercise and compare your creative processes.

*What were the main differences between your partner's creative strategy and your own?

*What were the similarities between your creative processes?

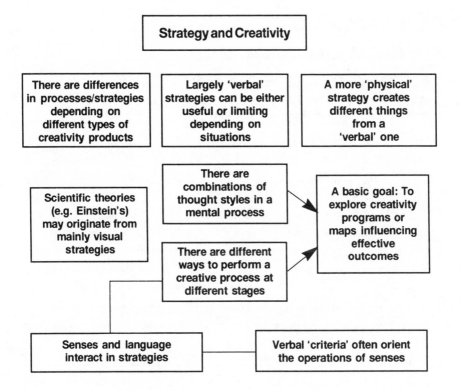

Key Points
There is a difference between the process and the content
results of creative strategies.

Activities
Make a list of some things that you would like to explore
further.
What, if anything, did you learn or confirm from this exercise
that you could immediately apply in your own working reality?
If you had it to do over again, what, if anything, would you
change about the way you approached this exercise?

Section 1.5
Macro Structure of
Experience and Creativity
The T.O.T.E. Model

While it is possible that there may be neurological processes that are random, most of what our nervous system does is highly organized. The T.O.T.E. model (Miller, et al, 1960) provides a way to define the structure of programs or maps that might facilitate or influence creative results. The basic structure of a program, whether it happens in a person or in a team or a group, is organized around a representation of a goal or an objective. Secondly, there is some kind of evidence or criteria that lets you know whether you're getting closer or moving farther away from the objective. Finally, you need some range of activities that you apply to attempt to accomplish the goals or objectives.

The term T.O.T.E. stands for the elements that make up this basic feedback loop—Test-Operate-Test-Exit. As you are trying to create something, you're continually testing your progress. "How far am I?" "Is it going in the direction that I like?" "Is it useful?" "Is it innovative?" And, based upon the result of that test, you operate, you do something, and then you test again to check the effect of the operation. You test. You operate, trying to change something or make a step in the right direction. Then you test again: "Was the result of this operation effective?" Based on the result of this test you either continue to operate or you exit, you're finished.

The test involves having a goal, an objective, and some sort of an evidence procedure for assessing progress toward the goal. In order to assess or to test you have to have a direction and some evidence or evidence procedures that lets you know whether or not you are accomplishing the goal. To operate effectively, you need a range or a series of choices of activities from which you can select to accomplish this goal.

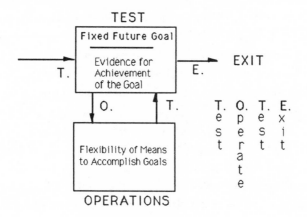

TEST

Figure 1.2   T.O.T.E.

The T.O.T.E. is a very basic process. Think of a child trying to walk. He has the goal of getting somewhere—say to a toy on a particular table or chair. He has evidence in terms of his relative distance from the toy, which can be seen and felt. He must then develop the skill and the flexibility necessary to get to his goal. Through many reiterations of testing and operating, his competency grows more and more. The child's goal, in this case, is fixed; get the toy. He has to have flexibility to accomplish that goal based on the potential flexibility and uncertainty within the system through which he is trying to move. If somebody moves the table or chair the toy is on, he has to readjust his operations. If he decided to fix his activity and just take a certain number of steps, he may reach his goal and he may not.

Consider the process of training. If you have a specific training goal, you have to vary the way that you do that training depending on the type of people in the training and the spontaneous situations that develop. If you fix a particular training procedure and stick to it no matter what happens, then you get variable results. You get a statistical distribution of success.

Of course, sometimes you want to produce varying results. In fact, when you were doing the creative exercise, you may not have even had an explicit goal at first. You may have just started a process and noticed what happened. That's one form of creativity. One of the simplest forms of creativity is a noise generator and a filter. A "noise" generator is something that just generates random possibilities. A filter selects only for certain results. You could have everybody brainstorming different ideas and then you filter the results. It's like panning for gold.

Another form of creativity would involve specifying a goal and then entering into an inventive kind of feedback loop, exploring the ways in which to accomplish that specific goal.

In either case, the T.O.T.E. defines the basic elements of the creative process. To have any kind of structured behavior you need to have goals, evidence for reaching the goals and ways of accomplishing the goals. NLP also adds that, on an individual level, the way that we make these cognitive guiding maps and execute these programs is fundamentally through neurological processes like the senses. Whether it's for an individual or a group, goals could be set through language. They could be established visually, by drawing diagrams for example. The goal could also be set in terms of emotional responses or feelings or even a physical demonstration, as in sports.

Then you have evidences and criteria for how well you're accomplishing your goal. Evidences especially are related to things that can be sensed and communicated. Evidence for the successful achievement of an objective will be seen, heard or felt in some concrete way. There is an important implication of this in terms of managing people. Two people can have the same goal but a different evidence. Sometimes one person is using a visual picture as an evidence and the other person is using a feeling, and they might not find the same results even though they share similar objectives.

For example, one TEST for creativity might be that an idea is "unique." If the concept you have come up with is not unique enough you will OPERATE or go through a procedure to make the idea more unique or to come up with a better concept. Individuals will have different ways to TEST for something like "uniqueness" based on personal representational system preferences or proclivities. For instance, something like uniqueness may be determined on the basis of:

1. What someone sees in the outcome.
2. What someone does physically as they are achieving the outcome.
3. What someone feels about the outcome.
4. What someone hears or says in relation to the outcome.

These variations may make a big difference in the kind of result produced by the creative process and in the audience to whom it appeals. Some ideas, for instance, may incorporate features of other products that already exist in the way that they are used but look very different. Other products may look very similar to others that already exist but have a different use.

In summary, in order to have the minimum information about how someone thinks we must identify:

1. The person's goals.
2. The evidence used by the person to determine progress toward the goal.
3. The sets of choices used by the person to get to the goal and the specific behaviors used to implement these choices.
4. The way the person responds if the goal is not initially achieved.

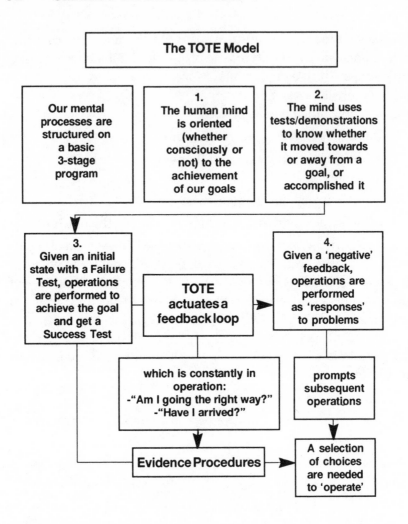

Key Points

According to the T.O.T.E. Model, intelligent mental processes are structured around a feedback loop made up of a basic 3-stage program: (1) setting goals (either consciously or unconsciously), (2) using tests or demonstrations to assess progress toward the goals, (3) operating to change something in order to move closer to the goal.

Different kinds of operations may be activated or mobilized based on the result of a particular test. A range of different operations may be required to successfully accomplish a particular goal.

A particular process may be made up of a number of macro and micro level T.O.T.E.s.

T.O.T.E. distinctions are relevant to the creative processes experienced and explored during the previous exercise.

Activities

Make your own personal representation or diagram of the feedback loop indicated by the T.O.T.E. Model.

What are some other process models that you know of that are similar to the T.O.T.E. Model or that seem to incorporate the elements of the T.O.T.E.?

What would you identify as being your overall goal while you were creating the concrete expression during the previous exercise?

What did you use as evidence to know if you were achieving that goal?

How would you classify the kinds of operations you engaged in during the exercise to attempt to achieve your goal? How well did you achieve it?

What were some of the micro goals you had during the exercise? What evidences and operations did you employ to accomplish those goals?

Take the T.O.T.E. distinctions and see if you can apply them to other activities and processes that you engage in during your working reality, both creative and otherwise. Are you able to sense that these are also organized around the feedback loop created by having goals, evidences and operations?

Section 1.6
Influence of Different Levels of Experience on Creativity

It is important to acknowledge that there are different levels of creativity and different kinds of influences on creativity. For instance, there's the *where* and the *when* of creativity. This relates to environmental influences, such as space and time constraints, that might influence creativity. For example, in the creativity exercise for this Chapter, you had to produce an object with limited external resources in a limited time frame.

There's also the *what* related to creativity. This refers to what kind of behavioral activities might influence creativity. Even if all readers were given similar environmental constraints, they would respond differently within these constraints. There would be a wide variety of behavioral outputs within the similar environmental constraints.

But what accounts for these behavioral differences? Differences on a behavior level are triggered by differences in cognitive processes. That is, by differences in *how* one is thinking about something or mentally representing it. The how level of creativity relates to the inner maps and the inner programs that trigger behavioral variations.

Creativity also relates to beliefs and values. These determine the *why* of creativity. "Why should I bother doing something innovative at all?" A person's degree of motivation will determine how much of his own inner resources he will mobilize. Motivation is what stimulates and activates the *how*s and the *what*s of our responses.

Finally, there's a *who* involved in creativity. "Am I a creative person or not a creative person?" "Should somebody in my function or my role be creative and in what types of activities?" *Who* is supposed to be creative? "If the idea came from the finance department it couldn't be creative, could it?"

Levels of Creativity and Innovation

People often talk about responding to things on different *levels*. For instance, someone might say that some experience was negative on one level but positive on another level. In our brain structure, language, and perceptual systems there are natural hierarchies or levels of experience. The effect of each level is to organize and control the information on the level below it. Changing something on an upper level would necessarily change things on the lower levels; changing something on a lower level could but would not necessarily effect the upper levels. Anthropologist Gregory Bateson identified four basic levels of learning and change—each level more abstract than the level below it but each having a greater degree of impact on the individual.

These levels roughly correspond to:

1. Who I **A**m—*Identity*   Who?
2. My **B**elief system—*Values and Meanings*   Why?
3. My **C**apabilities—*Strategies and States*   How?
4. What I **D**o or have **D**one—*Specific Behaviors* What?
5. My **E**nvironment—*External Constraints*   Where?
                                                        When?

The environment level involves the specific external conditions in which our behavior takes place. Behaviors without any inner map, plan or strategy to guide them, however, are like knee jerk reactions, habits or rituals. At the level of capability we are able to select, alter and adapt a class of behaviors to a wider set of external situations. At the level of beliefs and values we may encourage, inhibit or generalize a particular strategy, plan or way of thinking. Identity, of course, consolidates whole systems of beliefs and values into a sense of self. While each level becomes more abstracted from the specifics of behavior and sensory experience, it actually has more and more widespread effect on our behavior and experience.

* *Environmental factors* determine the external opportunities or constraints a person has to react to. Answer to the questions **where?** and **when?**

* *Behavior* is made up of the specific actions or reactions taken within the environment. Answer to the question **what?**

* *Capabilities* guide and give direction to behavioral actions through a mental map, plan or strategy. Answer to the question **how?**

* *Beliefs* and *values* provide the reinforcement (motivation and permission) that supports or denies capabilities. Answer to the question **why?**

* *Identity* factors determine overall purpose (mission) and shape beliefs and values through our sense of self. Answer to the question **who?**

Each of these processes involve a different level of organization and evaluation that will select, access and utilize the information on the level below it. In this way they form a hierarchy of "nested" T.O.T.E.s as shown in Figure 1.3.

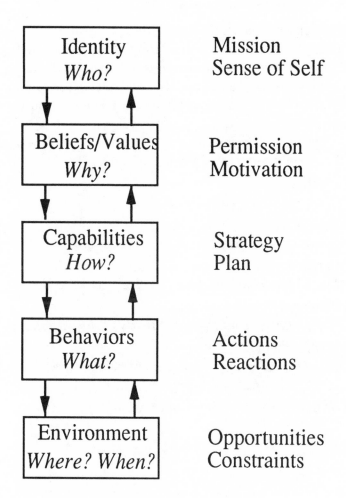

Figure 1.3   Nested TOTEs

Creativity is clearly a multi-level process and requires support from all these levels to be completely effective. Any level that is not aligned with the others can produce an interference to the creative process. As an example, someone may have been able to do something new in a specific context (specific behavior) but not have a mental model or map that allows them to know how to continue doing new things or to innovative things in a different environment (capability). Even when someone is capable of generating creative options, they may not value creativity as an important or necessary function so they rarely use it. Even people who are able to be creative and believe it is an important function do not always perceive themselves "innovators" or "inventors."

For instance, the following statements show how limits to creativity could come from any one of the levels.

1. Identity:
   "I am not a creative person."

2. Belief:
   "Creativity can be difficult and disruptive."

3. Capability:
   "I don't know how to think creatively consistently."

4. Behavior:
   "I don't know what to do differently in this situation."

5. Environment:
   There wasn't enough time to do something innovative."

Review the exercise and notice: Which levels most influenced your own personal experience of creativity?

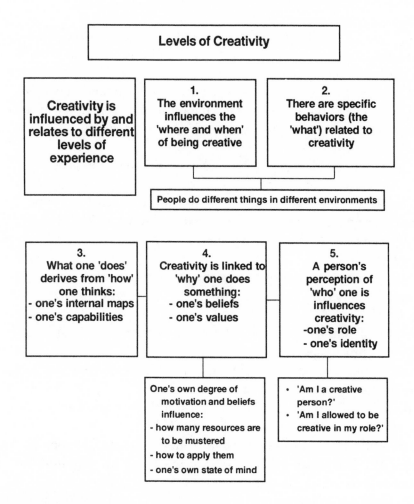

SECTION 1.6 / MAP A

Key Points
There are different levels of processes that influence creativity and other human activities:

(1) environmental processes influence the *where* and *when* of being creative.

(2) it is through behavioral processes that the *what* of creativity is manifested in the environment.

(3) behavioral actions and responses derive from *how* one thinks—one's internal maps, strategies and mental capabilities.

(4) creative thinking is influenced and directed by processes relating to beliefs and values which determine *why* one is being creative to begin with.

(5) self referential processes relating to one's perception of *who* one is in relation to one's personal identity and role determine which kinds of beliefs and values will be selected and implemented.

These different levels of processes exert different kinds of influences on creativity.

These different levels of processes mutually interact with one another and may either support or interfere with processes on other levels.

Activities

Review your experience during the previous exercise.

In what ways did the environment influence your creative process?

Which of your own behavioral actions seemed most significant to your process of creativity?

What mental processes and mental capabilities were most relevant to your creative process?

What beliefs and values had the most influence on your creative process, behavior and results?

How did your sense of who you are effect your creative process?

Are you able to sense how these various levels are different but interrelate to one another?

Think of several examples of each of the different levels for processes other than creativity.

Are you able to intuitively sense the different kind of impact and influence that each level exerts on a situation?

In what ways is your creative process within your own working context influenced by each of these different levels?

Which levels are most supportive of creativity in your own work context? Which levels are not supportive?

Which level(s) do you personally think are most significant for effective creativity for an individual? for a group?

Chapter 2

Structure of the Creative Process

Overview of Chapter 2

General objectives for Chapter 2

1. Introduce some basic principles and types of NLP modeling processes.
2. Assist readers to understand the cognitive micro structure of their own creative strategies.
3. Draw out and define basic types and phases of the creative process with respect to the readers' reference experiences.
4. Define some basic principles and methods to increase creativity.

Sections and goals for each Section

Section 2.1 Modeling and Creativity

Distinguish between the micro and macro aspects of behavior modeling and describe how the T.O.T.E. may be used as the basic paradigm for modeling.

Section 2.2 Defining the Structure of a Past Effective Creative Experience

Assist readers to fill out T.O.T.E. questionnaire for creativity.

Section 2.3: The Structure of Cognitive Processes in Creativity (The R.O.L.E. Model)

Introduce the basic cognitive distinctions of the R.O.L.E. Model and assist readers to relate them to their answers on the creativity T.O.T.E. questionnaire and other reference experiences.

Section 2.4 Types of Creativity

Define the three basic types of creativity (Innovation, Discovery and Invention) and relate them to the elements of the T.O.T.E.

Section 2.5 Increasing Creativity

Explain types of influences on cognitive strategies and their effects on creativity. Define the three ways of increasing personal creativity.

Section 2.1
Modeling and Creativity

The purpose of this Chapter is to focus on some of the elements of the modeling process. In NLP, the process of modeling revolves around the elicitation of the program an individual uses to accomplish an effective performance. The basic structure of this program is related to the elements of the T.O.T.E. What are the goals that an effective performer has? What are the evidences that an effective performer uses to access progress toward his or her goals? What sort of range of activities or operations does an effective performer have available to accomplish his or her goals?

And there is one other very important part of modeling an effective T.O.T.E.: What does an effective performer do when an operation or action doesn't work? Competence and excellence are not necessarily about being correct the first time. Competence often has to do with adapting to problems introduced by the environment or other parts of the system.

It is said that you don't really start managing until you run into a problem or into resistance. Until then, you're just giving instructions. It's not until there's a problem that you actually have to "manage." It is said that you don't really start selling until you run into a problem or a resistance. Until then, you're just taking orders. It is said that you don't really start teaching until you run into a problem or a resistance. Until then, you're just giving information. How you respond to difficulties is an essential element to an effective program.

These are the elements that we start with in modeling. The creative process can be modeled on a micro or a macro level. Micro modeling in NLP involves identifying specific but relevant details of a person's cognitive process. Macro modeling in NLP involves identifying general patterns relating to a style or approach to creativity.

Micro modeling has to do with issues such as what kind of representational systems you are using at which steps in a mental program or strategy. For example, a basic micro modeling procedure for creativity involves specifying the cognitive patterns accompanying each element of a person's T.O.T.E. for creativity. A macro modeling procedure would be to identify which classes of goals, evidence procedures or operations are associated with particular types or stages of creativity.

We are going to start with micromodeling and move to macromodeling in the following Chapters. [Note: Some good examples of micro modeling creativity strategies with NLP are in *Tools for Dreamers*.]

```
┌─────────────────────────────────────────────────┐
│              Modeling and Creativity              │
└─────────────────────────────────────────────────┘
```

```
┌──────────────────┐  ┌──────────────────┐  ┌──────────────────┐
│   An excellent   │  │  Micromodeling:  │  │  Macromodeling:  │
│  person can be   │  │   identify what  │  │  identifies how  │
│   modeled in     │  │      types/      │  │the different levels│
│ different ways   │  │ combinations of  │  │   of a creative  │
│   to transfer    │  │    senses and    │  │     process      │
│    his/her       │  │   language (or   │  │  (where/when -   │
│ creative skills  │  │ representational │  │    what - how -  │
└──────────────────┘  │    systems) are  │  │    why - who)    │
                      │   used for each  │  │ interact during  │
                      │   element of the │  │     general      │
                      │   TOTE program   │  │   procedures     │
                      └──────────────────┘  └──────────────────┘
```

```
┌──────────────────┐  ┌──────────────────┐  ┌──────────────────┐
│   One can also   │  │  micro-aspects   │  │  macro-aspects   │
│   self-model     │  │  of creativity   │  │  of creativity   │
│ in order to better│  └──────────────────┘  └──────────────────┘
│  'manage' one's  │
│  own creativity  │
└──────────────────┘
```

```
          ┌──────────────────────────────────────────┐
          │  There are different types of 'clues'    │
          │   one can observe in the persons         │
          │            to be modeled                 │
          └──────────────────────────────────────────┘
```

SECTION 2.1 / MAP A

Key Points

An individual's strategy or T.O.T.E. can be modeled and transferred as a skill.

The NLP modeling process may be applied to one's own creative strategies to identify the structure of other people's strategies.

The creative process can be modeled on a micro or a macro level.

NLP identifies different types of "clues" for the different levels of modeling.

TOTE identifies a mental
program that results in
behaviors according to a
3-element structure
  • Goals
  • Evidence
  • Operations

To each element
in the structure
correspond sensory
representations and
their combinations

in an individual

in a group

A goal can be defined
in terms:
• visual,
• verbal,
• physical, or
• of physical feelings

A 'verbal' goal - e.g.
"quality" - can produce
evidence ('how well it
was accomplished') of
different types:
• physical
• sensory

Operations can
be of different
types:
• visual (diagrams)
• physical (actions)
• linguistic (words), or
• emotional (feelings)

SECTION 2.1 / MAP B

Key Points

A basic micro modeling procedure for creativity involves
specifying the cognitive patterns accompanying each element
of a person's T.O.T.E. for creativity.

Activites

Which parts of your own creative process do you think involve
the most skill?

What would you most like to model about your own creative
strategy?

What would you most like to model about the creative
strategies of your collaborators?

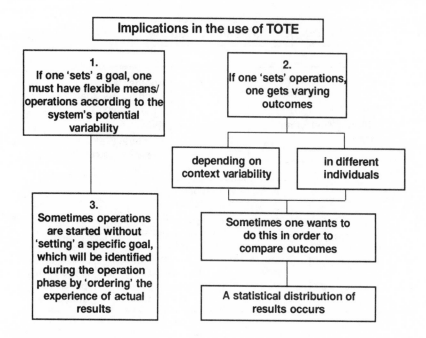

SECTION 2.1 / MAP C

Key Points

A macro modeling procedure would be to identify which parts of a T.O.T.E. are held constant and which are left flexible

Activites

Would you say that your creative process is more like brainstorming or more like a "guided missile" that goes toward a specific result.

Think of some examples in your professional reality where goals are fixed but operations are flexible.

Think of some examples in your professional reality where operations are fixed and produce variable results.

```
┌─────────────────────────────────┐
│        TOTE and Creativity       │
└─────────────────────────────────┘
```

```
┌──────────────────────────┐            ┌──────────────────────────┐
│ One way to create is      │            │ Another way:             │
│ • 'doing' brainstorming,  │            │ • setting the goal       │
│ then                      │            │   (as a 'given')         │
│ • 'filtering'/'selecting' │            │ then                     │
│   results                 │            │ • 'entering' the creative│
│                           │            │   process to reach the   │
│                           │            │   goal                   │
└──────────────────────────┘            └──────────────────────────┘
```

```
┌──────────────────────────────────┐
│  Basic elements of creativity     │
│          as it applies to:        │
└──────────────────────────────────┘
```

```
┌────────────┐  ┌────────────┐  ┌────────────────┐  ┌────────────┐
│ how to     │  │ how to     │  │ how to set the │  │ how to     │
│ set        │  │ define/    │  │ range of       │  │ respond to │
│ goals      │  │ perceive   │  │ operations and │  │ problems/  │
│            │  │ evidences  │  │ alternatives   │  │ difficulties│
└────────────┘  └────────────┘  └────────────────┘  └────────────┘
```

```
┌────────────────────────────────────────┐
│ Different people can have the same       │
│ thought modes for one element and        │
│ different ones for others                │
└────────────────────────────────────────┘
```

SECTION 2.1 / MAP D

Key Points

Macro modeling in NLP involves identifying how different levels of the creative process interrelate.

Micro modeling in NLP involves identifying specific but relevant details of a person's cognitive process.

Activites

Review the creative process you went through in the exercise in the previous chapter. What cognitive distinctions seem most relevant to your creative process?

Where did you have the most flexibility: goals, evidence or operations?

What micro and macro patterns stand out to you about your co-learners' creative processes?

Section 2.2
Defining the Structure of a Past Effective Creative Experience

In this Section you will be filling out a questionnaire for defining a creativity T.O.T.E. The questionnaire relates to a context in which you are already able to be creative. It poses a set of questions relating to goals, evidences and operations as a self-modeling exercise.

The first question asks for a brief description of a context in which you personally feel that you are already able to be creative. Choose something that's relevant to you personally. Optimally it would be something that is relevant to your professional reality.

The next question is, "What are the goals or objectives that you're attempting to accomplish by being creative in that context?" Creativity is triggered and mobilized by goals, and these goals might be on any number of levels. They might be on a *why* level or a *how* level or *what* level. Rather than try to consciously figure out at what level your goal is at this point, just answer the question out of your own intuition for now.

Question 3 asks, "What do you use as evidence to know if you are accomplishing these goals?" These don't have to be extremely detailed answers. However, it is good practice to describe it in enough detail that somebody else could understand what you mean.

Question 4 is, "What do you do in order to get to your goals? What kinds of steps or activities do you go through to be creative?" Think in terms of the specific cognitive and behavioral processes you engage in be creative in the context you have identified.

Finally, Question 5 asks, "If you experience unexpected problems or difficulties, what is your reaction?" How do you respond to problems? What kind of actions do you take to correct problem situations that arise in this context?

This set of questions will give you an interesting insight into the the elements that make up a personally effective performance. Even if you've performed creativity in this context many times, you may discover some additional insights about your process by organizing your experience of it into these kinds of chunks.

To model a T.O.T.E. relating to a past event, it is important to be able to think about the structure of the process "as if" you were reliving the experience. Your goal is to try to put down as much of what it is like when you're actually engaged in this creative activity. At the same time realize that you may also have to be doing a fair amount of guessing in retrospect. Since you will be answering these questions from memory, you may have never thought about some of these things before. So you might have to make a decision in retrospect about what your inner experience would have most likely been.

Exercise:
Exploring the Structure
of Your Creative Process

Take a few moments and, on a separate piece of paper, fill in answers to the following questions as completely as you can.

1. What is a context in which you are already able to be creative or innovative?

2. What are the goals or objectives that you are attempting to accomplish by being creative or innovative in this context?

3. What do you use as evidence to know you are accomplishing those goals?

4. What do you do to get to the goals—what are some specific steps and activities that you use to creatively achieve your goals in this context?

5. When you experience unexpected problems or difficulties in achieving your goals in this context, what is your response to them? What specific activities or steps do you take to correct them?

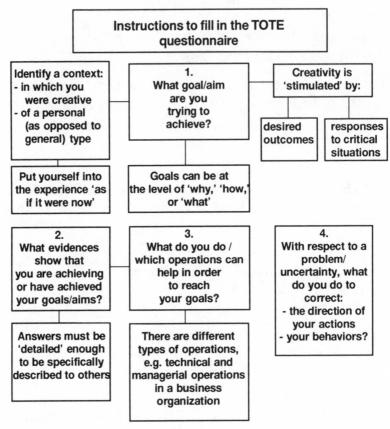

SECTION 2.2 / MAP A

Key Points

You can model your own creative process by specifying your T.O.T.E. for an event in your past in which you were able to be effectively creative.

To model a T.O.T.E. relating to a past event, it is important to be able to think about the structure of the process "as if" you were reliving the experience.

Activities

Practice associating yourself back into some past examples of creativity by mentally reliving them.

Contrast "reliving" the past experiences with simply "thinking about them" from a disassociated perspective. What different kinds of information do you get from the two ways of remembering?

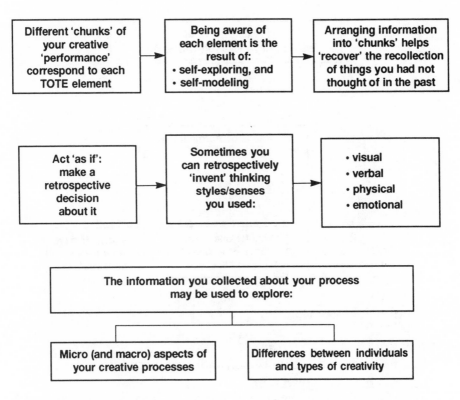

SECTION 2.2 / MAP **B**

Key Points

Chunking and organizing a past experience as a T.O.T.E. can give you new insights into it.

Even guesses made in retrospect can provide useful information about your creative process.

Activities

Think of a number of past examples in which you were able to be creative. Intuitively, what seems to be common to all of them?

Try to reconstruct details relating to several past instances in which you were creative. Guess or make up any pieces you cannot directly remember.

What do you learn from your guesses? In what way is guessing different and similar to actually remembering?

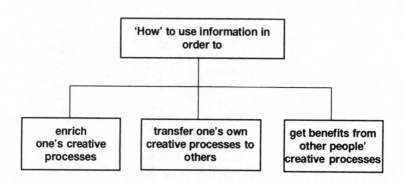

SECTION 2.2 / MAP C

Key Points
Self modeling can enhance personal creativity by:
(1) enriching one's awareness,
(2) facilitating the potential transfer of key elements to other personal contexts, and
(3) having a vocabulary to compare your creative process with others.

Activities
Make a note of:
(1) what new awarenesses you've gained about your own creative process from the questionnaire,
(2) what elements might be most useful to transfer to other contexts in which you need to be creative or to transfer to people you work with,
(3) in what ways do you imagine your process is different from other people that you know or work with.

Section 2.3
Structure of Cognitive
Processes in Creativity
The R.O.L.E. Model

You will discover that the answers on your questionnaire provide quite a bit of valuable information about your creative process. There are some other filters that we are going to use to derive information about the cognitive structure of your creative process. These filters will allow you to find both micro and macro level patterns.

This set of distinctions will help you to explore the creativity strategy that you've outlined on the questionnaire and draw out certain details about it that could be very relevant to:

1. Understanding your own process of creativity more fully, and

2. Helping you understand differences between people and different types of creativity and creative processes.

This will be a continuation of the process of personal exploration and self-discovery that we began in the previous Section. Then, in the next Sections we will shift our focus to applying the results of these explorations to develop ways to:

1. Widen or enrich your creative abilities;

2. Transfer creative abilities to other contexts where it would be valuable to have more creative potential;

3. Benefit from the creative processes of other people.

The next exercise relates to what is called the R.O.L.E. Model in NLP. Before we go over this material, realize that the purpose of this book is not for you to become experts at NLP but rather to draw relevant distinctions or tools from NLP that facilitate your creative abilities. Some of the information in this Section is presented at a level of detail that isn't necessary for you to master in order to derive benefits from it. Thus, as we approach this material, if certain elements of it seem intuitively enlightening or obvious to you, or seem to add something to your understanding, then take them in. If they don't seem so relevant to you, don't worry about it. In a standard NLP training, we take 20 to 25 days to teach people to consciously master the basic NLP skills. Our learning frame here is to offer you some key NLP distinctions we believe will enhance your unconscious competence. We do believe you will find many of them stimulating, relevant and easy to grasp intuitively .

The R.O.L.E. Model

In English, a person who is a 'role model' is somebody that people look up to and want to learn from. So, there's an intended ambiguity in the term. But more importantly, the letters stand for a set of distinctions that give you a deeper level of insight into the structure of your own thinking process. The letters R.O.L.E. are related to the first letters of the four major categories of micro level cognitive distinctions we will be exploring.

The "R" stands for "Representational system," which relates to the senses. This distinction relates to the type of sensory modality or representation a person is employing for a particular step in his or her strategy. For example, when you are setting your goals, are the goals represented visually? Are they represented as actions, physically? Are they represented verbally? Perhaps they are represented simply as a kind of feeling.

Similarly, you might ask whether the evidence you used to know if you were accomplishing the goals was verbal, visual, emotional or physical?

There are only a few basic representational system distinctions: seeing, hearing, feeling. Smell or taste could play a role in some strategies.

Later on, you are going to review your answers to the T.O.T.E. questions—your goals, evidences, and operational steps—and to explore what types of representation or sensory modality you used during each step. You might find that one of these representational modalities clearly stands out as being related to that step. You might also find that there are several representations or senses associated with a particular step in the strategy. For example, you might have had a cluster of goals instead of a single goal. And different goals might be associated with different senses. For example, your goal on a task level might have been represented in terms of a picture or image of the desired result, but your goal on a relational level might have been represented verbally or emotionally. Certain processes may be represented in terms of multiple senses such as feelings and imagery.

Which senses we use to cognitively represent desired future events and potential consequences is not simply a trivial detail. For example, some people run into problems accomplishing tasks because they have great visions but no comprehension of the feelings of effort that it might take to accomplish the vision, or no realization of the logical sequence of activities leading to the goal.

The "O" in the R.O.L.E. relates to the "Orientation" of the sensory modality or representation. For example, in terms the sense of vision, you could look out at something in the external world using your visual sense to scan the environment. Or you could use your visual sense in an internal way, remembering a past event or fantasizing about the future. If you were asked, "Do you remember the way you got to the room you are presently in from your home or office?" you would probably fashion some visual memories into a kind of internal map. On the other hand, if you were asked, "Imagine what you'll be doing three weeks from now?" you would probably use your imagination instead of your memory and form your internal map out of mental projections. For certain things, this kind of cognitive orientation can be very important strategically. Some people are very externally oriented in their creative process and use a lot of experimentation or go through trial and error methods to innovate. Others may be more internally oriented and take a lot of time to think things through before they act. Some people might rely alot on fantasy during their creative thinking process, while others piece together memories.

On a micro level, for instance, a person might:

1. Represent a goal by holding a memory of it;
2. Use perceptions of the external environment for evidence;
3. Fantasize about possible operations and variations to reach the goals.

For another person, goals might be represented as projected or constructed images, but evidences might be results that you observe in the outside world. In both cases the test in the T.O.T.E. would be a comparison of ongoing reality to the internal image.

Of course, language can be oriented internally, as a kind of an inner dialoguing, or externally as dialogue with another person. In NLP, touch is considered the external orientation of feeling. Emotions would be feelings that are represented internally. In NLP we use the term *kinesthetic* for feelings in general. The term stands for general body sensations; which could be sensations anywhere in the body: a muscle, the skin, the stomach, etc.

The "L" of the R.O.L.E. Model has to do with "Linking" or the connection between cognitive elements. Processes such as learning and creativity come as the result of our ability to associate and link cognitive processes. Some people, for example, may have a very strong link between images and emotions. Others have strong links between sound and emotion. It is these kind of links that allow us to enjoy art and music. Some people might have a strong link between actions and images. A dancer, for example, might be able to watch somebody dancing and actually internally feel as if she is making the movements she is observing.

Often it is the strength of these links that determine personal aptitudes. For example, Einstein had a very strong link between his inner fantasies and his feelings. His mental projections were very real to him. Other people have no feeling about their fantasies—their imagination is not connected to feelings of reality. So this will be another potentially significant micro level cognitive pattern to explore in your own strategy.

The "E" in the R.O.L.E. Model has to do with the "Effect" or function of a particular cognitive process. The effect of the cognitive steps in your own creativity strategy have, in fact, already been suggested by where it fits in the questionnaire. Effects are essentially about which function in the T.O.T.E. a cognitive process is serving. Is it a goal? Is it an evidence? Is it an operation? The function of each step is determined for the most part, by where it appears in the T.O.T.E.

Exercise:
Mirco Analysis of the
T.O.T.E. Questionnaire

The goal of this exercise is to explore:

1. Which of the senses, or which cluster of senses, you used for each step in the creativity strategy you outlined in your answers to the T.O.T.E. questionnaire;

2. What was the orientation of each of the senses;

3 What sort of links there were between the senses.

Referring to the checklist provided in this Section, determine which of the senses you associate most with your definition of the context. Obviously context is something that is external to you. Context has to do with your perception of *where* and *when* creativity is required.

Then explore the way you represented your goal or goals. Was it in pictures, feelings, words or actions? And, how was it oriented? Were you remembering something or imagining something? Did your goal involve the combination and linking of the senses?

Continue this micro-analysis for each of the questions: in which sensory modality is it primarily represented? Where is that modality oriented? Is the primary modality linked to any others?

It is best to approach this exercise with an attitude of self-curiosity and self-discovery. One thing that is true of creative people is that they are interested in the creative process. They are interested in their own thinking. This allows them to develop what is called a "meta-cognition" of their own cognitive strategies. This awareness of their own internal process allows them to continually evaluate and update their creative abilities.

Determine your primary sensory modality and its orientation for each of the T.O.T.E. questions. Then define any links between the senses. If you are confused or uncertain about a particular step, put a question mark there. That might be an important place for you to focus later on in order to improve your meta-cognition of your own thought process. That question mark may be just as valuable to improving your creativity as finding a specific answer.

R.O.L.E. Model Questionnaire

Note: The following questions relate to the answers on the Creativity T.O.T.E. questionnaire.

1. Context:
    What perceptual aspects of the context were most involved in stimulating you to be creative?
    Something you saw?
    Something you heard?
    Something you felt?
    Something someone said?
    Something you said to yourself?

2. Goals:
    How did you cognitively represent your goals in this context?
    Visualized them in imagination?
    Remembered them visually?
    Drew them?
    Verbalized them to someone else?
    Verbalized them to yourself?
    Recalled something verbally?
    Felt them?

3. Evidence:
    What cognitive or sensory processes did you use to asses your progress toward your goals?
    Something you saw?
    Something you imagined?
    Something you heard?
    How you felt?
    Something someone said?
    Something you said to yourself?

4. Operations:
    Which cognitive or perceptual processes did you use in relation to achieving your goals?
    Fantasizing?
    Self talk (inner dialogue)?

Intuitive Feelings?
Visual memory?
Recalled words or instructions?
Emotions?
Drawing?
Discussing?
Touching?
Watching?
Listening?
Moving/Doing?

5. Response to Problems:
   Which cognitive or perceptual processes did you activate in response to problems?
   Imagining options?
   Self talk (inner dialogue)?
   Intuitive Feelings?
   Visually remembering options?
   Recalled words or instructions?
   Emotions?
   Drawing?
   Discussing?
   Touching?
   Watching?
   Listening?
   Changing Actions?

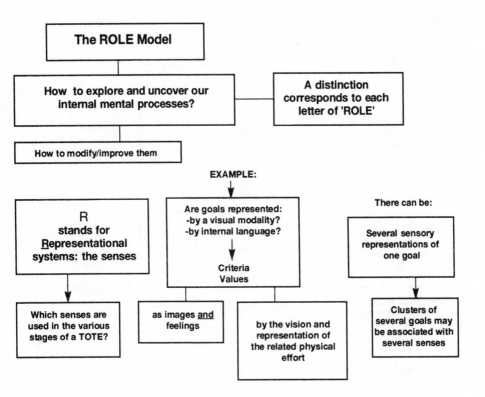

SECTION 2.3 / MAP A

Key Points
The R.O.L.E. Model provides further micro distinctions to enrich your awareness of the structure of your creative process.
The "R" in the R.O.L.E. Model relates to sensory Representational systems; corresponding to the five senses.

Activities
Find an example in your own personal history when you clearly relied on or emphasized one of your senses over the others. Find examples for each of the senses.

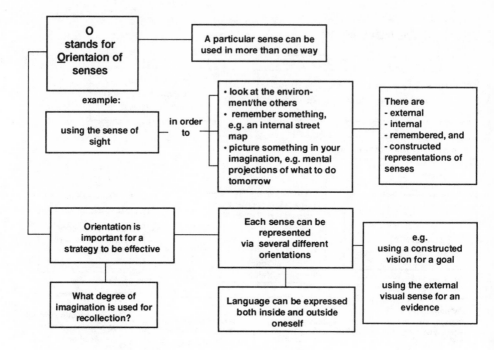

SECTION 2.3 / MAP **B**

Key Points
The "O" in the R.O.L.E. Model relates to the Orientation of a representational system; whether one is (1) directing a sense toward the outside world or one's inner reality; or (2) building an inner map from memory or fantasy.

Activities
Think of a time when your senses were fully oriented externally.

Think of a time when your senses were fully oriented internally.

Practice shifting the orientation of each of your senses from external to internal.

Practice shifting the orientation of each of your senses from memory to imagination.

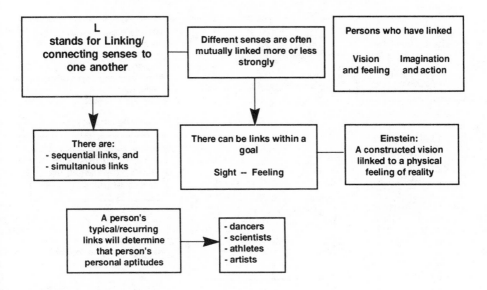

Key Points

The "L" in the R.O.L.E. Model relates to the way in which
different representational systems are Linked to each other
and influence each other.

Activities

Which of your own representational systems are most linked
together?

Practice purposefully linking your senses together:

  *Imagine that touching different parts of your arms or hands
   produced different tones.

  *Imagine colors had different sounds associated with them
   and that sounds produced specific colors.

  *Imagine shapes had different feelings associated with them
   and that feelings produced specific shapes.

  *Imagine you could link tastes and smells to colors and
   sounds.

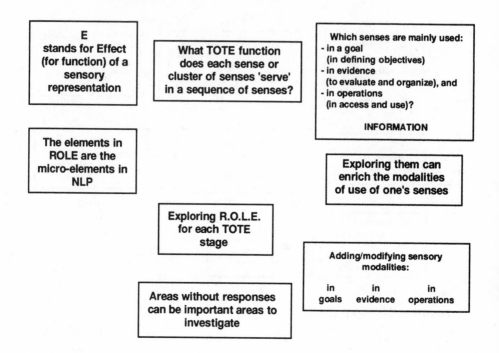

The boxes contain the following text:

E stands for Effect (for function) of a sensory representation

What TOTE function does each sense or cluster of senses 'serve' in a sequence of senses?

Which senses are mainly used:
- in a goal
  (in defining objectives)
- in evidence
  (to evaluate and organize), and
- in operations
  (in access and use)?

INFORMATION

The elements in ROLE are the micro-elements in NLP

Exploring them can enrich the modalities of use of one's senses

Exploring R.O.L.E. for each TOTE stage

Adding/modifying sensory modalities:

in   in   in
goals   evidence   operations

Areas without responses can be important areas to investigate

SECTION 2.3 / MAP **D**

Key Points

The "E" in the R.O.L.E. Model relates to the Effect or function
a representational system serves in a mental program or
cognitive strategy; which part of the T.O.T.E. is being used for.
Exploring the cognitive micro structure defined by the
R.O.L.E. Model for each step in one's creativity T.O.T.E. can
open up new awareness and insight.

Activities

What new awarenesses did you get from analyzing the micro
cognitive structure of your creativity T.O.T.E.?
Which of the questions were the most easy to answer? Which
were the most difficult?

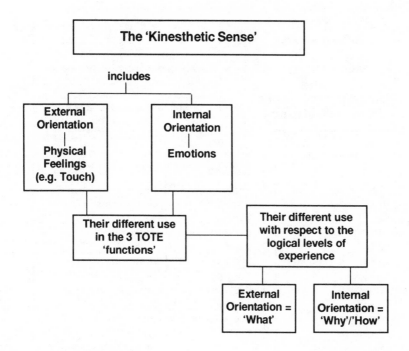

SECTION 2.3 / MAP E

Key Points
The senses pick up different kinds of information depending on their orientation.
Different orientations of the senses may be more associated with different levels of process.

Activities
Which of the micro level cognitive patterns or features you defined do you most associate with creativity?

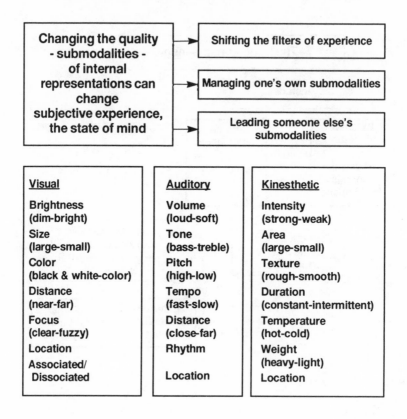

SECTION 2.3 / MAP F

Key Points

There are qualities or "sub-modalities" of each sensory modality that serve as filters for our experience and influence our perceptions.

Activities

What cognitive features or patterns would you need to change in order to make your management of the situation you chose to analyze in the T.O.T.E. questionnaire less creative?

Which of the submodality qualities seem most significant to you in relation to your recollection of that situation.

Section 2.4
Types of Creativity

One implication of NLP is that certain kinds of strategies might allow effective performance in certain kinds of contexts but be less effective in others. Mozart probably had a different strategy than Leonardo. Both were creative, but the micro aspects of their strategies lead them to be effective in different areas.

People are creative in different ways. In fact, on an interactive level, differences between individual creativity strategies is in itself another source of creativity. The fact that people have different maps of the world is a factor that can either be a positive factor or, if mismanaged, a negative one in an organization.

One conclusion that we might begin to draw from what we have covered so far is that different contexts, functions and roles might require different strategies for creativity. So that people who have certain kinds of representational proclivities, or aptitudes, might find themselves more suited to certain kinds of contexts. Their way of thinking might naturally fit the strategies and skills required for a certain function. This is something positive, in that these differences allow people to effectively serve different functions. The challenge then becomes unifying these different ways of thinking, through some kind of a macro level strategy, which manages these differences towards some kind of common goal or shared vision.

There are also macro level expressions of these different types of strategies, even in cultures. For example, in the past several decades there has been a big difference between American and Japanese creativity strategies in the development of technology. American technology companies tend to be oriented toward big breakthroughs and visions of new and innovative technologies. The creative style of Japanese technology companies, on the other hand, has been to incrementally refine something to make it better and better. Both are creative, but in different ways.

The belief system of NLP is that creativity is a process that has structure. The paradox of creativity is that you, in fact, need structure to generate new possibilities. The structure of the creative process is related to the T.O.T.E. Any structured activity is oriented around a goal and an ongoing feedback loop directing us toward the goal.

On a micro level we've said that the effectiveness and richness of the functioning of this feedback loop depends on certain fundamental neurolinguistic processes: how information is represented and how information is processed in the nervous system on a micro level.

On a macro level, there are different kinds of creativity that might be associated with processes related to the different elements of the T.O.T.E. structure. One type of creativity involves formulating goals. Others relate to implementing operations or evaluating results. These different types of creativity often lead to conflicts about the nature of creativity by people in different roles. For example, designers and engineers often argue about who is really doing the creative work. The engineers say, "I don't know what's so special about the designers. Why do they get paid so much? If you just tell me what to invent, I'll invent it." Their implication is that the actual creation of the physical expression of an idea involves the the real creativity. But, of course, telling someone what to invent presupposes that some form of creativity has already been used that is very important.

The American inventor Thomas Edison is often quoted as having said, "Invention is one percent inspiration and 99 percent perspiration." But the one percent inspiration has got to make it worth the 99 percent perspiration. So in this case, the one percent 'inspiration' might be associated with formulating the goal. The 'perspiration' is associated with the operations that physically realize the goal.

Changes in goals could be called "innovations"—a change in the *what*. Creativity relating to "invention" or "implementation", on the other hand, involves changes or refinement in the *how* of the operation.

"Discovery" involves changes in the filters that we apply to our experiences. In order to discover you do not necessarily need to do anything different from what you always do, but to apply a different set of filters. Discovery involves looking at something from different perspectives until you discover something new about it.

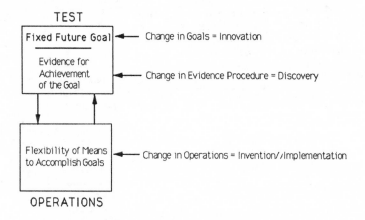

Types of Creativity and Innovation

1. **Innovation**—Coming up with a completely new idea—relates to goal setting.

2. **Discovery**—Changing your perceptual filters to experience something familiar in a different way—relates to evidence procedures.

3. **Invention/Implementation**—Operating within a set of parameters to achieve a specified goal—relates to means for accomplishing goals.

Figure 2.1   Types of Creativity

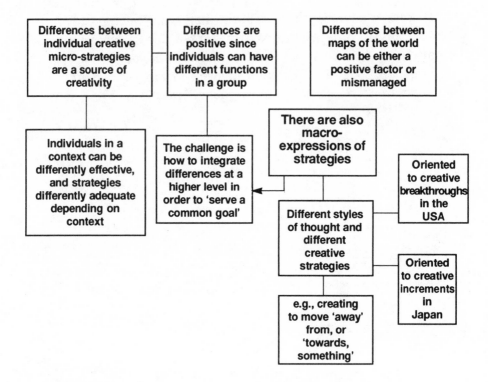

SECTION 2.4 / MAP **A**

Key Points
The difference between people's creativity strategies is in itself a source of creativity.
Different kinds of creativity strategies are effective for different contexts.
Different micro strategies are indicative of different general thinking styles.
The effective management of creativity involves the coordination of different thinking styles.
Activities
In what ways have the differences you have discovered so far between your creativity strategy and the strategies of others stimulated more creativity in you?
In which contexts is your creativity strategy most effective? Not so effective?
What general patterns of how you think can you relate to your micro strategy for creativity?

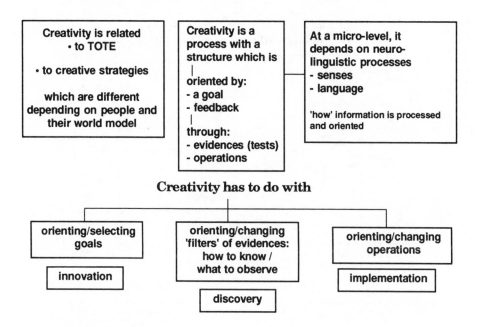

SECTION 2.4 / MAP B

Key Points
There are different general types of creativity related to the
different elements of the T.O.T.E.
Innovation has to do with changes in goals.
Discovery has to do with changes in filters and evidence
procedures.
Implementation / invention has to do with changes in
operations.

Activities
Identify specific examples of people you work with that seem
to emphasize one type of creativity.
What kinds of functions and/or roles would require which
types of creativity?

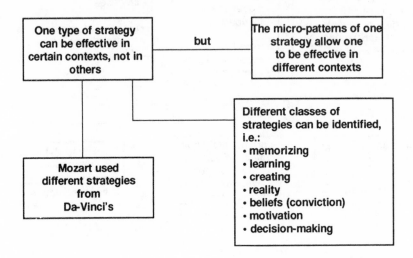

The effectiveness of a strategy will depend on the context in which it is applied

One type of strategy can be effective in certain contexts, not in others

but

The micro-patterns of one strategy allow one to be effective in different contexts

Different classes of strategies can be identified, i.e.:
• memorizing
• learning
• creating
• reality
• beliefs (conviction)
• motivation
• decision-making

Mozart used different strategies from Da-Vinci's

SECTION 2.4 / MAP C

Key Points

One type of creative strategy is often effective in certain contexts but not in others.

Creative strategies can be enhanced and adapted to be more effective in more contexts by enriching and adjusting micro level patterns and features.

Activities

What might prevent your creativity strategy from being effective in other contexts?

What micro or macro features of your strategy might you be able to adjust to make it more effective in other contexts?

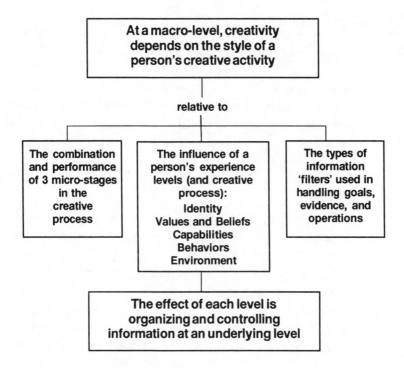

At a macro-level, creativity depends on the style of a person's creative activity

relative to

The combination and performance of 3 micro-stages in the creative process

The influence of a person's experience levels (and creative process):
Identity
Values and Beliefs
Capabilities
Behaviors
Environment

The types of information 'filters' used in handling goals, evidence, and operations

The effect of each level is organizing and controlling information at an underlying level

SECTION 2.4 / MAP D

Key Points

On a macro level, a person's creative ability relates to
(a) the management and balance of the different types of creativity;
(b) the degree of influence of different levels of creativity—
where and *when, what, how, why, who*;
(c) the types of information filters used in setting goals, defining evidences and selecting operations.

Activities

How well do you balance the different types of creativity in your own macro creative process?

Which levels seem to most influence your creative process when you are effective?

What sort of information do you pay attention to when your creative process is most effective?

Section 2.5
Increasing Creativity

Knowing about the cognitive structure of creativity opens the possibility of enhancing and managing the creative process to make it more effective. There are three key processes involved in enhancing and managing creativity.

The first one is *adding*. One way to enhance is to add. You could ask, "What could I add to what already exists, that is already working?"

The second process is *transferring*. There might be some aspect of a creativity strategy that was developed in one context that, on a process level, might have value in other contexts. Thus, you might be able to transfer elements of an effective strategy from one context to another.

The third process for increasing creativity is *coordinating*. In this case the question would be, "How might I coordinate my strategy with creative strategies of others so that they're complementary instead of conflicting?" For example, in NLP one of the classic kinds of communication problems is where you have a visually-oriented person trying to coordinate with an orally-oriented person or a feeling-oriented person. The visual person says, "I don't see what you're saying. Can you show me what you mean?" The verbal person says, "I told you a hundred times." The visual person says, "Well, I'm just not clear." The feeling-oriented person responds, "I just can't get in touch with what the problem is. I can't grasp it." In this case there would be an issue relating to the coordination of basic channels of communication and representational modalities.

In the coming Sections we will be exploring each one of these ways of enriching creativity in more detail.

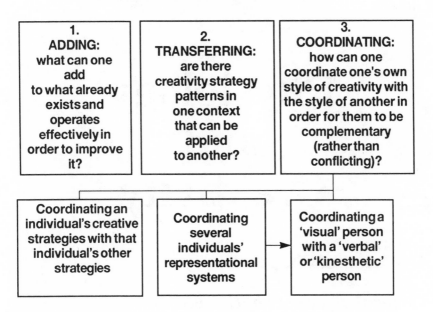

SECTION 2.5 / MAP A

Key Points
NLP identifies three basic ways of enhancing creativity.
Adding: What other processes or filters can be added to the process that is currently being used?
Transferring: Which patterns of a creative process that is effective in one context can be transferred to another context?
Coordinating: How can different kinds of creativity strategies, cognitive patterns and thinking styles be coordinated together within oneself or between oneself and others?

Activities
What could you add to your creative process to make it more effective?
Which patterns of your creative process could you transfer most easily to other contexts in which you would like to improve your creative ability?
How could you improve the coordination of the different phases of your own creative process?

Chapter 3

Physiology and Creativity

Overview of Chapter 3

General objectives of Chapter 3

1. Introduce readers to the relationship between physiology and the cognitive processes associated with creativity.
2. Define and demonstrate some basic connections between micro behavioral cues and specific cognitive patterns and processes.
3. Assist readers to develop basic observational skills.
4. Define some basic strategies for using physiology to enhance one's own personal creativity and manage the behavior of others.

Sections and goals for each Section

Section 3.1 Creativity and Personal States
Introduce the importance of physiology and internal states as influences on the cognitive processes associated with creativity.

Section 3.2 Influence of Micro Behaviors
on Creativity (The B.A.G.E.L. Model)

Present the basic micro behavioral distinctions of the B.A.G.E.L. Model and relate them to the R.O.L.E. Model and reader's reference experiences.

Section 3.3 Exploring Micro and
Macro Cues of Creativity

Lead readers through an exercise contrasting behavioral cues associated with a creative with cues associated with a state of being stuck or distracted.

Section 3.4 Managing Physiology
to Enhance Creativity

Describe the basic ways physiology may be used to enhance one's own creative state and help manage the creativity of others.

Section 3.1
Creativity and Personal States

How do we purposefully trigger or operationalize cognitive processes? Creativity is a mental process. How does someone go about getting access to mental process in a concrete way?

In this Chapter we will address some ways of beginning to operationalize the information we've been exploring about creativity. We are going to explore some tools to enhance personal creativity and to capture or focus moments of creativity. These same tools can also be used to re-access a creative state if you've been distracted or interrupted.

A good deal of what happens with creativity is unconscious. The key aspects often happen outside of conscious awareness. In addition to instruments and tools that allow us to bring unconscious thoughts into awareness, it is also useful to have some ways of encouraging and actually directing or utilizing unconscious processes as well.

A core contribution of NLP has been in defining the connection of behavioral cues and patterns to internal cognitive structures and unconscious processes. In addition to the mental strategies and programs related to creativity there are also physiological and behavioral aspects to creativity. Certainly, there are language cues that might be used to stimulate, trigger or encourage creativity. There are also purely behavioral cues.

For example, the founder of a large shipping company claimed that he used physical activities to help him solve problems. For certain problems he would have to go out and play golf to get in the frame of mind required to deal with the issues. For other problems he would go out and ride his bicycle in order to think about it effectively. He was so specific about which type of physiology to use that he would say, "You can't golf on that problem. That's one that you have to ride your bicycle on."

The point is that physiological activities stimulate and organize other neurological activities. Riding a bicycle is a macro level activity. There are also micro physiological and behavioral cues and processes that accompany cognitive processes.

Creativity is a function of a person's state as well as his or her mental processes. Neuro-Linguistic Programming acknowledges the influence of behavior, even very subtle aspects of physiology, on performance. If you observe athletes getting ready to perform, they clearly prepare their state through certain kinds of physical cues. Similarly, effective creativity is influenced by a person's state which can be adjusted through certain kinds of macro and micro level behavioral cues.

Sometimes creativity is state-dependent, too state-dependent. This is illustrated in the American movie *Butch Cassidy and the Sundance Kid*. The Sundance Kid was a gunfighter who was a great shot, but he could only shoot if he was moving. If he tried to stand still, he couldn't hit anything, he had to be jumping or falling or twisting in order to aim. This is an advantage but also a limitation. Similarly, some people can only be creative when they're under stress.

Different people have different motivations for being creative. Some people are creative when they are going towards something. Others are more creative when they are trying to avoid something. There is a saying that, "When the going gets tough, the tough get going." The implication is that a difficult situation forces strong people to draw more fully on their inner resources. The problem arises for these kinds of people when there is no difficult situation. They have to create one in order to get going. The physiological cues identified by NLP give us tools to influence our state as well as the cognitive processes associated with creativity.

NLP has developed a system of identifying certain kinds of cues. There are macro cues like body posture and gestures, and there are more subtle micro or minimal cues.

In this Chapter we will investigate the relationship between physiology and creativity. The exploration of the influence of physical state on the creative process is important to both complete and balance our micro analysis of creativity.

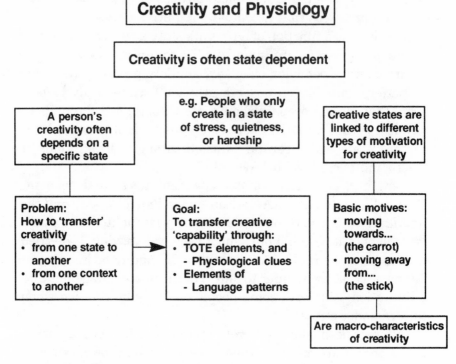

SECTION 3.1 / MAP A

Key Points

In addition to cognitive processes, the ability of an indiviudal
to be creative is influenced by that person's physiological state.
Like cognitive patterns, physiological states can be linked to
micro and macro characteristics of creativity.
Creativity can be enhanced and transferred throught physical
cues.

Activities

Think of some examples of how your state has influenced your
ability to be creative both positively and negatively.
In what ways does your state influence your general attitude
in realtion to creativity?
Review the exercises you have done during the previous
Chapters. What micro or macro level physical patterns can
you find that might be associated to your creative ability?

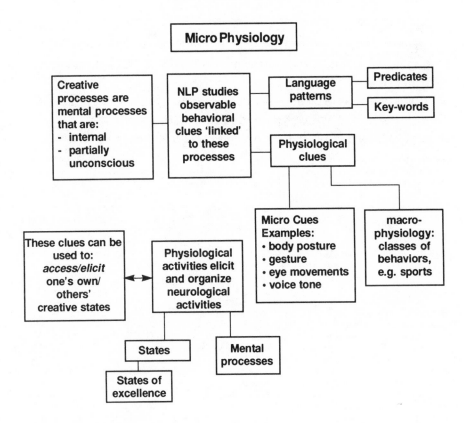

SECTION 3.1 / MAP B

Key Points

Physical activities influence neurological activities and vice versa.

NLP has identified micro behavioral cues that are associated to cognitive processes.

These micro behavioral cues can be used to (1) identify certain aspects of uncoscious mental processes and (2) mobilize or reactivate processes related to cognitive patterns or physiological states connected to creativity.

Activities

Explore changing some aspects of your micro and macro physical behavior and notice how they effect the way you think, feel or perceive.

If you were able to significantly enhance your creative ability in a context in which you would like to think more innovatively, what behaviors do you think would be most different?

Section 3.2
Influence of Micro
Behaviors on Creativity
The B.A.G.E.L. Model

This Section refers to what is known as the B.A.G.E.L. Model. The B.A.G.E.L. Model identifies types of behavioral cues associated with cognitive processes. As with the R.O.L.E. Model, the B.A.G.E.L. Model distinctions do not need to be understood or learned in detail. Feel free to incorporate only those distinctions which seem most intuitively meaningful and useful with respect to your understanding and experience of creativity.

B.A.G.E.L. stands for the first letter in a group of English words identifying key categories of behavioral patterns. (A bagel is also a kind of role ['roll']—another intended ambiguity.)

The letter "B" is related to Body posture. Body posture is an important influence on creativity. For example, most people would probably find it very difficult to be creative with their head down and their shoulders hunched forward. If you put yourself into that physiology you will find it's going to be difficult to be inspired. NLP has discovered that when people are visualizing they tend to be in an erect posture. When people are listening, they tend to lean back a bit with their arms folded or head tilted. When people are having feelings, they tend to lean forward and breathe more deeply. These cues won't necessarily tell you if the feeling is positive or negative; only that an individual is accessing feelings. So somebody might be feeling very relaxed and have the same general posture as somebody who's feeling depressed.

The letter "A" refers to types of non-verbal Accessing cues. For example, voice can be a very powerful cue. When people are visualizing, they will tend to speak in a slightly higher and faster tone of voice. When people are into feelings, their voices are often lower and slower in tempo. These types of vocal patterns can effect people's states. For example, if someone said in a low slow voice, "Now I want you to watch this complex movement very carefully," you would probably feel more like going to sleep than observing. On the other hand, if someone said, "Okay everybody, really get relaxed and comfortable!" in a very rapid and high pitched voice, you might experience a different kind of incongruity. Voice tone and tempo can serve as a cue to trigger cognitive processes. Attention to the sense of hearing is often triggered by melodic voice changes and fluctuations of tone, tempo and rhythm.

The letter "G" refers to Gestures. People often gesture to the sense organ that is most active for them in a moment. People will touch or point to their eyes when they are attempting to visualize something or when they get an insight. People gesture toward their ears when they are talking about something they heard or are trying to hear. Likewise people will touch their mouth when they are thinking verbally (like Rodin's *The Thinker*). When people touch their chest or stomach it generally indicates feeling.

The letter "E" relates to Eye movements. Eye movement patterns are one of the most interesting micro behavioral cues, and the one most associated with NLP. It has been said that "The eyes are the windows of the soul." In NLP, the eyes are considered a window to the mind. Where a person's eyes are looking can be an important cue. Eyes up tends to accompany visualization. Eyes to the left and right go along with listening. Eyes down accompany feeling. An eye position to the left is often indicative of memory, while a movement to the right indicates imagination. These cues are covered in more depth in later Sections.

The letter "L" refers to Language patterns. People often give clues or cues about their thinking process through language. For example, somebody might say, "I just *feel* that something is wrong." This statement indicates a different sensory modality than somebody who says, "I'm getting a lot of *static* about this idea," or somebody who says, "It's not very *clear* to me." Each statement indicates the cognitive involvement of a different sensory modality.

The B.A.G.E.L. Model

Classes of clues
 - physiological
 - linguistic
and typical connections of them with internal sensory representations

Body posture		

Representation	Body	Head and shoulders	Breathing
Visual	Leaning back	Up or rounded	Shallow Short
Auditory	Straight	Head cocked Shoulders back	Diaphragmatic
Kinesthetic	Leaning forward	Down	Deep Abdominal

Representation	Accesssing Cues	
Visual	Squinted eyes	Voice: High pitch, faster tempo
Auditory	Knitted brow	Voice: Fluctuating tone and fast tempo
Kinesthetic	Hands at breast/ heart	Voice: Deep, with slower tempo

SECTION 3.2 / MAP A

Key Points

The B.A.G.E.L. Model provides a set of micro behavioral
distinctions, defined by NLP, that can be used to identify and
enhance cognitive and physiological states related to creativity.
The "B" in the B.A.G.E.L. Model relates to Body posture.
Different body postures are associated with the accessing of
different sensory processes and physiological states.
The "A" in the B.A.G.E.L. Model is related to Accessing cues in
the form of breathing patterns and non-verbal vocal cues
which are indicative of cognitive patterns and internal states.

Activities

Practice shifting your body posture and notice which body postures produce which kinds of effects on your perceptions and internal state.

What body posture would you associate most with your personal process of creativity?

Experiment by shifting between different breathing patterns and trying out different tonal and tempo patterns of your voice.

How do the different patterns effect the way you think, feel or perceive?

Representation	Gestures: Indicating the sense organ one is thinking of	
Visual	Touching the eyes	Gesture above eye level
Auditory	Touching or pointing toward the ear	Touching the mouth or jaw
Kinesthetic	Touching the chest or stomach	Gestures below the neck or down

SECTION 3.2 / MAP B

Key Points

The "G" in the B.A.G.E.L. Model is related to Gestures which give clues as to the orientation of a cognitive process as well as its sensory source.

Activities

Identify some common gestures that you use when you are thinking creatively.

Touch or point to your eyes, ears, mouth, chest and stomach. What do these different gestures trigger in you or symbolize to you?

| Unconscious eye movements: indicate the use of a class of sensory representations and their sequences | | One can observe typical eye movements in order to understand people's internal thought patterns, and 'pace' and 'lead' them |

Eye Positions and the Senses

Subject's Right   *Subject's Left*

Constructed Visual

Constructed Auditory

Kinesthetic

Constructed Visual

Remembered Auditory

Auditory 'Digital' (Verbal)

SECTION 3.2 / MAP C

Key Points

The "E" in the B.A.G.E.L. Model relates to Eye movements. In NLP eye movements indicate the internal orientation of micro cognitive patterns as well as which representational system is being accessed.

Activities

Try some of the "Exercises for the Mind's Eyes" listed in Chapter 3 of *Tools for Dreamers*. Notice how they influence your perceptions and internal state.

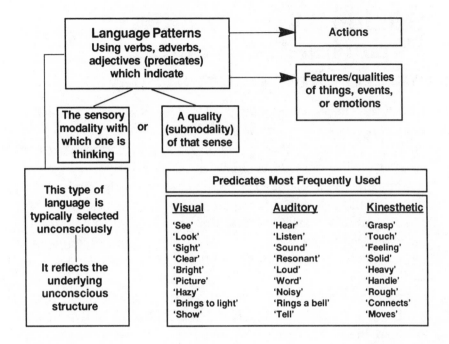

SECTION 3.2 / MAP D

Key Points

The "L" in the B.A.G.E.L. Model is related to Language patterns which indicate types and qualities of cognitive processes.

Clusters of physical clues give indications about which micro cognitive patterns are being mobilized and linked during a person's thinking process.

Activities

What kind of language patterns do you think you use most often?

What kind of language patterns do you think you use when you are being creative?

Take an experience or event that you would typcially describe in terms of one of the sensory modalities and describe it in terms of a different sense. How does it change your experience?

Section 3.3
Exploring Micro and
Macro Cues of Creativity

One of the simplest and most profound ways of finding relevant behavioral cues is through what we call "contrastive analysis" in NLP. In this case, this would involve contrasting states of creativity with states of being stuck or distracted.

For example, think of a time you were creatively inspired and put yourself back into that experience as fully as possible. Then contrast that state with a time that you wanted to be creative but were either distracted or interrupted. Notice which behavioral cues, both obvious and subtle, change between the two states.

In NLP we suggest that even very subtle behaviors can make a difference in performance. If you can find some of these cues, you can help to reaccess that state in a more conscious and purposeful way.

Of course, some cues are going to be idiosyncratic. They are unique to a certain person, like some of the cognitive aspects of a person's creativity strategy. There are other kinds of cues that are shared by many people. You might find, for example, that certain kinds of gestures might vary in their meaning from culture to culture but other kinds of physiology and physiological cues might also be shared from culture to culture like facial expressions.

In terms of our own personal process of creativity, what's important is developing as much meta-cognition or awareness of our idiosyncratic cues as we can. This can provide us with a way to tell if we are in a state conducive to creativity and offers a tool to get back into the state of creativity when we need to. The more you know about both the cognitive and physiological aspects associated with your own creativity, the more chance that you have of being able to re-access it at will.

In terms of managing the creativity of others, many people have a tendency to assume that others are creative in the same way they are and that behavioral cues mean the same thing for everybody. This can create problems, especially with people that you work with. Developing an awareness of shared and idiosyncratic cues can help avoid problems of interpretation of the behavior of others.

The goals of the exercise we are going to do next are to:

1. Discover something about your own cues for creativity.

2. Learn to observe and read other people's cues more effectively.

You might discover something that you haven't been aware of related to the physiology associated with personal states that effect your ability to think creatively. You will also begin to develop an awareness about the kind of cues that might be valuable in terms of recognizing and managing the states of other people.

If possible, this exercise is best done in a group of three. One person is in the role of an "explorer." The explorer is the person who's reliving the different experiences of creative *versus* stuck states. A second person is an observer of the explorer's physiology. The third person is a kind of a guide who will be giving the explorer directions and collaborating the observations of the observer.

Using the guidelines provided in this Section, the guide would direct the explorer to think of a time when he or she was able to be creative. The explorer is to relive an example of a personal creative state as fully as possible. Both the observer and the guide observe for significant behavioral cues using the guidelines provided in this Section. The guide would then ask the explorer to think of an experience in which he or she was stuck or distracted. Again, using the guidelines provided in this Section, observer and guide are to compare the behavioral cues for the two states.

Observer and guide should then make comments to the explorer on what they have observed. It is important for this exercise to remember the difference between observing and interpreting. Saying, "You looked comfortable," is not an observation, that's an interpretation. The skill here is to actually describe the behavior you observed, such as, "Your eyes were up and to the right;" "Your hand was on your face;" "You were leaning forward;" etc. Otherwise, you're going to get into disagreements based on personal interpretations.

To test your observational skills, the guide can then ask the explorer to pick a different situation in which he or she was either creative or stuck but not to verbally reveal which one it is. The guide and observer will try to guess whether it is an example of the creative state or not. Once they have guessed, the explorer can validate or correct the guess.

Keep in mind that the purpose of this test is not to try to hide the answer but to learn to read each other better. One of the biggest problems that creative people have in working together is they often interrupt each other's process. It is important to be able to have the awareness to tell when somebody is available to be interrupted or not, so that you're not interfering with or interrupting an important process.

You might also want to consider which kinds of macro behaviors you typically use to be creative. Do you ride a bicycle like a shipping company executive? Some people take a shower. Others get up and walk around a bit. What are some some of the different ways you stimulate creativity through macro behaviors in addition to micro behaviors?

Body Posture and Creativity

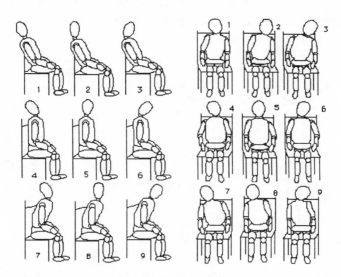

Circle the pictures that most represent your posture when you are being creative. Put a square around the pictures that most represent your posture when you are stuck or distracted (choose both a front and a side view).

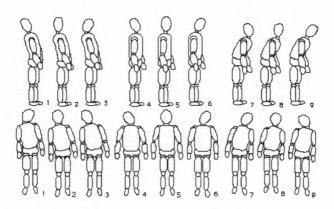

Gestures and Creativity

Circle the picture that most represents the gestures you most
often use in a creative state, or draw the gestures on the picture
provided.

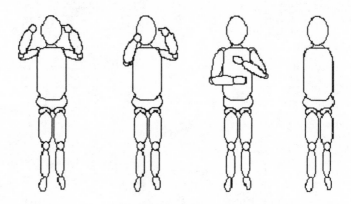

Creative State

Circle the picture that most represents the gestures you most
often use in a stuck or distracted state, or draw the gestures
on the picture provided.

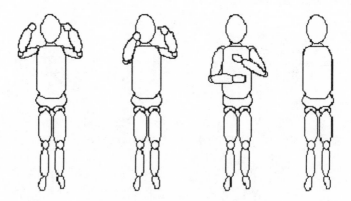

Stuck or Distracted State

Eye Position and Creativity

On the diagram below indicate which eye position(s) are most associated with your creative state. If there is more than one, indicate the sequence or order the eye movements typically follow. You may use either numbers or arrows.

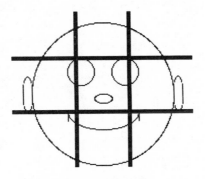

Creative State

On the diagram below indicate which eye position(s) are most associated with a stuck or distracted state. If there is more than one, indicate the sequence or order the eye movements typically follow. You may use either numbers or arrows.

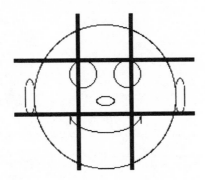

Stuck or Distracted State

Language Patterns and Creativity

In the table below, mark or write down the language patterns that seem most associated with your creative state.

Visual	Auditory	Kinesthetic
"see"	*"hear"*	*"grasp"*
"look"	*"listen"*	*"touch"*
"sight"	*"sound"*	*"feeling"*
"clear"	*"resonant"*	*"solid"*
"bright"	*"loud"*	*"heavy"*
"picture"	*"word"*	*"handle"*
"hazy"	*'noisy"*	*"rough"*
"brings to light"	*"rings a bell"*	*"connects"*
"show"	*"tell"*	*"move*
_____	_____	_____
_____	_____	_____

In the table below, mark or write down the language patterns that seem most associated with a stuck or distracted state.

Visual	Auditory	Kinesthetic
"see"	*"hear"*	*"grasp"*
"look"	*"listen"*	*"touch"*
"sight"	*"sound"*	*"feeling"*
"clear"	*"resonant"*	*"solid"*
"bright"	*"loud"*	*"heavy"*
"picture"	*"word"*	*"handle"*
"hazy"	*'noisy"*	*"rough"*
"brings to light"	*"rings a bell"*	*"connects"*
"show"	*"tell"*	*"move*
_____	_____	_____
_____	_____	_____

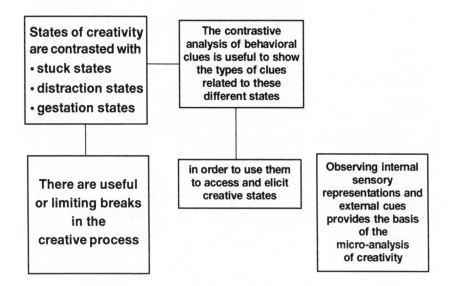

SECTION 3.3 / MAP A

Key Points

Contrasting different states is a powerful way of identifying which kinds of physical cues and cognitive patterns are most relevant.

Relevant behavioral cues and cognitive patterns for personal creativity can be discovered by contrasting states of creativity to stuck states or states of distraction.

Activities

Think of examples of situations in which you have been highly creative and contrast them with situations in which you have been stuck or distracted. What differences are you aware of in terms of cognitive and physical patterns?

What is the difference for you between being distracted and stuck?

What is the difference for you between 'gestation' and 'procrastination'?

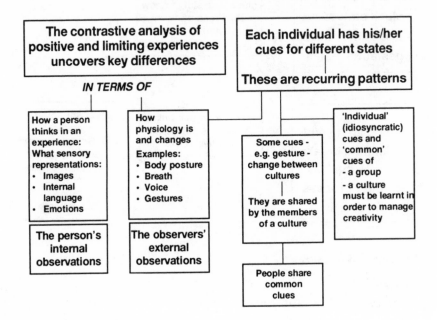

SECTION 3.3 / MAP **B**

Key Points

The combination of sensory representations and micro behavioral cues constitute the basis of micro analysis in NLP. Comparing the cues associated with creative states and stuck or distracted states highlites the key micro behavioral and cognitive differences.

There are both individual "idiosyncratic" cues and global common cues associated with creativity.

Activities

Which aspects of your own experience of creativity do you think are personal and idiosyncratic to you?

Which aspects of your own experience of creativity do you think are common with the creative processes of all people?

```
                    ┌──────────────────────────┐
                    │      Micro-Behavioral     │
                    │         Analysis          │
                    └──────────────────────────┘
```

```
┌────────────────────┐ ┌────────────────────┐
│ Step 1:            │ │ Step 2:            │
│ (A) thinks of a    │ │ (A) thinks of a    │
│     creative       │ │     limiting       │
│     experience     │ │     experience     │ ┌──────────────────┐
│ (B) observes       │ │ (B) observes       │ │ Step 3:          │ ┌────────────────────┐
│     physiological  │ │     physiological  │ │ (A/B) Contrastive│ │ Step 4:            │
│     cues           │ │     cues           │ │       analysis of│ │ (B)'guesses' a    │
│ (A) reports what   │ │ (A) reports what   │ │       the two    │ │     state based    │
│     happened       │ │     happened       │ │       experiences│ │     on person      │
│     'inside' his/  │ │     'inside' his/  │ └──────────────────┘ │     (A)'s non-     │
│     her mind       │ │     her mind       │                      │     verbal cues    │
└────────────────────┘ └────────────────────┘                      └────────────────────┘
```

```
         ┌────────────────────────────────────┐
         │ Step 5:                            │
         │        Macro-Analysis              │
         │     A and B describe their         │
         │  respective macro-behaviors        │
         │   that make them 'creative'        │
         └────────────────────────────────────┘
```

SECTION 3.3 / MAP C

Key Points

"Calibration" involves the connection between observable behavior and internal subjective experience.

Having an awareness of the micro and macro behaviors associated with your creative process is a valuable tool for increasing creativity.

Being able to observe the micro behavioral cues of others provides insight into their creative abilities and is an important tool in facilitating and managing the creativity of others.

Activities

What did you discover about your cognitive and physical patterns from the exercise?

How were your cognitive and behavioral patterns different from your partner's?

How well were you able to 'calibrate' the creative and stuck or distracted state of your partner?

Which cues were easiest for you to observe? Which were the most difficult?

In what ways could you use these observational skills in your everyday working reality?

Section 3.4
Managing Physiology
to Enhance Creativity

Physiological cues are 'anchors' to manage one's own state in order to reproduce or access a particular state at will. By having an awareness of your own physical cues you have a tool to help you enter a state of creativity regardless of the context.

Physiology also provides a powerful leverage to change peoples' states and thinking processes. It is important to have the skill to observe without interpreting when managing others. You may have noticed during the exercise that it can be difficult to appreciate the differences in the micro physiology of the two states unless you are very accurate in your observation because many behaviors are often more or less similar. This kind of accuracy involves a certain commitment of observation which in daily reality you don't always have time for. On the other hand, there might be certain contexts where it's worth the investment of precision—for example, with somebody that you have to work with intensely or in a moment where it becomes very important in terms of what's happening in your interactions. A top manager once made the comment that, "There are moments where a leader has to have the ability to change the second half of his sentence based on the feedback he received to the first half of the sentence." Not that you would always do that; but sometimes circumstances require that commitment of observational skill.

It is important to realize that in situations in which you experience stress or conflict, you might express those attitudes even though you're not aware of it. And, as you become aware of these kinds of cues, some of them become quite obvious, especially in situations where people are acting spontaneously.

You may have also observed during the exercise that, at times, people tend to imitate the behaviors of another person. This is actually a significant point in NLP. When people interact and begin to actually establish rapport with each other, oftentimes there's a kind of matching of certain behaviors that starts to happen. This process is called "pacing" in NLP. If you begin to watch people you will notice that when they are really in rapport with each other, they do a lot of mirroring of each others' behaviors. This is a basic principle of communication that can be used as a tool to help manage people more effectively.

For instance, one way to develop rapport is by listening to the kinds of language patterns a person uses and doing a kind of "active listening" by matching some of their words. So if somebody says, "I *feel* that we need to go more deeply into this," you might say, "Yes, I understand that you have a *feeling* that we need to explore this," instead of saying, "*Looks* to me like you want to *focus* on this more fully."

Another observation that you may have made is that there are some people who are physically still when they are creating and other people who are more animated and use more gestures. One question this may raise is whether or not there is a basic type of attitude that is common to creativity. Certainly there are basic types of attitudes, but these attitudes can be expressed through different organizations of thinking and behaviors. Attitudes relate more to the level of beliefs and values than to specific behaviors. Thus, there can be different specific micro behavioral and cognitive processes through which attitudes are expressed. In a very challenging context, a particular attitude might be expressed one way through one kind of behavior and one kind of thinking. In another, more relaxed context, these more micro level processes might change.

In fact, one way of insuring that you don't interfere with somebody's creative process when you're talking to them is to assume elements of their behavior, to sort of 'put yourself in their shoes.' Of course, it is easier to do this with people that know each other and already have rapport. It's almost like an acknowledgment of rapport in that case. But in situations involving people that you're not familiar with, it might be difficult; and it might even be disrespectful. One suggestion in that kind of situation would be to do it in stages such that you pace one element at a time. Perhaps voice tone first and then gestures, etc.

In summary, physiology can be used help manage the creative processes of others by:

1. Establishing rapport with people through the process of pacing and matching their general behavioral patterns;

2. Understanding or feeling peoples' world views more fully by mirroring key elements of their physiology;

3. Drawing information about peoples' internal processes from their physical cues and helping to reaccess or add to states and cognitive patterns associated with creativity.

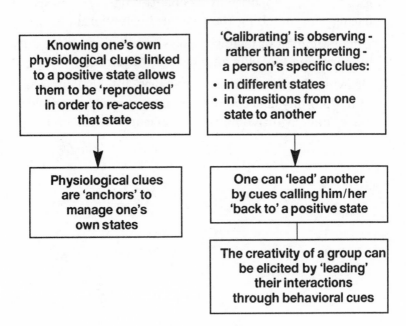

SECTION 3.4 / MAP A

Key Points

It is important to have the skill to observe without
interpreting when managing others.

Physiological cues are 'anchors' to manage one's own state in
order to reproduce or access a particular state at will.

Behavioral cues can be 'paced' or matched in order to establish
rapport with someone.

Activities

Practice reproducing or reaccessing a creative state by
reproducing the physical cues associated with it.

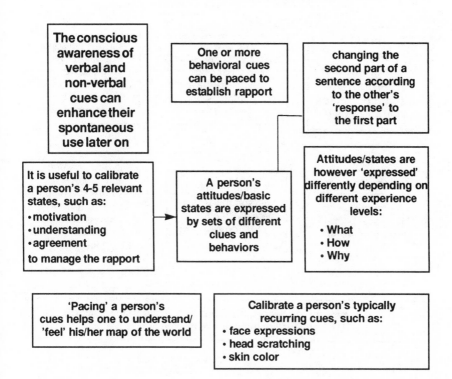

SECTION 3.4 / MAP B

Key Points

Because a person's internal states, cognitive processes and attitudes are expressed through micro and macro physical cues, the pacing or mirroring of physical cues helps to gain an understanding or feeling of another person's world view.

Activities

What are some common internal states which arise in people that influence situations you need to manage? What are some typical micro or macro behavioral cues associated with those states?

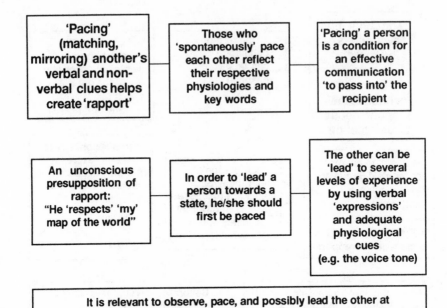

| 'Pacing' (matching, mirroring) another's verbal and non-verbal clues helps create 'rapport' | Those who 'spontaneously' pace each other reflect their respective physiologies and key words | 'Pacing' a person is a condition for an effective communication 'to pass into' the recipient |

| An unconscious presupposition of rapport: "He 'respects' 'my' map of the world" | In order to 'lead' a person towards a state, he/she should first be paced | The other can be 'lead' to several levels of experience by using verbal 'expressions' and adequate physiological cues (e.g. the voice tone) |

It is relevant to observe, pace, and possibly lead the other at important moments of an interaction

SECTION 3.4 / MAP C

Key Points
Physiology provides a powerful leverage to change peoples' states and thinking processes.

Activities
Practice pacing and matching some else's physical cues. What do learn about that person's state, attitude and thinking style? Practice pacing the micro behaviors of others in order to establish rapport with them.

What do you think you can learn most about people by observing them?

A Summary

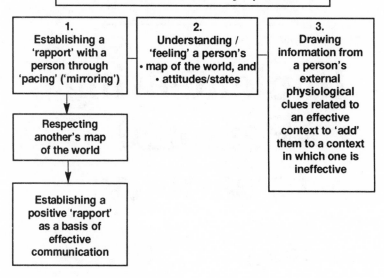

How to use the information from the external 'clues' sent out by a person?

| 1. Establishing a 'rapport' with a person through 'pacing' ('mirroring') | 2. Understanding / 'feeling' a person's • map of the world, and • attitudes/states | 3. Drawing information from a person's external physiological clues related to an effective context to 'add' them to a context in which one is ineffective |

Respecting another's map of the world

Establishing a positive 'rapport' as a basis of effective communication

SECTION 3.4 / MAP D

Key Points

Physiology can be used to help manage the creative processes of others by:

(1) establishing rapport with people through the process of pacing and matching their general behavioral patterns,

(2) understanding or feeling peoples' world views more fully by mirroring key elements of their physiology,

(3) drawing information about peoples' internal processes from their physical cues and helping to reaccess or add to states and cognitive patterns associated with creativity.

Activities

Think about how you can use calibration, pacing and leading, and the observation of physical cues to help you to manage your own creativity and the creativity of others in your working reality.

Chapter 4

Implementing Personal Creativity

Overview of Chapter 4

General objectives for Chapter 4

1. Introduce readers to the basic phases of the creative process.
2. Assist readers to apply NLP skills and distinctions to establish a personal creativity strategy by linking the basic phases of creativity together in a feedback cycle.
3. Define the set of 'well-formedness conditions' for evaluating new ideas related to the different phases of creativity.
4. Define basic principles of creativity and how they relate to the reference experiences and models explored during Part One.

Sections and goals for each Section

Section 4.1 Walt Disney and the
 Three Phases of Creativity
Describe and relate the three basic phases of creativity (Dreamer,

Realist and Critic) to the three types of creativity and the reader's reference experiences.

Section 4.2 Establishing a Personal Creative Cycle
(Disney Strategy)

Lead the readers through a demonstration and exercise applying NLP tools and skills to establish a strategy for personal creativity based on the creative process of Walt Disney.

Section 4.3 Well-Formedness Conditions for
Evaluating New Ideas

Define a set of general 'well-formedness' conditions for evaluating creative ideas and relate them to Disney's phases of creativity.

Section 4.4 Principles of Creativity

Summarize basic principles of creativity and their relation to the reader's reference experiences.

Section 4.1
Walt Disney and the
Three Phases of Creativity

Walt Disney's ability to connect his innovative creativity with successful business strategy and popular appeal allowed him to establish an empire in the field of entertainment that has survived decades after his death. Disney embodies the ability to make a successful company based on creativity. He represents the process of turning fantasies into concrete and tangible expressions. In a way, Disney's chosen medium of expression, the animated film, characterizes the fundamental process of all creative genius: The ability to take something that exists only in the imagination and forge it into a physical existence that directly influences the experience of others in a positive way.

The simple yet worldwide appeal of Disney's characters, animated films, live action features and amusement parks demonstrate a unique ability to grasp, synthesize and simplify very basic yet quite sophisticated principles. Disney was also responsible for a number of important technical and organizational innovations in the fields of animation and film-making in general.

The tools and distinctions of NLP make it possible to create explicit maps of the successful thinking strategies of people with special talents like Walt Disney. NLP explores the way people sequence and use fundamental mental abilities such as sight, hearing and feeling in order to organize and perform in the world around them. One of the major elements of Disney's unique genius was his ability to explore something from a number of different **perceptual positions**. An important insight into this key part of Disney's strategy comes from the comment made by one of his animators that, "...*there were actually three different Walts: the **dreamer**, the **realist**, and the **spoiler**. You never knew which one was coming into your meeting.*"

This is not only an insight into Disney but also into the process of creativity. Creativity as a total process involves the coordination of these three subprocesses: dreamer, realist and critic. A dreamer without a realist cannot turn ideas into tangible expressions. A critic and a dreamer without a realist just become stuck in a perpetual conflict. A dreamer and a realist might create things, but they might not be very good ideas without a critic. The critic helps to evaluate and refine the products of creativity. There is a humorous example of a boss who prided himself on his innovative thinking abilities but lacked some of the Realist and Critic perspective. The people who worked in the company used to say, "He has an idea a minute... and some of them are good."

The point is that creativity itself involves the synthesis of different processes or phases. The Dreamer is necessary for creativity in order to form new ideas and goals. The realist is necessary for creativity as a means to transform ideas into concrete expressions. The critic is necessary for creativity as a filter and as a stimulus for refinement.

Certainly, each one of these phases represents a whole thinking strategy all on its own—strategies that more often tend to conflict with each other rather than support each other. Of course, the specifics of how Disney used and coordinated his imagination (the *dreamer*), methodically translated those fantasies into a tangible form (the *realist*) and applied his critical judgment (the *critic/spoiler*) are something that we need to explore in more depth.

In this Section we will apply the NLP distinctions and tools that we have developed so far identify and 'install' a creativity strategy based on Disney's creative process.

Micro Analysis of Disney the *Dreamer*

The descriptions of Disney's physiology at the time he was thinking creatively present a classic portrait of the micro behaviors or 'accessing cues' associated with deep visual fantasizing. For example, one of his associates reports:

"When Walt was deep in thought he would lower one brow, squint his eyes, let his jaw drop, and stare fixedly at some point in space, often holding the attitude for several moments... No words could break the spell..."

This description could easily be of a hypnotic subject having a positive hallucination. The trance-like quality attributed to Disney's behavior while 'dreaming' in the description above indicates just how fully he committed his entire neurology and attention to the creative process. This same kind of 'hypnotic' quality has been observed in many other creative geniuses throughout history.

The caricature of Disney's "most typical expression" below (Thomas and Johnson, 1983) adds further confirmation to the observation cited above. The picture shows Disney looking up and to the right. According to the model of NLP this indicates that he is fantasizing, or constructing internal visual images (V^c). The fact that the picture also illustrates him as touching his left hand to his face is significant as well. In NLP this gesture is known as the 'telephone position' and accompanies internal verbalization (A_d), indicating that Disney is using at least two of his sensory representational systems simultaneously.

Figure 4.1   Walt Disney

This brings up an important key in modeling Disney's impressive creativity: the linking process is known as *synesthesia*— literally *'a synthesizing of the senses.'* A synesthesia occurs when someone overlaps two or more of the senses together, as when one feels what they see, or sees images of sounds that they hear, etc. This process of linking the senses was a common one in Disney's creative thought process and was most likely at the basis of many of his creative inspirations. In his introductory notes to the film *Fantasia*, for instance, Disney wrote:

"When I heard the music it made pictures in my head... here are the pictures."

"We take music and visualize the stories and pictures which that music suggests to our imaginations. It is like seeing a concert."

From an NLP standpoint, Disney is describing a strategy sequence in which:

1. The external auditory input (A^e) of music directly causes

2. constructed internal imagery (V^c) through the process of synesthesia.

   Disney would then

3. transform these fantasies into external images (V^e) via the process of animation. Disney reveals the involvement of another representational system when he claims:

"There are things in that music (Bach's Toccata and Fugue in D Minor) *that the general public will not understand until they see things on the screen representing that music. Then they will feel the depth in the music."*

Here, Disney is indicating that to 'see' something is to 'understand' it, again confirming that his primary representational strategy is visually oriented. He is also indicating that seeing something allows one to 'feel' its depth. This would tend to indicate that Disney also used a synesthesia between seeing and feeling—that he would immediately feel what he saw.

Disney's major representational system as a Dreamer, however, was his vision. But it was not necessarily specific pictures of things. As he maintained in response to a question about the future:

> *"What I see way off is too nebulous to describe. But it looks big and glittering."*

Micro Analysis of Disney the *Realist*

As important as his ability to dream, was Disney's expertise at forging those dreams into reality. Like Leonardo da Vinci, Disney seemed to have an intense commitment to visually understand the deepest nature of whatever he was exploring, claiming, *"Animation can explain whatever the mind of man can conceive."*

And, as with Leonardo, Disney seems to have been as committed to being a 'realist' as he was to being a 'dreamer:'

> *"Our work must have a foundation of fact in order to have sincerity."*

> *"I definitely feel that we cannot do the fantastic things based on the real, unless we first know the real."*

> *"When we consider a new project, we really study it... not just the surface idea, but everything about it."*

Clearly, Disney, like Leonardo, felt that to be truly inventive one needed to have a feedback loop between the 'dreamer' and the 'realist.' It is this combination that allows one to truly impact the world. Disney believed he was doing something more than simply making cartoons. During work on his ambitious and innovative animated feature *Fantasia* (a film that is still as popular today as it was when it was released over fifty years ago), Disney stated to the animators:

> *"This is not 'the cartoon medium.' We have worlds to conquer here."*

Disney, of course, is primarily famous for his creation and portrayal of characters and stories. The special quality and appeal of Disney animation comes from a strategy by which characters were developed, and illustrates a second important aspect of Disney's creativity strategy. Disney was able to associate *into* his characters, take on their persona and view the world from their perspective. In the language of NLP, this would be called the ability to take *'second position'* (DeLozier and Grinder,1987). *'First position'* involves seeing, hearing and feeling a particular event from one's own perspective. 'Second position' involves seeing, hearing and feeling an event from someone else's perceptual position, including their values, beliefs and emotions. For example, if you were in 'first position' imagining a character riding a bicycle, you would be seeing it from the point of view of a bystander. Being in 'second position' would involve looking from the perspective of the rider, being on the bicycle seat, looking down at your hands on the handlebars, etc.

Disney seemed to have had a unique ability to assume 'second position'.

> *"Mickey's voice was always done by Walt, and he felt the lines and the situation so completely that he could not keep from acting out the gestures and even the body attitudes as he said the dialogue."*

By associating himself into his characters' perceptual positions, Disney experienced his imaginary characters' motives and behavior more intimately. It probably also enhanced his creativity by allowing him to spontaneously discover how the character might act in a particular situation, rather than having to figure it out analytically.

The fact that Disney used the processes of synesthesia and the physical identification of himself into second position with his characters during his creative process no doubt made the products of Disney's creativity quite robust and compelling. As one of his associates commented, *"Snow White existed in Disney's head as a very real thing and... he was determined it should reach the screen just as he conceived it."* In addition to being a major part of his creativity strategy, this process of physically associating into characters also seems to have played an important role in Disney's abilities as a 'realist.' If you can act something out or role-play it you have begun to make it tangible and real.

Disney's primary strategy, however, and his major strength, as a realist was the ability to chunk and sequence his dreams into pieces of a manageable size. In fact, Disney was the innovator of the process of *story-boarding*. A story-board is like a visual table of contents—it is a set of still drawings that represent the sequence of critical events to take place in the storyline of a film. Story-boarding is an extension of the process of animation to a larger scale.

Animation takes place through a process that involves starting with the drawing of still pictures representing the critical events of a particular movement. These drawings are typically done by the chief animator. Once the critical chunks have been defined, the individual drawings connecting these pictorial "milestones" are filled in by the secondary animation team. Disney simply extended this process of chunking and sequencing to a larger level—becoming a kind of "meta" animator.

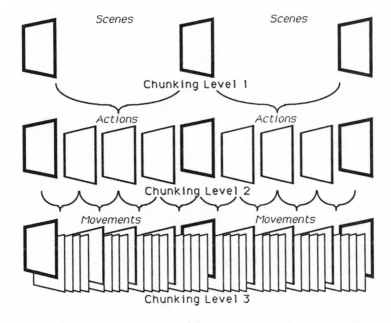

Figure 4.2   Story-Boarding/Animation Process

The "story-boarding" process, which is a very powerful way of organizing and planning, can be applied at any level of the film-making procedure. It may be applied at chunk sizes ranging from the smallest details of actually animating a particular movement of a particular character (at 32 individual pictures per second), to a particular action or event in a scene, to a scene itself, to the sequencing of the entire film.

From the point of view of strategy, the story-boarding process of chunking and sequencing the critical pieces required to achieve a particular result is not limited to film making but can be used for any kind of planning. It can be used to chart and organize a business project, a training seminar, a book, a counseling session, a computer program and so on.

Micro Analysis
of Disney the *Critic*

Because of Disney's intense commitment to his work, his critical judgment about it was also intense. In fact, Disney's critical evaluations were so formidable that his animators nicknamed the screening room in which their work was first viewed the "sweatbox:"

> *"The animators saw Walt at the story meetings where he acted out everything as it should be, and then again in the 'sweatbox,' when they showed him the scenes as they had animated it."*

While Disney the dreamer was excited and stimulated by ideas, Disney the critic had different criteria.

> *"He expected everyone to work as hard as he did, and to be as interested and excited about what we were doing. He never spared feelings, because his interest was in the product and not in who had the best idea or who made a poor suggestion or expected applause. We were all in it together and the fellow who went off on his own, developing an idea that Walt had not approved, was asking for trouble, and received it."*

The 'spoiler' critically evaluated the fruit of the realist's labor. The focus of the critic shifted from the spontaneous creativity of the dreamer and the organization and exploration of the realist to the qualities of the end result. In the 'sweatbox' new ideas and innovative explorations were not highly valued, as they were to the dreamer and the realist, but rather the "product."

There is an interesting anecdote about Disney that illustrates some key elements of the cognitive strategy of his 'critic.' Just prior to the opening of the ride, *Pirates of the Caribbean*, at Disneyland, Disney was making a last minute inspection of the scenes along the ride. He was dissatisfied with the one depicting New Orleans. He felt something important was missing that would make the ride more authentic but could not put his finger on what it was. Much effort had gone into every detail of the scene and his designers were exasperated. It seemed that the 'spoiler' was out and about. Finally, Disney gathered around him as many people as he could locate, including the maintenance and food service employees. He asked everyone to effectively go to 'second position'—that is, imagine they were one of the characters in the scene, participating in what was taking place. Disney then systematically took everyone through each of the sensory representational systems. He asked, " Does it look right?" He had spent a lot of time and money on authentic costumes and foliage and had modeled his buildings from New Orleans' French Quarter down to the wrought iron decorations. "Does it sound right?" he queried. He had installed the most modern audio technology with multiple sound tracks, each timed and positioned perfectly to provide the sounds of music, voices, boats and even animals. He then asked, "Does it feel right?" He had controlled and adjusted the temperature and humidity to exactly match that of a sultry New Orleans night. He next asked, "Does it smell right?" He had created an elaborate setup by which he could infuse and intermingle smells of spicy Cajun food with the smells of gunpowder, moss and brine. Everything checked out, but he still felt something was missing. "What is it?" he asked. Finally, a young man who had been sweeping one of the floors said, "Well Mr. Disney, I grew up in the South, and what strikes me is that on a summer night like this there ought to be lightning bugs." Disney's face lit up. "That's it!" he exclaimed. The young man was given a handsome bonus and Disney actually imported live lightning bugs, at a considerable cost, until he could work out a scheme to imitate them.

The success of
an organization   │   or a person
system
depends on their ability to fulfill
('give body to') fantasies

Walt Disney's experience:
Being able to be 3 'types of
man' -
- a dreamer
- a realist
- a critic

that is

connect thought with action

Creativity as a total process
involving the coordination and
synthesis of three sub-processes

A critic without a
realist is not
productive

A realist without a
dreamer has no
direction

A critic is necessary as a
drive to 'refine' and
control

THREE PROBLEMS

1
How to elicit
creativity?

2
How to make
creativity
concrete?

3
How to deal with
interferences with, and
obstacles to, creativity?

SECTION 4.1 / MAP A

Key Points

The success of a person or organization depends upon the
ability to manifest dreams—to move from thoughts to actions.
Creativity is a total process that involves the coordination of
three sub-processes or phases. These phases may be generally
designated as (1) Dreamer, (2) Realist and (3) Critic.
Each phase serves an important purpose and is necessary for
the others to function effectively. Each phase may be
associated to a different type of creativity:
Dreamer: innovation—reformulation of goals
Realist: implementation/invention—reformulation of
operations
Critic: discovery—reformulation of filters and evidence
procedures

Activities

Think of some examples in which you have had ideas and been successfully able to bring them into action.

Think of some ideas that have not been brought into action. What has made the difference?

Think of some good examples of situations in which you have been a strong dreamer. Do the same for times you have been a realist and critic. Get a sense for how your cognitive processes are different in the different situations.

What is it like to have a dreamer but no realist or critic?

What is it like to have a dreamer and critic but no realist?

What is it like to have a realist and critic but no dreamer?

Think of a time in which you formulated a new goal. In what ways were you innovative?

Think of a time in which you successfully implemented something. In what ways were you inventive?

Think of a time in which you evaluated something. What did you discover?

How were the processes different? In what ways can you relate them to dreamer, realist and critic?

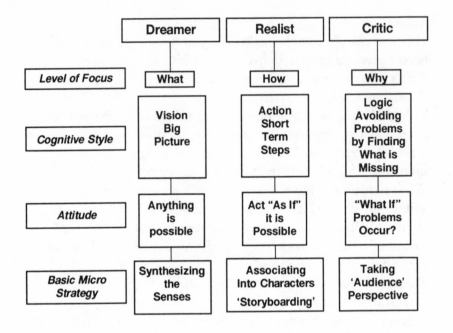

	Dreamer	Realist	Critic
Level of Focus	What	How	Why
Cognitive Style	Vision Big Picture	Action Short Term Steps	Logic Avoiding Problems by Finding What is Missing
Attitude	Anything is possible	Act "As If" it is Possible	"What If" Problems Occur?
Basic Micro Strategy	Synthesizing the Senses	Associating Into Characters 'Storyboarding'	Taking 'Audience' Perspective

SECTION 4.1 / MAP **B**

Key Points

The tools and distinctions of NLP can be used to model the specific cognitive patterns used by exceptional people such as Walt Disney in such a way that they may be transferred to others.

Disney's process of creative dreaming primarily took place through visual imagination but also involved the overlapping and synthesizing of the senses.

The Dreamer focuses on the 'big picture' with the attitude that anything is possible.

Disney's process of 'realizing' his dreams took place through Disney's physical association into the characters of the dream and through the 'storyboarding' process of chunking the dream into pieces.

The Realist acts "as if" the dream is possible and focuses on the formulation of a series of successive approximations of actions required to actually reach the dream.

Disney's process of critical evaluation involved the separating of himself from the project and taking a more distant 'second look' from the point of view of his audience or customers. The Critic seeks to avoid problems and ensure quality by logically applying different levels of criteria and checking how the product under various "what if" scenarios.

Activities

Review a successful project involving creativity and innovation in which you participated. Identify the Dreamer, Realist and Critic phases of the project

Section 4.2
Establishing a Personal
Creative Cycle
Disney Strategy
Overview of Disney's Creativity Strategy

Perhaps the most comprehensive description of how Disney's 'Dreamer,' 'Realist' and 'Critic' operated in conjunction with each other comes from Disney's statement that:

> *"The story man must **see clearly** in his own mind how every piece of business in a story will be put. He should **feel** every expression, every reaction. He should get **far enough away** from his story to take a **second look** at it... to **see** whether there is any dead phase... to **see** whether the personalities are going to be interesting and appealing to the audience. He should also try to **see** that the things that his characters are doing are of an interesting nature."*

The first part of the description focuses on the interaction between the dreamer and the realist. It is clear that the "second look" is the domain of the 'spoiler' or critic.

Certainly, the statement defines three distinct perspectives.

1. The 'Dreamer'—Vision, whole story:
"The story man must see clearly in his own mind how every piece of business in a story will be put."

2. The 'Realist'—feeling and action, first position, associated, moving:
"He should feel every expression, every reaction."

3. The 'Spoiler'—second position, distant:
"He should get far enough away from his story to take a second look at it.

   a. Whole story:

"To see whether there is any dead phase."

b. Individual character, disassociated, still:

"To see whether the personalities are going to be interesting and appealing to the audience."

c. Individual character, disassociated, moving:

"He should also try to see the things that his characters are doing are of an interesting nature."

Disney's "Second look" provides what is called a *double description* of the event. This 'double description' gives us important information that may be left out of any one perspective. Just as the differences in point of view between our two eyes gives us a double description of the world around us that allows us to perceive depth, Disney's double description of his own creations served to give them an added element of depth.

Of particular interest in NLP is that the "second look" involves a specific reference to being 'far enough away.' If it was too close it could be overly influenced by the other perceptual positions. Similarly, it could also overly influence them. If the critic is too close to the dreamer, it may inhibit those dreams.

Application Exercise:
Disney Creativity Strategy

One of the goals of NLP is to make an explicit and operational map of the inner strategies of successful people like Walt Disney. Using NLP we can synthesize our information about Disney's creative thinking strategies into a set of steps that may be used by anybody desiring to employ some of the creative processes that contributed to Disney's genius:

1. From Meta Position select three physical locations and label them:

   (1) Dreamer   **(2) Realist**   **(3) Critic**

2. Anchor the appropriate strategy to each physical location. Use Meta Position to make sure the physiological state associated with each state stays 'pure.'

   a. Think of a time you were able to creatively dream up or fantasize new ideas without any inhibitions; step into location (1) and relive that experience.

   b. Identify a time you were able to think very realistically and devise a specific plan to put an idea effectively into action; step into position (2) and relive that experience.

   c. Think of a time you were able to constructively criticize a plan—that is, to offer positive and constructive criticism as well as to find problems. Make sure the location is far enough away from the others that it doesn't interfere. Step into location (3) and relive that experience.

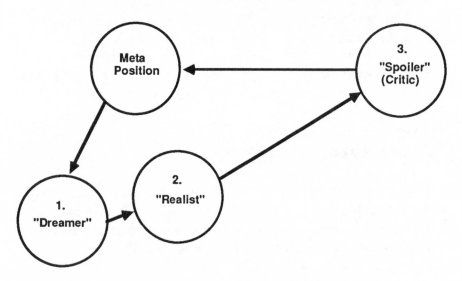

Figure 4.3 Disney Cycle

3. Pick an outcome you want to achieve and step into the dreamer location. Visualize yourself accomplishing this

goal as if you were a character in a movie. Allow yourself to think about it in a free and uninhibited manner.

4. Step into the realist location, associate into the "dream" and feel yourself in the positions of all of the relevant characters. Then, see the process as if it were a 'storyboard' (a sequence of images).

5. Step into the critic position and find out if anything is missing or needed. Then, turn the criticisms into 'how' questions for the dreamer.

   a. Remember, the critic is to criticize the plan, not the realist or the dreamer.

   b. It is often helpful to have the critic initially acknowledge which elements of the plan are satisfactory before asking questions.

6. Step back into the dreamer position to creatively come up with solutions, alternatives and additions to address the questions posed by the critic. If the critic's questions seem too harsh or it is difficult to think of the questions without accessing the critic state, go through Meta Position before returning to the dreamer location. You may even wish to rephrase the critic's questions from Meta Position.

7. After you have repeated this cycle several times, consciously think of something else that you really enjoy and are good at but continue to walk through the dreamer, realist and critic locations. This will promote lateral thinking and unconscious gestation.

8. Continue to cycle through **steps 4, 5** and **6** until your plan congruently fits each position.

Example of Installing Disney's Creative Cycle

I think that everybody already has the dreamer, realist, critic in them. Unfortunately, what usually happens is that the dreamer and the critic get into a fight. If you take a typical business meeting, you can have a dreamer, a realist and a critic in this meeting. Rather than functioning in some organized strategy, the dreamer says something, the critic argues against it, then the dreamer has a polarity reaction to the critic. The dreamer and critic go in conflicting directions until, finally, the realist says, "We're out of time." And you get this mass of chaos as opposed to saying, "How can we structure this so that these strategies support each other?"

One of the biggest problems is that the critic doesn't just criticize the dream. The critic criticizes the dreamer. It is different to say, "That idea is stupid," than to say, "You are stupid for having that idea." Part of why Disney could function so effectively is that he didn't criticize his team or himself, he criticized the plan to accomplish the dream. I think that what keeps the critic and the dreamer from being stuck in a polarity response is the realist.

It is important to structure the relationship between these stages of creativity so it creates a harmonious process. The key is to acknowledge that there will be multiple perspectives of the same thing—double or triple descriptions. You need to see a plan from the critic's point of view as well as from the realist's point of view and the dreamer's point of view.

In this Section we are going to explore the process of installation. Once you have identified an effective strategy the next question is, *"How do you install it so it functions naturally on its own?"*

Dreamer

First, we know from Disney that we have a 'vision space,' the dreamer. We know some of the micro-aspects of the dreamer. He is trying to visualize the gestalt. And, from basic NLP principles, we know that vision is going to be a particular physiology—remember the caricature that the animator drew of Walt Disney; he was looking up to the right.

Realist

Then we want to establish the realist. And as we know, the micro-strategy of the realist involves:

1. Chunking into sequences, a story-board,

    and

2. Identifying with the characters in the dream.

Critic

Lastly there is the critic. The critic is going to be distant. We are going to have to make enough distance, not only so that the critic can see the whole thing, but if the critic was right up close he might interfere.

Transcript of Demonstration

R.D.: We know some of the steps of Disney's strategy. We also want to draw out of you some of your own natural strategies. Installation is both pacing and leading. Who would like to volunteer as the demonstration subject?

(Person X comes up)

Here is the first step. Find a location for your dreamer.

Put aside any content for now. We want to set up the states without content. We want to first focus on only the process. So, here I would like you to think of the time when you were really able to dream freely, when your mind could cover an incredible amount of space, and it didn't matter if it were real. In fact, what was really great about it, was that it was a kind of escape to a fantasy world, away from the real world. It was your own world that you could make up.

Then step into this location—experience that state.

(X steps into the location, body erect but relaxed, eyes straight ahead)

And maybe to enhance it even a little more, put your head and eyes up just a little bit. So your vision can reach a little farther.

When you really feel that you have been able to get to it you can step back out.

(X smiles and hesitates before he steps back from location)

R.D.: (To audience) Sometimes people don't want to leave that space!

(To X) Somewhere about here, a little bit behind that dreamer location, I would like you to think of a time you were planning, you were making something concrete as much as you could. You are a realist when you are thinking, "What has to be done to make this happen?" "What steps will reach that goal"?

It is important that you use this micro-strategy to identify the realist because some people confuse the realist with the critic. And believe me critics are not realistic. They can be just as out there as a dreamer. "This *could* go wrong, that *could* go wrong."

When you are the realist you are future pacing yourself through the steps to the dream and creating an action plan for the steps.

(To X) Get into that state of mind and step into the realist location.

(X steps into the realist space, body tilted slightly forward, eyes pointing ahead but slightly down)

And when you have a good sense of it there you can step back out.

(To audience) Since I do computer programing, I know this state very well. You start planning this thing and getting into it. The next thing you know is that it is five o'clock in the morning!

(To X) Now, over here I want to find a location some distance from both your dreamer and your realist. Here is where we are going to put your critic. And to me the physical distance is important. Disney said, "I have to get far enough away and take a second look... so that I am looking at it as my audience would." You want to think about judging something as if it is not your own idea.

The critic is generally highly auditory and rules oriented. If you are really good at criticizing other people's ideas, then, you can use that for yourself.

You might also want to think about it from the point of view of your own worst critic. If you are working on a particular project, lets say designing a training program, I would suggest that you put yourself into the perspective of the person who is most likely to be resistant. Find your worst critic because, if that person can't find any problem with it, then it is going to be a fairly solid plan.

That is what I would like you to do; have a cold and piercing examination of something at the time when you were really critical. I don't mean just negative. And then step into the critic location.

(X steps into critic location, leaning to side, head is cocked, hand on his chin)

Alright, now step away from that space and come back here to meta position.

Now we have our three locations. By the way, you can always use additional strategies to enhance the locations. For instance, if you are in the dreamer position you can use a metaphor, an image of somebody else who was successful and model them, you can even pretend that you are Walt Disney himself.

"How would Walt Disney respond to this problem?"

"How would Leonardo da Vinci approach it?"

You might also choose to just dream about the first step of something instead of the whole thing. But I suggest you keep a broad view. Usually the problem that we have in pursuing an idea isn't because we don't think about it precisely enough, it is because you don't have a broad enough vision.

(To X) Now I want you to think of the content of that idea or problem you were working on. Is it possible to say the general area? Is it personal?

X: It is a lot about my metaphor of how things happen.

R.D.: In other words, it is a sort of inner personal issue. So what is your goal?

X: To find another process that I would fancy more which would include more tolerance.

R.D.: OK. Here is the starting point. First start here in the dreamer location and dream up a miraculous world where there would be all these things that were so seductive to you that they could draw you into them. As if you waved a magic wand and you could have a world that you would like.

(To audience) Now I see something that might be significant already. This physiology wasn't there the first time (X has his hand on his chin). I saw this physiology when you were in the critic spot.

(Laughter)

This is where NLP can be very useful. Step back out and acknowledge the critic, but let him know he will have his say later. Now step in and just be the dreamer for a moment.

(X steps in with dreamer physiology this time)

So, here there is just this space. See the whole thing, what does it look like?

You have that sort of seductive tolerance.

Maybe you can have a metaphor or even a fantasy, some kind of vision.

This is not about how to solve a problem, this is about how to have a vision. So you don't have to check if the vision is going to work, just have it.

OK, have you got something?

(X nods)

Good. Take this vision, step into the realist location and ask yourself, "OK. What would happen if that was the case?" What are the steps it would take to manifest this vision? Who are the characters that are involved? For instance, if there are parts of you, how would these parts interact with each other? Would it be like Mickey Mouse and Goofy? Maybe it would be more like

Indiana Jones? *(Some laughter in the room)* But it doesn't have to be a metaphor.

You don't have to get the whole movie. This is like the first cut. You just go, "How am I going to make this work?"

(X's hand begins to move toward his chin. Robert grabs the hand)
You will have your chance critic!

(Laughter from the participants)

At least let him get some good stuff you can tear in to.

(X returns to realist physiology)
You can get a few of the steps that might be necessary to carry out that dream....

Good. *Now* we can let the critic out. Come way over here to the critic location.

(X steps into critic location in critic's physiology)

So what do you think of those steps? What is missing? Is it going to work or is it simple still?

You don't have to find the solution, all you have to do is find what is wrong?

This is the person who does problem finding, not problem solving. The problem finding is as an important part as problem solving.

X: I don't know for instance how I can know that I have reached the first step.

R.D: OK. So, this is one question that this critic has.

X: And it can't work if I can't check anything.

R.D.: Great. These are very important issues relating to evidence procedure. Now, take those concerns and walk up over there to the dreamer location and the dreamer is going to dream up a way that you are going to know how it got to the first step. The dreamer might say, "Oh, yes, the first step, I know how!" "What a neat challenge!"

You can make a metaphor. It could be crazy. It's just a dream.

(X's physiology changes. He breaks into a broad smile)

X: Mm... *(Laughter in the crowd.)*

R.D.: Einstein used to try to visualize what it would look like to ride a light beam. This is a little crazy, isn't it? Of course, it upset our concept of the universe.

Now, take that enriched vision and step over here to the realist location.

(X moves to realist location. His physiology shifts to that of the realist state)

How are you going to implement that? Say to yourself, "Alright, I've got to do this, I've got to do that!" "What are the steps?" "How am I going to know it?" "Maybe come up with some clever way of figuring that out!"

Put yourself into it. You are at the first step and you know that you are at the first step. What pieces are there?

Do you have something?

X: Ah-hum...

R.D.: Alright. Now over to the critic again.

(X moves into critic location and physiology)

Well, what do you think?

(X hesitates, then starts to smile.)

(Bursts of laughter from audience)

It is getting hard to be staying so critical, eh?

Let us go to the next part for a moment. Without thinking about anything in particular consciously, I want you to walk to the dreamer location, pause for a moment, then walk to the realist location, and then return again to the critic spot. And do that three times without anything in particular in mind.

X: Am I supposed to see the vision?

R.D.: You can or you may let your mind wander to something else for a moment.

(X. walks through the locations according to R.D.'s instructions)

(To audience) Have you ever seen people pacing up and down when they are trying to solve a problem? We do that kind of thing all the time.

(X finishes the three loops)

R.D.: (To X) Now, come to meta-position and consciously think for a moment about the vision. Right now. Has it changed at all since you last checked in on it?

X: Yes, it did. Each step has a complementary function. Other options came out. It has become more congruent and stronger.

(To Audience) In other words, all he was supposedly doing was walking, but the strategy continued to run because it was anchored to the locations.

He is starting to put the pieces together and more in balance. The states are anchored to physical spaces and they don't care about what your conscious mind is thinking at that moment. These states are going to have an effect on what is happening even if you were thinking of what you had for dinner last night.

Again, you keep taking three perspectives. You will align them to a common vision. When you are aligning all the functions literally and physically in the same direction, you get yourself out of the way. When I step out of the realist location, all that is left there to criticize is the plan, not me. I am not in that plan. There is no person there, it is the steps of the plan.

Then you have set up an aligned strategy that is going to create a positively reinforcing feedback loop. It uses all of your neurology in coordination.

These physiological states are literally accessing a few billion brain cells at a time. You could visualize the activity as lights which go through the body, so that you hear this brilliant, bright light coming down and it is very focused. You kind of watch the nervous system, twinkling as all different parts light up and you get that system working on something. As Mozart said, "It eventually becomes a pleasant lively dream that magically produces something concrete."

(To X) May Walt Disney be with you!

(To audience) By the way, notice the importance of setting the first couple of loops through the locations. If I get the critic physiology in the dreamer's location, I contaminate this space. This is probably going to happen 90% of the time when people try to solve a problem. They start off immediately by contaminating the space—whether it is a single person or a group of people.

If you can sequence it and chunk it then you are going to have something that works smoothly. So your first couple of loops are really important. After that it becomes desirable for the physiology to start to integrate together because eventually you might find that all of those three functions form one larger macro-strategy that happens at the same time—remember the caricature of Disney. But it is important to the installation to start very cleanly.

I always find it amazing that people don't have any places for creativity in their homes, or in their companies. I find sometimes when I am working on a problem, if I really want to dream it, it is as if my dreamer lives out in the woods near my house. So I go out into this forest full of gnomes and fairies.

Then my office is sort of my realist place. I get there and I work away on my computers. Then I have to leave it and go down to my kitchen or living room and I've got to think about that idea that I had from the critic position. Is it really going to work?

Sometimes the more you can initially separate these when you first start solving the problem and get the circuit going, the more trouble and confusion it saves you later on.

Are there any questions?

Q 1: Is it important that it begins with vision in the dreamer and auditory in the critic?

R.D.: This has to do with the degree to which it is your own *versus* Disney's strategy that you want to install. My answer is:

Having a choice is always better than not having it. If you start up with something that's auditory you might want to add vision just to see how it would enhance the process. So I would keep the choice at least.

Q 2: Can we use it for something we want to achieve in the future?

R.D.: Yes. What you work on doesn't have to be a problem you are trying to solve. I suggest you all just start with some vision you have. If the circuit works you may surprise yourself.

After the Exercise

Q 1: It was very powerful. Can you do it with more than one person at a time?

R.D.: You can take a whole group through it. You can cover a much broader space that way.

I use this process in my own computer company. We have actually different rooms where we can go to think different ways: one to brainstorm, another to plan and another to evaluate. When we brainstorm we most often sit in a circle. But when we start planning we all sit next to each other and look at the plan on a board. And when we are evaluating we sit around a table with the plan in the center and ask: "Is this really going to work?" So you can also set up the environment to support a multi-person circuit as well.

Q 2: Where is the decision point then?

R.D.: It is at the critical evaluation.

Q 3: Could we consider that at the evaluation time there is one person in charge of the decision process?

R.D.: In some companies where you have a hierarchical structure, yes. But what they call "buy in" management is based on group consensus rather than on hierarchy. It all depends on the kind of evidence procedure you are using.

Q 4: I was surprised that it changed my whole relationship with time. I have a project due three years from now that I am going to start tomorrow night, and after this, there is no limit in time because now I dreamed that I could always dream and realize what I dream!

R.D.: Sometimes people start with a dream that literally is very distant in their minds, maybe in terms of years from now. And after going through the Disney strategy it is right here and not in the distance anymore.

Q 5: In the critic state, I was often quite negative and sad; but now, knowing that I can go afterwards to the dream state, I feel much better.

R.D: The whole dynamic of the circuit shifts if the critic knows that I will go to him for advice, and that he can seek help from the other functions as well. Then it is not like being so lost or alone.

Sometimes the magic that happens here is that it really starts to become constructive criticism. The critic begins to give positive feedback as opposed to negative. And when your own worst critic says, "Go for it!" you know nothing can stop you.

Q 6: I noticed that the critic part actually gave a feeling of security.

Q 7: We felt after finishing the three part round that we needed to bring in a fourth part—which was the "will" part that the subject felt like putting in front of the dreamer's part.

R.D.: At some stage you want to take the dream and connect it to your mission. I think this is what you are talking about with the "will." So once I attached the vision, the dream, to the mission then it becomes a commitment. This is a nice next step.

I want to say one thing about potential problems with this process.

The thing that we have to realize with any strategy is that the chain is no stronger than the weakest link. In other words, if some part of the strategy is weak it can throw the whole thing out of balance. Sometimes a person says, "I can't visualize, I can't do the dreamer's step." And clearly the ability to be creative is going to be relative to your ability to develop and utilize your senses. Some people are much more comfortable as the critic, they spend 90% of their lives in that position. This is where developing flexibility with micro-strategies is so crucial.

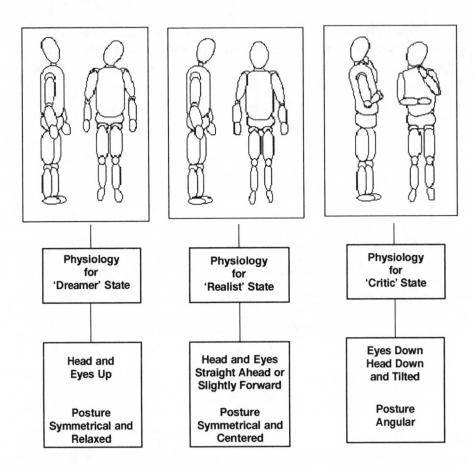

SECTION 4.2 / MAP A

Key Points
There are micro and macro level behavioral cues that
accompany the Dreamer, Realist and Critic states.
Activities
Think of what it is like when you are 'dreaming.' What kinds
of cognitive patterns and behavioral cues do you think are the
most significant for your 'dreaming' process?
Think of what it is like when you are 'realizing' an idea or
'dream.' What kinds of cognitive patterns and behavioral cues
do you think are the most significant for your 'realizing'
process?

Think of what it is like when you are thinking 'critically.'
What kinds of cognitive patterns and behavioral cues do you
think are the most significant for your 'critical' thinking
process?

Which of the three types of thinking styles—Dreamer, Realist
or Critic—seems to be the most natural for you?

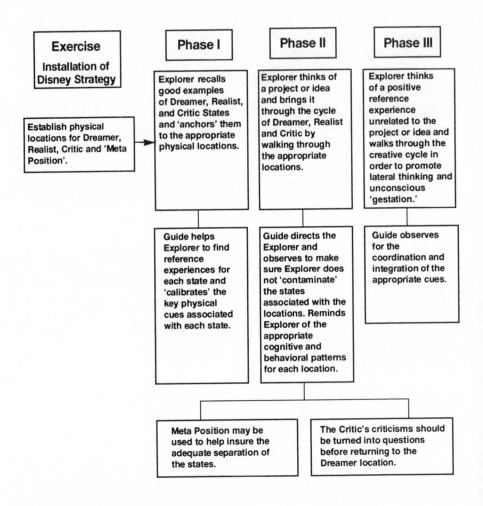

SECTION 4.2 / MAP **B**

Key Points

The locational sorting of the different processes helps to organize and coordinate them and avoid interferences or 'contamination' between the states.

Turning a criticism into a question helps to avoid the 'negative' effects of the critic and stimulate the Dreamer.

Once a creative cycle is robustly 'installed' it can be enriched by processes which stimulate lateral thinking and unconscious gestation.

Activities

What is the relationship between your Dreamer and Realist?
Your Realist and Critic? Your Critic and Dreamer?

During the exercise, notice how easy or difficult it is for you to
keep the three states sorted out.

What cognitive and behavioral cues can you use to know if the
states are getting mixed or contaminated?

How does the sorting and coordinating of the different states
change the role of your internal Critic?

Think of some ways in which you could use the process of
'storyboarding' in your professional reality.

Think of some ways in which you could use the process of
taking the audience perspective in your professional reality.

Think of how you could spatially sort and 'anchor' your own
Dreamer, Realist and Critic in your working environment.

Section 4.3
Well-Formedness Conditions for Evalutating New Ideas

(From *Tools for Dreamers*, pp. 60-62)

The criteria used for the test phase of each of the stages of creativity roughly correspond to what are called *Well-Formedness Conditions* in NLP. These conditions are used to identify the minimum set of requirements an idea or outcome has to satisfy in order to be "well-formed." The standard set of NLP well-formedness conditions is listed below.

Dreamer

1. Outcome is stated in positive terms. That is, it states, 'what you do want' as opposed to 'what you don't want.'

   Questions: *What do you want? What is possible? What is the payoff?*

Realist

2. Can be initiated and maintained by the person or group desiring it.

   Question: *What specifically will **you** do to achieve this goal?*

3. Testable in sensory experience.

   Questions: *How, specifically, will you know when you achieve the goal? What are the performance criteria? How will they be tested?*

Critic

4. Preserves the positive by-products of the current behavior or activity.

   Questions: *What positive things, in any way, do you get out of your present way of doing things? How will you maintain those things in your new goal?*

5. Is appropriately contextualized and ecologically sound.

Questions: *Under what conditions would you not want to implement this new goal? Who and what else could it effect?*

I have organized them into the various phases of creativity to which they are relevant. What makes something well-formed is different at different stages. The criteria of the dreamer T.O.T.E. are primarily organized around possibility and desirability. The criteria of the realist T.O.T.E. are organized around feasibility and workability. The criteria of the critic T.O.T.E. are organized around acceptability and 'fit' in relation to the larger system.

The following Exercise demonstrates how well-formedness conditions may be combined with logical levels and elements of the Disney strategy to form a powerful creativity 'engine' that may be either used by oneself or with a 'coach.'

Story Boarding Exercise

Pick a project or idea that you would like to "story-board."

1. For each phase of the creative cycle (Dreamer, Realist and Critic), ask the questions relevant for that phase (listed below). A coach may be helpful to prompt the explorer and help keep track of his or her answers.

2. While answering the questions, the explorer is to assume and maintain the appropriate physiology and thinking style defined in the guidelines below.

Note that it is the combination of the appropriate verbal question *and* physiological state that produces the appropriate answer. Asking a dreamer question while you are in a critic state of physiology will produce a 'contaminated' answer. If the question is not processed through the appropriate 'circuitry' the answer will begin to become confused. This combining and congruence between language, cognitive process and physical states is the essence of Neuro-Linguistic Programming.

3. Coach and explorer should both ensure that the explorer maintains the appropriate state and does not 'contaminate' it.

When you have finished going through the complete Exercise:

4. Keep cycling through the phases to make successive approximations of the plan.

"WANT TO" PHASE—Dreamer

Objectives:

State the Specific Goal in Positive Terms; Establish the Payoffs of the Idea.

*"**What** do you want to do? (As opposed to what you want to <u>stop</u> doing, <u>avoid</u> or <u>quit</u>.)"*

*"**Why** do you want to do it?" "**What** is the purpose?"*

*"**What** are the payoffs?" "**How** will you know that you have them?" "**When** can you expect to get them?"*

*"**Where** do you want the idea to get you in the future?"*

*"**Who** do you want to be or be like in relationship to the idea?"*

Level of Focus: What.
Cognitive Style: Vision—Define the 'big picture.'
Attitude: Anything is possible.
Basic Micro Strategy: Synthesizing and combining the senses.
Physiology: Head and eyes up. Posture symmetrical and relaxed.

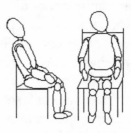

Figure 4.4   Dreamer State Physiology

"HOW TO" PHASE—Realist

Objectives:

Establish Time Frames and Milestones for Progress; Make Sure It Can Be Initiated and Maintained by the Appropriate Person or Group and That Progress is Testable Through Sensory Experience.

*"**How** specifically will the idea be implemented? **How** will you know if the goal is achieved? **How** will the performance criteria be tested?"*

*"**Who** will do it?"* (Assign responsibility and secure commitment from the people who will be carrying out the plan.)

*"**When** will each phase be implemented?" "**When** will the overall goal be completed?"*

*"**Where** will each phase be carried out?"*

*"**Why*** is each step necessary?"

Level of Focus: How.

Cognitive Style: Action—Define the short term steps.

Attitude: Act 'as if' the dream is achievable.

Basic Micro Strategy: Associating into characters and 'storyboarding.'

Physiology: Head and eyes straight ahead or slightly forward. Posture symmetrical and slightly forward.

Figure 4.5   Realist State Physiology

"CHANCE TO" PHASE—Critic
Objectives:
Make Sure It Is Ecologically Sound and Preserves Any Positive By-Products of the Current Way(s) Of Achieving the Goal.

"*Why might someone object to this new idea?*"

"*Who will this new idea effect and who will make or break the effectiveness of the idea and what are their needs and payoffs?*"

"*When and where would you not want to implement this new idea?*"

"*What positive things do you get out of our current way(s) of doing things?*"

"*How can you keep those things when you implement the new idea?*"

Level of Focus: Why.

Cognitive Style: Logic—Avoid problems by finding what is missing.

Attitude: Consider 'what if' problems occur.

Basic Micro Strategy: Taking 'audience' perspective.

Physiology: Eyes down. Head down and tilted. Posture angular.

Figure 4.6   Critic State Physiology

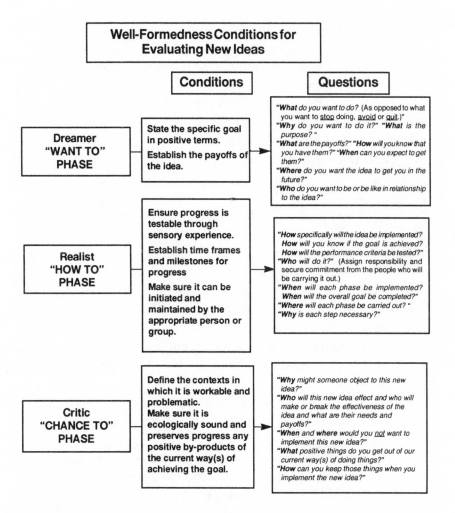

Well-Formedness Conditions for Evaluating New Ideas

Conditions   **Questions**

Dreamer "WANT TO" PHASE

State the specific goal in positive terms.

Establish the payoffs of the idea.

*"**What** do you want to do?* (As opposed to what you want to *stop* doing, <u>avoid</u> or <u>quit</u>.)"
*"**Why** do you want to do it?" "**What** is the purpose? "*
*"**What** are the payoffs?" "**How** will you know that you have them?" "**When** can you expect to get them?"*
*"**Where** do you want the idea to get you in the future?"*
*"**Who** do you want to be or be like in relationship to the idea?"*

Realist "HOW TO" PHASE

Ensure progress is testable through sensory experience.

Establish time frames and milestones for progress

Make sure it can be initiated and maintained by the appropriate person or group.

*"**How** specifically will the idea be implemented? How will you know if the goal is achieved? How will the performance criteria be tested?"*
*"**Who** will do it?" (Assign responsibility and secure commitment from the people who will be carrying it out.)*
*"**When** will each phase be implemented? When will the overall goal be completed?"*
*"**Where** will each phase be carried out? "*
*"**Why** is each step necessary?"*

Critic "CHANCE TO" PHASE

Define the contexts in which it is workable and problematic.
Make sure it is ecologically sound and preserves progress any positive by-products of the current way(s) of achieving the goal.

*"**Why** might someone object to this new idea?"*
*"**Who** will this new idea effect and who will make or break the effectiveness of the idea and what are their needs and payoffs?"*
*"**When** and **where** would you <u>not</u> want to implement this new idea?"*
*"**What** positive things do you get out of our current way(s) of doing things?"*
*"**How** can you keep those things when you implement the new idea?"*

Section 4.3 / map A

Key Points

NLP has identified certain 'well-formedness' conditions with which to evaluate new ideas.

According to NLP, when establishing new ideas it is important to:

(1) State ideas in positive terms. That is, to define what is desired as opposed to what is to be avoided.

(2) Specify the evidence for the expression of the idea in sensory based terms. That is, evidences should be defined in terms of factors that are tangible and directly perceivable by one of the five senses.

(3) Ensure that the operations required to achieve the ideas should be within the capabilities and motives of those responsible for manifesting the idea.

(4) Define the contexts in which the idea is valuable and useful, and also those contexts in which it could be problematic.

(5) Assess the impact and 'fit' of the idea within the ecology of the current system.

Different well-formedness conditions are more associated with different phases in the creative cycle.

Well-formedness conditions may be assessed on different levels (i.e., *who, why, how, what, where, when*).

Activities

Think of an idea or project on which you are currently working. Check it against each of the well-formedness conditions.

Think of some reference experiences in which ideas were not stated in terms of what was actually desired. What kinds of problems did it create?

Think of some reference experiences in which the evidence for the expression of an idea was not specified in some tangible, mutually perceivable form. What kinds of problems did it create?

Think of some reference experiences in which the people responsible for manifesting an idea did not have the capabilities or motivation to achieve it. What kinds of problems did it create?

Think of some reference experiences in which the contexts in which an idea was valuable were not distinguished from those in which it might be problematic. What kinds of problems did it create?

Think of some reference experiences in which ideas did not fit into the current system. What kinds of problems did it create?

Section 4.4
SUMMARY: Principles of Creativity

A core presupposition of NLP is that the map is not the territory. The objective for Part One has been to explore some of the principles and patterns related to how we make these maps; in particular in relationship to creativity. According to Neuro-Linguistic Programming these maps are essentially formed from our inner representations and from language. By identifying key patterns relating to internal representations, language and physiology we have developed a set of tools with which to define and influence the creative process on a personal level.

As situations change we need to adjust how we deal with them in order to respond effectively. Processes that produce a result creative in one situation, may not produce a creative result in a different context. Elements of the process need to be added or adapted. So, a certain minimum amount of flexibility is needed to manage change within the systems of which we are a member.

In Chapter 1 we explored some of the micro elements of personal creativity. You created something tangible with whatever materials you could find. The purpose of this was to bring out the fact that there was a structure to creativity and to the thinking process. We concluded that thinking in general, and creativity in particular, involved setting goals. If there's no direction or outcome for one's actions it's difficult to be creative. If you only know what you don't want, and you don't know what you do want, it is difficult to be creative. Creativity involves proactivity.

We further concluded that thinking and creativity also involve establishing evidences for the achievement of goals. Sometimes we're only limited in creativity because our perceptual filters are screening out possible answers and signs of success. Creativity takes place through a feedback loop between goals, ideas, actions and perceptions.

The purpose of the T.O.T.E. questionnaire in Chapter 2 was to find a reference experience involving a situation in which you were creative or had responded innovatively, and to organize that experience in terms of the goals, evidence procedures, operations and response to problems that characterized the effective process. We then made a cognitive micro analysis of the T.O.T.E. elements to explore some of the specific aspects of the inner representations associated with that creative reference experience—processes such as visualizing, verbalizing, feeling, etc. The different channels by which we make our inner maps can either open up spaces or constrain our perceptions of alternatives.

In Chapter 3 we went on to explore some of the micro level physiological aspects of creativity and the influence of creative states. Creative processes themselves might not be activated unless some kind of a creative state is mobilized. We examined some of the subtle but influential physical cues that might promote or inhibit creativity such as eye position, body posture and language patterns. The purpose of the exercise was to demonstrate that there are certain patterns of mental and physical processes that each person has associated with his or her own creative processes that are different from others.

In this Chapter we addressed the fact that there are different stages in the creative cycle that involve different types of strategies. A key skill in managing creativity involves coordinating different types of creativity. Particular creative processes may be effective for certain situations and not for others.

One goal of this book is to provide ways in which we can enhance and increase the creative process of ourselves and others. By interacting with other people who have different strategies, you can find elements that enrich your own creativity. NLP provides tools and distinctions that allow us to identify specific elements of peoples' creative thinking processes. By modeling exceptional individuals, such as Walt Disney, we are able to identify and transfer key cognitive and behavioral patterns that can enrich the creative processes of others.

In addition to the identification of micro level patterns that characterize and enhance individual creativity, NLP has identified general types, phases and well-formedness conditions for creativity that are significant for understanding and managing the global process of creativity.

As a summary of Part One, we can define three general principles of creativity:

1. **Outcome Frame**

   Maintain an orientation toward the future goal that you want to achieve rather than away from the problem to be avoided. Even if you are trying to get around a problem, it is important to do it within the broader vision and context of the goal state.

2. **Feedback *versus* Failure Frame**

   If an idea doesn't work, the way in which it failed will give you feedback as to what to do to succeed (learn from your mistakes). Sometimes you even need to do something which you know will not work in order to get the feedback necessary to take the next step.

3. **Flexibility Frame**

   a. Always have at least two other choices to fall back on before you start implementing a particular operation.

   b. "If what you are doing isn't working, do something different—do anything different." Almost anything is a better choice than what you are doing if you've already demonstrated that it won't work.

The first general principle is that there has to be an outcome for creative thinking to occur. Even if you're avoiding something, you need to avoid it with reference to some kind of goal space. In other words even if you try to get around a problem, it needs to be done in a wider context of a desired state. Thus, creativity is always proactive in that sense.

The second general principle is that creativity takes place within a feedback *versus* a failure frame. Creativity is an ongoing process. Depending upon the nature of the outcome, it may take months or even years to accomplish a particular goal. It is important to distinguish between the process and products of creativity. Creativity isn't just related to immediate results, it is a function of an ongoing feedback loop. Sometimes you even need to do something that you know probably won't work in order to get the feedback necessary to progress.

A good illustration of this is the example of an inventor who had developed a very complex three dimensional imaging device. It had taken him years to complete it and he made many versions that had not worked. During an interview he was asked, "How did you manage to deal with all of the failures you encountered along the way?" Initially the inventor was kind of confused by the question. Finally he said, "I guess I didn't consider them failures. I just considered them to be a solution to a problem other than the one I was working on at the time." And, in fact, something that hadn't worked at one stage in the development of the device, was often a legitimate solution at another stage.

Another example is that of the man who invented xerography, Chester Carlson. In an interview he said that at several points he had to make a machine that he knew would not work in order to get the feedback he needed to know what to do next. You might say he had to make a 'grander failure' than the earlier version.

The third general principle is that of flexibility. It's often useful to have choices already planned before you start something, so you're not having to reflexively respond to problems. Effective creativity involves having a range of possibilities before you begin. The flexibility principle is also related to the *Law of Requisite Variety*. It is important to have a degree of variability proportional to the possible change or uncertainty in the system.

Stated simply, "If what you're doing isn't working, do something different." Do anything different, because if you have already demonstrated that what you're doing is not working, there is no creative purpose to continue proving it to yourself. Almost anything is a better choice than what you're doing.

There's a humorous story that illustrates all three principles. It is about a young American fellow who gets a job working in a store. He's very motivated and he really wants to do his best for his organization and the people he's trying to serve. One day he's over working with the fruits and the vegetables and an elderly man comes in and wants to buy a half a head of lettuce. The young fellow says, "I'm sorry sir, but the store doesn't allow us to sell it in half a head. We can only sell it whole." The old man gets very irate and starts yelling, "I don't care. I want a half a head of lettuce!"

The lad doesn't want to disturb the other shoppers so he says, "Well, let me go check with my boss." So he goes to the back of the store where is boss is working and says, "Some old jerk out here wants a half a head of lettuce..." Suddenly, he notices that the old man has followed him back and just heard every word that he said. But, instead of panicking, the young fellow gestures elegantly and continues, "...and this fine gentleman would like the other half." The crisis is averted. Afterwards, the lad's boss is talking to him and he says, "That was really good. You're very clever. I think you have a creative way of handling problems. I'm opening up a new store in Canada and I'd like you to be the manager." But the young fellow is less than enthusiastic and says, "Oh, I don't know." And the boss says, "What's the problem?" The young fellow finally responds, "I hear all that's in Canada is whores and hockey players." All of a sudden the boss becomes very angry and says, "My wife is from Canada, I'll have you know." After a brief pause the young fellow says, "Oh, really? What team did she play for?" Sometimes even something that seems to be a disaster can be turned around with enough creativity.

To recap:

The map is not the territory: explore by what information/ elements people 'make'/construct their maps	Maps are made of sensory and language representations	'How to make maps' in the case of creativity must be explored

As situations change, we need to align our maps with creative processes	Processes that provide results in one context fail to do so in others	Accordingly, there is a need to adjust thought patterns	Any thought pattern - even a creative one - has a structure: one has to have a goal, evidence (assessments as to the outcomes), and operations

Unless there are goals, we are stuck, and there is no creativity	Information about a creative process must be organized according to the TOTE structure, and the senses/sensory channels being used in accessing/operating this process must be found

SECTION 4.4 / MAP A

Key Points

Creativity relates to how we construct our maps of the world.
Because situations change, we must change our maps.
Maps that are effective in one context may be ineffective in another.
Our maps have a structure based on cognitive, linguistic and physiological patterns.
Our thinking processes are oriented a basic goal oriented feedback loop called a T.O.T.E.

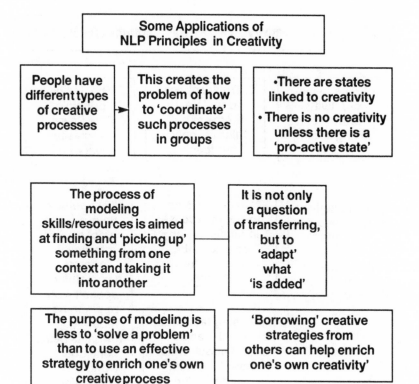

SECTION 4.4 / MAP **B**

Key Points

People are creative in different ways.

There are different types of creativity related to different stages of the creative process.

A key issue in creativity is how to coordinate different creative processes in individuals and groups.

NLP provides tools and skills by which we can model and transfer the creative thinking processes of other individuals.

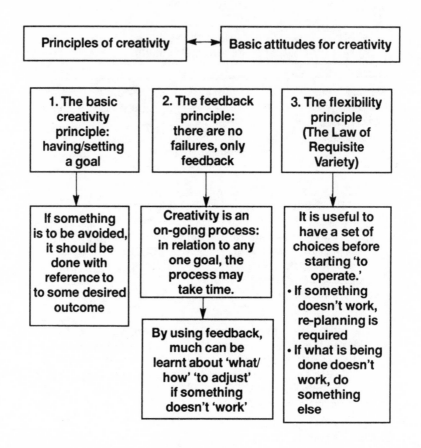

SECTION 4.4 / MAP C

Key Points

On a macro level there are some basic principles and attitudes related to the creative process.

While the stimulus for creativity may either be to achieve or to avoid, the creative process always occurs in seeking a positive outcome or a solution space.

Within the frame of creativity there are no failures. Rather, lack of success is perceived as either (a) a solution to different problem, or (b) feedback providing information about what needs to be adjusted or how it needs to be adjusted.

Creativity is deeply related to choices. Having several options before starting something is important. Having a choice is always better than not having one.

If what you are doing is not working, then do something different.

Activities

Think of a time you creatively avoided something. In what way did you need to have some sort of outcome or direction in mind in order to be creative?

Think of something that you creatively accomplished but did not succeed at initially. How did you respond to the lack of success? In what ways did the initial lack of success provide feedback for your eventual success.

Think of a task that you undertook in which you had several options about how to achieve it. Compare that with one in which you had only one option to achieve it. How did the difference effect your ability to respond creatively?

Think of something you approached unsuccessfully in one way repeatedly but then decided to approach differently and were successful. What did it feel like to try something new? How did you come to realize that you needed to try something new?

Think of something you are approaching inflexibly in your present professional context. What would happen if you were to try something different?

part two

Co-Creativity

Creativity and Problem Solving

Developing Multiple Perspectives

Promoting Lateral Thinking

Overview of Part Two

Co-Creativity

The purpose of Part Two is to:
1. Connect creative thinking abilities to problem solving contexts.

2. Enrich creative problem solving abilities through the exploration of several interactive tools and strategies for innovative thinking.

Part Two is made up three chapters:

Chapter 5   Creativity and Problem Solving
Defines the relationship of creativity to problem solving and provides a method to improve creative problem solving ability by transferring the process elements of an effective problem solving strategy from one context to another.

Chapter 6   Developing Multiple Perspectives
Assists readers to develop visual mapping strategies as a tool for interactive problem solving and for uncovering unconscious assumptions.

Chapter 7   Promoting Lateral Thinking
Introduces lateral thinking strategies, such as analogies, metaphors and symbols, and explores their influence on creative problem solving.

Overview of Part Two

Co-Creativity

The material to be covered in Part Two is based on a set of assumptions about creativity and problem solving.

Assumptions

Problems are primarily created by our perceptions of a situation and the choices we perceive possible or available in that situation.

Our perceptions of a problem are primarily a function of our cognitive map of the problem space. These internal maps guide or limit us more so than the external 'reality' of the problem.

There is a difference between the form and content of our thinking strategies.

Our modes of thinking create problems that the same mode of thinking will not solve.

Creativity in problem solving is primarily about widening or 'repunctuating' our perceptions and cognitive maps of a problem space, in terms of the mode of representation of the problem and basic assumptions about the problem space.

Certain process elements of a strategy that is effective in one context may also be effective in other contexts.

Different people have different maps of the world, and different modes of representing and punctuating problem spaces. This diversity of perception is inherently useful for creativity and problem solving.

Creative thinking strategies may be enhanced or transferred by the identification and manipulation of cognitive patterns and micro behavioral cues.

184

Chapter 5

Creativity
and
Problem Solving

Overview of Chapter 5

General objectives for Chapter 5

1. Define the concepts of 'problem space' and 'solution space' and their relationship to creativity.
2. Provide models and distinctions for readers to (a) define and widen perceptions of a problem space and (b) open up adequate solution space.
3. Assist readers to apply NLP skills and models to identify and transfer an effective creative process from one problem solving context into another.
4. Help readers to understand the benefits of different ways of thinking in the process of problem solving.

Sections and goals of each Section

Section 5.1 Defining Problem Space and Solution Space
Define the relationship between 'problem space' and 'solution space' and establish the principle that a problem cannot be

185

solved with the same thinking that is creating it.

Section 5.2 Punctuating Key Elements of a
Problem Space (The S.C.O.R.E. Model)

Present the S.C.O.R.E. Model and its relationship to defining problem and solution spaces.

Section 5.3 Creativity and Widening the
Perception of a Problem Space

Explain the process and key considerations involved in identifying and transferring the relevant elements of an effective T.O.T.E. for creativity to a situation requiring more creativity.

Section 5.4 Basic Co-Coaching Skills

Define the basic conceptual, observational and interactive skills involved in coaching creativity for problem solving.

Section 5.5 Transferring an Effective
Creativity Strategy Across Contexts

Guide readers through the process of identifying and transferring relevant elements of an effective T.O.T.E. for creative problem solving to a problem situation involving communication.

Section 5.6 Assessing Improvement in Creativity

Present some ways in which improvement in creativity may be assessed for an individual and a group.

Section 5.1
Defining Problem Space
and Solution Space

One of the most common applications of creativity and innovation is problem solving. A key element of effective problem-solving is defining the 'problem space.' Problem space is not just the physical space associated with a problem. Relationships, values, perceptions and beliefs might all contribute to the problem space. The problem space is defined by the elements, both physical and non-physical which create or contribute to the problem.

In order to solve a problem it is necessary to find a 'solution space.' A solution space contains alternatives and resources that allow us to either overcome, transform or avoid the problem. If, however, the alternatives and resources available in solution space are not enough to address all of the elements of the problem space, an insufficient solution will arise. The solution space needs to be broader than the problem space. It is possible to find inadequate solutions because they don't address all of the elements of the problem.

One application of creative thinking is to help widen the available solution space; but a certain amount of creativity might be necessary to uncover and define the problem space to begin with. Thus, creativity serves two basic functions in problem solving:

1. To enrich and clarify our perception of the problem space, and

2. To define or create some area of solution space that is broad enough to address all of the relevant aspects of the problem space.

Before we can find a solution, we have to first comprehend the variables that are creating the problem space. The basic principle of finding solution space is that you can't solve the problem with the same kind of thinking or the same map that is, in fact, creating the problem. In the words of Albert Einstein, "Our thinking creates problems that the same thinking can't solve." A map that leads us into a problem space may not show the way out.

The whole goal in creative problem solving is to find a way of thinking that is not the same thinking that is creating the problem. Then, hopefully, this other way of thinking will lead to a solution space, that is at least as broad or broader than the problem space, in which the appropriate alternatives and resources can be found.

Creativity and Problem Solving

(From *Tools for Dreamers*, pp. 258-260)

Probably the majority of creative activity goes into problem solving. In NLP the word "problem" falls into a class of language known as "nominalization." A nominalization is a process or relationship that is being talked about as if were an object. In NLP, no particular thing or object can be a problem. A problem is a relationship. Specifically, NLP defines a problem as the difference or the gap between your present state and your desired state.

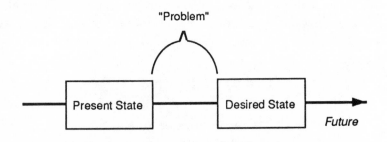

Figure 5.1   Problem Space Flowchart

If there is no difference between where you are and where you want to be, you have no problem. If there is a small gap between where you are and where you want to be, you have a little problem. If there is a large gap, you have a big problem.

In fact, given this definition, you could say that almost all creativity and innovation is directed toward solving or *creating* a problem of some kind. It is important to realize that as soon as you set an outcome, you've created a problem for yourself. As soon as you define a goal or desired state, you have made a problem out of thin air, because you are not at that state yet. That's why so many people are afraid of their 'Dreamer'—the dreamer creates problems by thinking up outcomes.

Of course, it's the map or model that you make to represent a problem that will determine whether it stays a problem or turns into an opportunity. How do you involve the 'Realist'? How do you involve the 'Critic'?

When you sit down and think, "What am I going to do about X? I have a problem. I have something I need to solve." How do you think about it? How do you organize it? The first thing is to take your problem and make it into a question. It's a lot easier to figure out an answer for a question than a problem. But, of course, answering your question can create more problems. "Is it the right answer?" "What do I do now that I have an answer?" "Is one enough?"

Of course, some people jump on the first answer they come up with and just go, "Aha, I got a gut response. I know this is what I should do," and go for it. Others sit and go over endless scenarios until the time they have to do the thing has passed and now they no longer have to bother with it because it is too late.

Let's say you wanted to solve a problem and you had three or four scenarios you came up with. How far do you run the scenarios out into the future? How much of past history do you include? How far back do you go? How many people do you include in the way in which you're going to impact them? For instance, do you make decisions creatively for yourself, or creatively in relationship to how many other people this decision is going to impact directly?

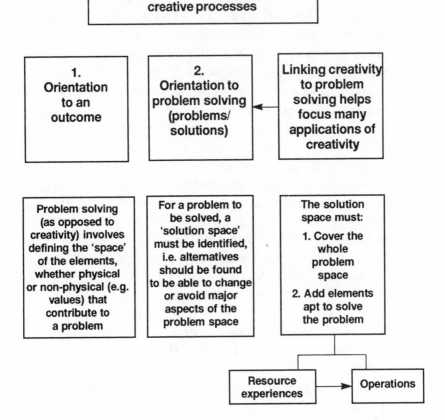

SECTION 5.1 / MAP A

Key Points

Problem space is defined by both physical and non-physical
elements which create or contribute to a problem.
Solutions arise out of a 'solution space' of resources and
alternatives.
A solution space needs to be broader than the problem space
to produce an adequate solution.

Activities

Review a problem that you are currently working on. Think about the physical and non-physical factors that make up the problem space; such as relationships, beliefs, values, history, context, cultural differences, etc.

Think of both effective and ineffective solutions that you have experienced to different problems. What made them effective or ineffective?

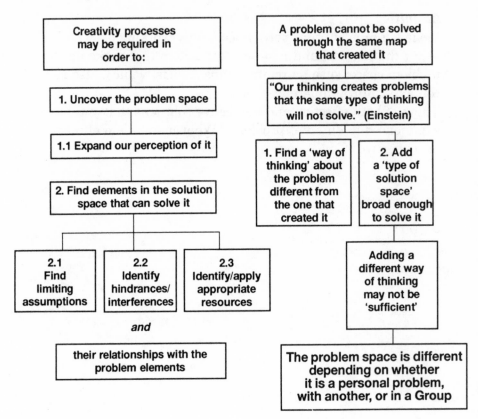

SECTION 5.1 / MAP **B**

Key Points

Creativity is needed to (1) uncover all of the elements of a problem space and (2) discover or create some area of solution space.

You cannot solve a problem with the same kind of thinking that is creating it.

Activities

Think of some examples of how you have used creativity to define a problem.

Remember a time in which you struggled with a problem for a long time and suddenly found a solution. How did your thinking change? What sort of 'solution space' did you discover?

Identify a good example of someone unsuccessfully trying to solve a problem with the same thinking that created it.

Section 5.2
Punctuating Key Elements
of a Problem Space
The S.C.O.R.E. Model

What is a problem? What makes something a problem? What are the important elements to define about a problem space?

First, it is important to realize that if you have no outcome, you have no problem. If you don't want to be anywhere other than where you are, you have no problem. In fact, often the process of establishing a goal actually creates a problem. A problem is the difference between your present state and your desired state and the issues that have to be dealt with in order to get to the desired state.

In the process of moving toward a desired state, symptoms come up in the form of constraints, resistances and interferences to reaching the outcome. Symptoms are typically the most obvious aspect of a problem. A typical kind of symptom in a company might be a drop in profits or productivity.

Of course, effective problem solving involves finding and treating the cause of a particular symptom or set of symptoms. Causes are often less obvious, broader and more systemic in nature than the particular symptom that is being manifested at the moment. A drop in profit or productivity may be the result of something related to competition, organization, leadership, change in the market, change in technology, communications channels, or something else. What you identify as the cause determines where you will seek to create the solution.

The desired effect of achieving a particular goal or outcome can also be a significant factor in defining a problem space. A specific outcome is generally a step along a path to longer range effects. It is important that the solution to a problem be congruent to the longer range desired effects. Sometimes the way in which an outcome is reached can actually interfere with reaching the longer term target; i.e., it is possible to "win the battle but lose the war."

Thus, a problem space is defined by the relationship between the goal or outcome, the kind of symptoms that are getting in the way of achieving the outcome, the causes of those symptoms and the longer range desired effects of reaching the outcome. In order to find the resources that will produce an effective solution for a particular symptom, it is necessary to know the causes of the symptom, the outcome and the ultimate desired effect to be reached. These are the primary elements of the S.C.O.R.E. Model (Dilts and Epstein, 1987, 1991).

Creativity may be required in defining any element of the S.C.O.R.E. space. In addition to finding potential resources and alternatives, creativity is required to establish outcomes, antici-pate effects, define and measure symptoms and uncover causes.

So, creativity has applications in different areas of problem-solving—not all of which will produce solutions but which may be required to get to a solution. Depending upon how specific or general a problem situation is, the process of creativity might produce an immediate result or it might only produce steps to results. Some solutions may require an intensive amount of creativity applied over a space of months or years. The process of defining symptoms, outcomes, causes and potential effects is an ongoing process.

In general, the need for creative problem solving arises in situations of change and transition. Creativity may be applied to:

1. Perceiving change and resistances to change, or

2. Managing change.

Creative problem solving ability involves defining the 'problem space' and identifying potential areas of 'solution space' by establishing the relationship between the various S.C.O.R.E. elements:

Symptoms

Typically the most noticeable and conscious aspects of a present problem or problem state; such as confusions or conflicts in relation to changes in policies or procedures.

Causes

The underlying elements responsible for creating and maintaining the symptoms; such as rigid or outdated cognitive maps or limiting beliefs and assumptions ('thought viruses') that lead to the conflict or confusion.

Outcomes

The particular goals or desired states that would take the place of the symptoms; such as the acceptance and implementation of the new policies or procedures.

Resources

The underlying elements responsible for removing the causes of the symptoms and for manifesting and maintaining the desired outcomes; such as tools and alternatives for communicating and clarifying the *where, when, what, how, why* and *who* of the change in policies or procedures.

Effects

The longer term results of achieving a particular outcome; such as the improvement in productivity, profitability or quality of working environment anticipated as a result of the change of policies or procedures.

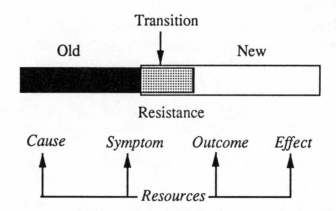

Figure 5.2   The S.C.O.R.E. Model and Change

In defining these elements of problem and solution space, creativity may be used to:

1. Cluster information into larger or smaller 'chunks;'
2. Focus on different aspects of the problem space;
3. Take different perspectives and perceptual positions, and
4. Create multiple descriptions of the problem and potential solutions.

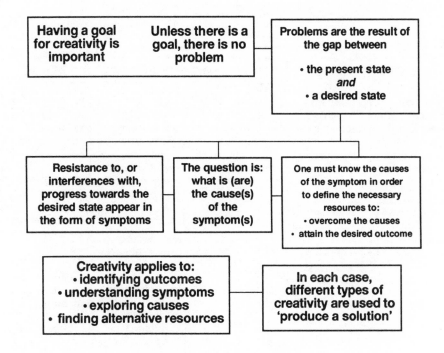

SECTION 5.2 / MAP A

Key Points

A problem space may be defined by the relationship between
several key dimensions defined by the S.C.O.R.E. Model.
The "O" in the S.C.O.R.E. Model relates to Outcomes.
Outcomes are an essential element of problem spaces because
they create a gap between where you are and where you want
to be.

Activities

Think of a problem you are currently working on.
What is your desired *outcome* for this problem? In what way
did creativity play a role in determining this outcome?
What do you anticipate will be the longer term *effects* of
reaching this outcome? How much creativity or imagination is
required to anticipate these effects?

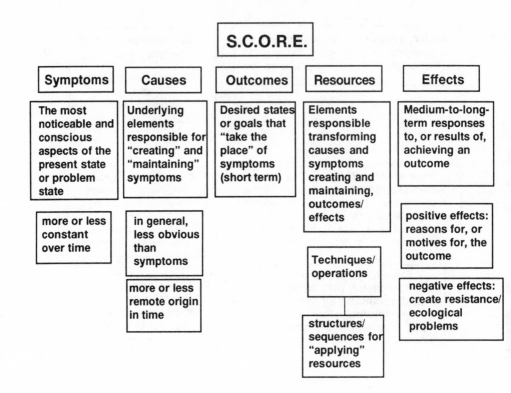

SECTION 5.2 / MAP **B**

Key Points
The "S" in the S.C.O.R.E. Model relates to Symptoms—which generally occur as a constraint, resistance or interference to reaching a desired state.
The "C" in the S.C.O.R.E. Model refers to the Cause or causes of the symptom. Causes are typically less obvious than symptoms.
The "E" in the S.C.O.R.E. Model relates to Effects, which are the longer term products of reaching an outcome.
Activities
Think of a problem you are currently working on.
What are the most obvious *symptoms*?
What do you think are the *causes* of those symptoms?
How might you use the process of creativity to identify or confirm causes and their relationship to the symptoms?

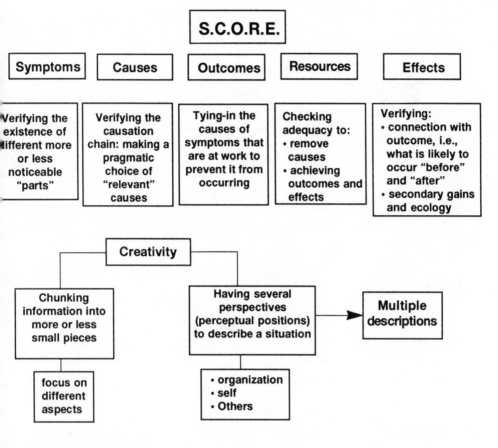

S.C.O.R.E.

Symptoms	Causes	Outcomes	Resources	Effects
Verifying the existence of different more or less noticeable "parts"	Verifying the causation chain: making a pragmatic choice of "relevant" causes	Tying-in the causes of symptoms that are at work to prevent it from occurring	Checking adequacy to: • remove causes • achieving outcomes and effects	Verifying: • connection with outcome, i.e., what is likely to occur "before" and "after" • secondary gains and ecology

Creativity

Chunking information into more or less small pieces

Having several perspectives (perceptual positions) to describe a situation → **Multiple descriptions**

focus on different aspects

• organization
• self
• Others

SECTION 5.2 / MAP C

Key Points

The "R" in the S.C.O.R.E. Model refers to Resources, which are the elements, choices or operations necessary to transform causes and symptoms and attain a desired outcome. Creativity can be applied in defining any element of the S.C.O.R.E. Model.

Activities

Think of a problem you are currently working on. What kinds of resources do you have access to or can you mobilize to address the symptoms and their causes and to achieve the desired outcome? How does creativity play a role in defining and mobilizing resources?

Section 5.3
Creativity and
Widening the Perception
of a Problem Space

In addition to the distinction between the process and products of creativity, there is a distinction between the process of creativity and the contexts or situations in which it is enacted. Thus, it is possible to extract elements of creative process that are effective in one context or situation and apply them with positive results in other contexts or situations.

Like all goal oriented activities, the process of creative problem solving is a T.O.T.E.—a feedback loop whose purpose is to converge on a solution that adequately addresses a problem space. Using NLP, key elements of the structure of the T.O.T.E. for an effective problem solving strategy can be modeled and transferred to other contexts and situations. This can help to:

1. Widen perception of a problem space, and

2. Introduce a form of thinking that is different from the one creating the problem.

The general framework for an effective transfer of T.O.T.E. elements is to:

1. Identify and apply lessons learned from past successes, and

2. Add new perceptions to a problem situation in order to 'reframe' difficulties into feedback as opposed to perceived failure.

The objective is to transfer processes that worked in an effective context into some other context where one is stuck.

The basic transfer process involves identifying cognitive and behavioral patterns which occur in an effective context and add them to, or enact them in, a context where you would like to have more access to your creative potential or to have an enriched process of creativity. The essential objective is to transfer some element from the effective context that might add more flexibility, create more choices or somehow mobilize more of the creative process in the challenging situation. In other words, you want to explore how you can transfer or adapt some effective elements from a positive situation into a currently negative or problematic situation.

The notion of "adding" is significant. Adding is different than replacing or discarding other processes or approaches. The essential presupposition of the T.O.T.E. transfer is that finding an appropriate solution is a function of the thoroughness of coverage of the problem space. Thoroughness leads to the possibility of many solutions, not only one. The goal of all NLP application procedures is to add choices, not take them away.

The first step for modeling and transferring a T.O.T.E. involves contrasting a T.O.T.E. for a problem situation that involved effective creativity with the T.O.T.E. for a situation that has been ineffective. The next step involves adding elements of the effective T.O.T.E. to the currently ineffective problem solving process. Essentially, you want to add something from an effective situation to the context in which you are experiencing difficulty.

Since different thought processes cover different types of perceptual space, you might find that some of the elements of the creative process that work well in one context are not relevant for the other situation. Sometimes elements need to be adjusted or adapted in order to fit. The process of transferring itself requires a certain amount of creativity.

Contrasting specific situations gives information about micro level patterns. Contrasting general classes of situations gives information about macro level patterns. The closer the contexts of the two situations being contrasted, the more the difference will be due to variations in micro level processes; i.e., representational systems, specific evidences and operations, etc.

If the contexts being contrasted are far apart from each other, the relevant patterns will typically be on higher levels; i.e., states of mind, beliefs and values, etc. Very often the biggest innovations in a particular field come from people who are outside of that field because they don't have the same sort of assumptions. So transferring from widely different contexts might involve more adapting, but the results of this effort could be quite fruitful.

Keep in mind that the goal of the process is not to produce a specific solution, but rather to widen one's map of a problem space in order to find other choices and to develop meta cognition about effective problem solving strategies. Obviously, any past situations that are being contrasted are already over. The benefits to be gained by contrasting them relate to the lessons that might be learned with respect to the problem solving process itself. We are not really concerned with particular situations themselves but rather with the creative process that was applied and the lessons that can be learned about effective creativity from those situations. The resourceful, creative reference experience is not supposed to provide a guaranteed solution, rather its purpose is to provide hints about what you might add into the creative process associated with the difficult situation.

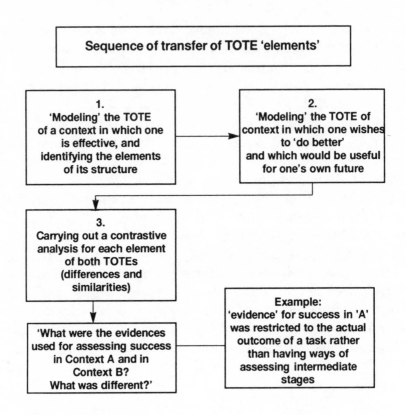

SECTION 5.3 / MAP A

Key Points

The process of creative problem solving is a T.O.T.E. made of goals, evidences and operations.

Key elements of the structure of a T.O.T.E. for effective problem solving strategies can be modeled and transferred to other contexts and situations to (a) help widen perception of a problem space and (b) introduce a form of thinking that is different from the one creating the problem.

Activities

Think of a problem solving situation in which you were effective and one in which you experienced difficulties. What are the differences in your T.O.T.E.s for the two situations? In the ineffective situation, were you constrained with respect to goals? evidence? operations? flexibility of response to problems?

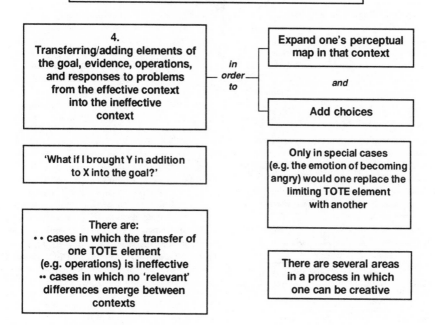

SECTION 5.3 / MAP B

Key Points

T.O.T.E. elements may be modeled and transferred by (a) contrasting a T.O.T.E. for a problem situation that involved effective creativity with the T.O.T.E. for a situation that has been ineffective and (b) adding elements of the effective T.O.T.E. to the currently ineffective problem solving process. Not all elements of a T.O.T.E. that is effective for one situation are relevant for another situation.

Activities

Imagine you could 'relive' the ineffective situation applying what worked in the effective situation.

Which aspects of what you did in the effective situation have the most relevance: goals, evidence, operations or response to problems?

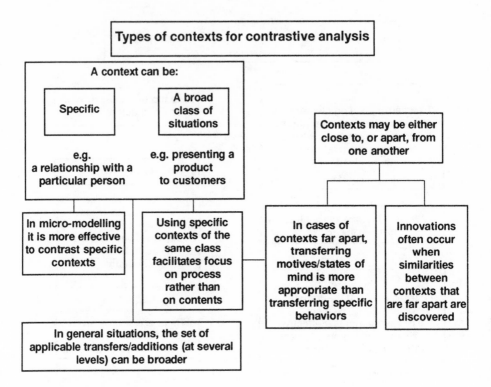

SECTION 5.3 / MAP C

Key Points

The closer the contexts of the two situations being contrasted are, the more the difference will be due to variations in micro level processes; i.e., representational systems, specific evidences and operations, etc.

If the contexts being contrasted are far apart from each other, the relevant patterns will typically be on higher levels; i.e., states of mind, beliefs and values.

Activities

Contrast two specific instances involving creativity and difficulty being creative—i.e., two particular interaction such as communicating with a certain individual at a meeting. What kinds of factors stand out to you as being significant in terms making the difference between your ability to be creative or not in the two situations?

Contrast two general classes of activities: one in which you are able to be creative and one in which you experience difficulties—e.g., making presentations to customers or colleagues, working with a boss, etc.

What kinds of factors stand out to you as being significant in terms of your ability to be creative or not in these two general contexts?

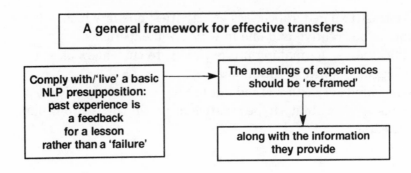

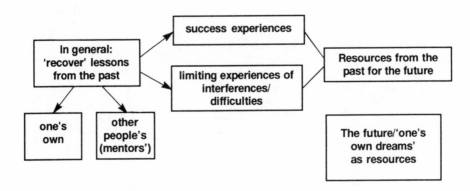

SECTION 5.3 / MAP D

Key Points
The general framework for an effective transfer of T.O.T.E.
elements is to (1) identify and apply lessons learned from past
successes and (2) add new perceptions to a problem situation
in order to 'reframe' difficulties into feedback as opposed to
perceived failure.

Activities
Think about the different kinds of lessons that may be learned
from past successes and failures.
Recall some experiences that you have considered 'failures.'
How can you use learnings from your past successes to shift
your map of these situations so that they too become
'feedback' that you are able to learn from?

Section 5.4
Creative Co-Coaching Skills

Assisting someone to transfer an effective creative process or
T.O.T.E. is a coaching activity that requires certain interactive
and observational skills. The application of these skills leads to
a type of co-creativity.

The basic operations of the coach are to:

1. Ask questions that elicit information about cognitive
   patterns related to effective and ineffective situations
   involving creativity;

2. Assist the 'explorer' to add and adapt relevant factors of
   the effective creative process to the ineffective situation
   through the frame of acting 'as if';

3. Help the explorer to identify any limiting beliefs or
   assumptions in the ineffective situation, and

4. Observe for changes in the behavioral cues of the explorer in response to the additions and changes being
   made.

The overall objective of the coach is to assist the explorer to
expand his or her perception of a problem situation (not to find
a guaranteed solution). Coaches should focus on elements of
process and structure as opposed to content. Remember that the
focus of NLP is on separating the process from the particular
situation or the products that are the context or result of that
creative process. The application of creativity to a problem
solving situation will not always produce a solution *per se*. Its
primary purpose is to find and explore other possibilities and
alternatives.

The process of transferring a T.O.T.E. is itself an operation in
the larger T.O.T.E. of the coaching process. From the point of
view of the explorer, the goal of this transfer is to try to widen
your maps of a problem situation; to find places that you might
be limiting yourself because of your map of that situation and
add something or open up something more. The evidence is

going to be in terms of the changes in your physiology, your emotional response to the situation and how you represent the problem space, and in terms of the choices and alternatives you perceive available to you. The evidence will not necessarily be that you've reached a solution, but rather that in some way you've enriched your perception of the problem space and possible solution space.

At the end of the exercise the problem situation you used as a reference for the difficult example may still be unsolved, but you will minimally have a wider perception of the issues that make it a problem. Depending on the nature of the problem and the problem space, it may not even be possible to find a good solution at this time. But the value of attempting to widen your map is that, in a future situation, resources that don't quite fit the specific reference situation you have chosen for this exercise might actually become viable alternatives. You may find a solution to a problem other than the one you are specifically working on.

In relation to a specific past situation, you may in fact confirm that you did the best that you could at that time. At the same time, you might find some particular assumption that you have been making about a certain situation, might actually not be necessary to make in the future. And that could be very valuable.

You might just simply find that what made the difficult context a problem was the goal that you had for that situation to begin with. Sometimes, if you change the goal, the situation is not a problem anymore. Again, the purpose is simply to enrich or widen your perceptual space of some context in which you would like to have more potential for creativity. You may never get into precisely that same situation again, but if you're in other situations that are somewhat similar your map already has new choices and alternatives available.

Choosing Which Contexts to Contrast

Choosing the contexts to be contrasted is an important decision because it will determine the degree of co-creative effort that has to be expended by the coach and the explorer in order to adapt the resources from the effective strategy to the problematic context. For instance, if the context in which a person is able to experience creativity is a personal situation as opposed to a relational one, or is a more generalized one (such as skiing) as opposed to a specific situation (such as delegating a particular task to a specific person), there will be additional contextual factors that may have made a significant difference. Sometimes, those differences are the reason why a person already has difficulty in transferring creative abilities.

For example, some people find that they are able to be creative when they are by themselves. That is, they are able to be creative when it is up to them to reach a particular goal on their own. They may find themselves less creative when they are expressing themselves in a more dynamic situation involving interactions with others. Initially when you attempt to transfer patterns from the solitary situation to a dynamic situation, you may have difficulty because the problem space is not related to managing the task as much as it is to managing the relationship. When a person is trying to be creative in a group, the difficulties may appear in terms of relational difficulties that inhibit creativity and that disturb the individual creative process. The challenge becomes one of extrapolating and transferring elements that are effective in a private situation to a social situation. The question becomes, "How can you adapt the creative process to situations in which it does not already transfer easily or function effectively?" You might find that something doesn't immediately fit but you could adapt it a little bit and it offers a potentially wider map.

Assessing What to Transfer or Add

One simple way to assess what might be added to the T.O.T.E. of a problem situation is to apply the basic principles of creativity:

1. In the problem situation, is there an outcome?

2. Does the evidence for success in the problem situation serve as feedback or failure?

3. In terms of the operation, is there flexibility? Should some other operation be added?

These three basic principles provide a set of basic guidelines for determining what might be transferred or added to the problem situation.

On a macro level, there will often be a very obvious difference just between types of attitudes or states. In general, you are more likely to be creative if you are being proactive in a situation than if you are being passive.

If the contexts are very different, the elements of their problem spaces might be quite different and, therefore, what works as a solution in one context will be either irrelevant or maybe even problematic in the other context. Yet, at the same time, transferring a process that is effective in one context to a very different one often the source of great innovation.

Transferring Different Levels of Resources

This is where the different levels of process that can be transferred becomes a significant distinction. The context of a situation relates to *where* and *when* it occurred; 'yesterday at the office' or 'a month ago on the ski slope,' for example. Some contexts might be very close together. The contexts for down hill skiing and water skiing may be closer to one another than either is to working in your office. What's implied by the model of levels is that in similar *where*s and *when*s one can use similar *what*s. A particular behavior might be easily enacted in very similar contexts. You can take the same behavior that you engage in on one ski slope and transfer it relatively easily to another ski slope. Likewise you can take the same behaviors you engaged in your old office and transfer them relatively easily to a new office. But it is more difficult to transfer the behavior of the ski slope to the office and *vice versa*.

In environmental contexts that are very far apart, the *what* begins to become less relevant. It can't be easily transferred. To draw a resource from a more distant context, you might look past the *what* to the *how*, which is more abstracted from the constraints of a particular environment. The coach will want to ask, "How are you thinking?" "Are you visualizing?" "Are you experiencing things in terms of emotions or words?" Some of these kinds of deeper NLP distinctions might then allow you to apply some aspect of a particular capability to a more distant context, even though the *what* is different.

If you are trying to bring resources into a context that is very different from the positive reference experience, you may not even be able to apply the same kind of thinking. In that situation you may have to move up to a higher level like beliefs or values to find a resource that may be transferred.

Thus, if you are trying to transfer a resource from a situation in which you were skiing to a situation in your office, you will only be able to transfer very limited elements of the *what*, the actual behaviors associated with skiing. There may be certain aspects of the micro physiology you use to prepare to ski that could be transferred, but the macro behaviors would be inappropriate for the office environment.

On the level of cognitive capabilities you might find that when you are skiing, you are able to form a very clear picture of the path you are going to take; but in your office you just have vague words you are using to represent your path. It may not be too difficult to transfer the cognitive process of 'visualizing' a path.

The next question is, "Does that shift or widen your perceptual map enough to produce an adequate solution?" Is visualizing a path enough of a resource or a different enough way of thinking to produce an adequate solution?

If not, you might return to the positive reference experience and search for patterns at the level of beliefs and values. Maybe the *what* and the *how* cannot be effectively transferred, but in the downhill skiing situation you believe you are going to make it and you trust in your unconscious skills to guide whatever moves you have to make. And that belief you can transfer. You might find that if you take this same belief in your own unconscious competence into the challenging office situation, all of a sudden, when you are confronted with constraints, more alternatives seem available.

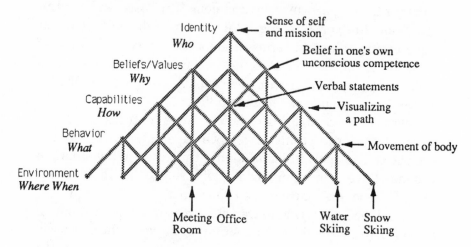

Figure 5.3   Levels of Resources

If the contexts are extremely different you might find that the best resource that you can take from one context to the other is your sense of your identity or mission. Perhaps in the resource situation you know exactly who you are and what your mission is. That same sense of identity and mission may be a very valuable resource in a challenging context.

The Importance of Physiology

It is important to remember, as a coach and as an explorer, that different types and intensities of behavioral cues are associated to different levels of process. The level of neurology that is mobilized when you experience a sense of mission and identity is much deeper than the level of neurology that is required to reflexively move your hand. To experience your environment, you can remain passive. You don't have to commit much of yourself. You can observe the environment without having to activate anything very deep. To take action in your environment, you have to mobilize more of your nervous system. To think about your actions, you have to mobilize and link another level of neurology to that involved in producing your actions. To access your beliefs and your values, you begin mobilizing things related to your heart, your guts. And, of course, your sense of self comes from a kind of a total mobilization. In general, higher levels of process mobilize a deeper commitment of the nervous system.

One of the purposes of NLP is to define through some of these kinds of distinctions—representational systems, physiology, programs, goals—ways in which we can mobilize more of this kind of neurology. The goal of the exercise is not necessarily, as we have said, to produce a solution, but is to open up more solution space. The first issue is, "What can be transferred and how?" The next issue is, "Does what was transferred open up enough perceptual space to produce an adequate solution?"

As a general strategy, the coach should start with more tangible and observable micro level patterns and then move to more macro level patterns. Behavioral cues are a tool and an evidence for the transfer of creative processes from one context to another. From the point of view of NLP, if the circuitry is not open to the new thinking or the new map, it won't come in.

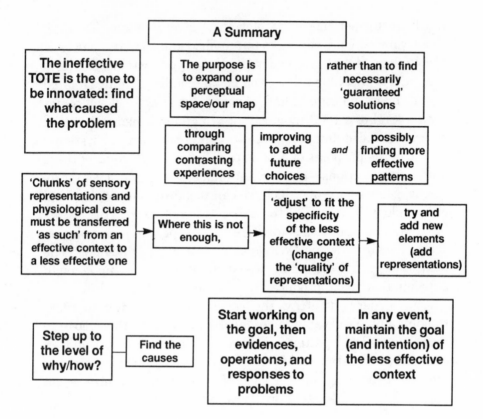

SECTION 5.4 / MAP A

Key Points

Assisting someone to transfer an effective creative process or T.O.T.E. is a coaching activity that requires certain interactive and observational skills.

The application of these skills leads to a type of co-creativity. The process of coaching is itself a kind of T.O.T.E.

The overall objective of the coach is to assist the explorer to expand his or her perception of a problem situation, not to find a guaranteed solution.

As a general strategy, the coach should start with more tangible and observable micro level patterns and then move to more macro level patterns.

Coaches should focus on elements of process and structure as opposed to content.

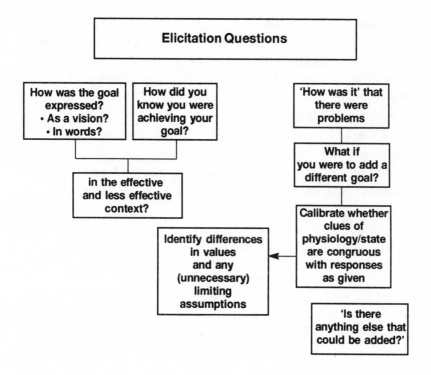

SECTION 5.4 / MAP B

Key Points

The basic goals of the coach are to (1) ask questions that elicit information about cognitive patterns related to effective and ineffective situations involving creativity, (2) assist the 'explorer' to add and adapt relevant factors of the effective creative process to the ineffective situation through the frame of acting 'as if,' (3) help the explorer to identify any limiting beliefs or assumptions in the ineffective situation and (4) observe for changes in the behavioral cues of the explorer in response the additions and changes being made.

Behavioral cues are a tool and an evidence for the transfer of creative processes from one context to another.

Activities

Think of situations in which you were able to be an effective coach (as opposed to boss or advisor).

Think of situations in which you have been able to help people solve problems by asking questions instead of telling them what you think they should do.

Recall the T.O.T.E., R.O.L.E., B.A.G.E.L. and Disney exercises from Part One. Review the skills you developed for (1) focusing on process as opposed to content, (2) identifying micro cognitive patterns and (3) observing behavioral cues.

In analyzing the thinking style, identify:
- what internal sensory representations (visual, auditory, kinesthetic)
- internal language

and

- the quality of internal representations (e.g. voice volume/tempo, image distribution)

Different types of resources can be added in limiting situations:
- sensory represen-tations
- state
- goals
- physiology
- values ('why') of the effective situa-tion

General presupposition: enriching the experience map changes the perception of 'what to do'

There is a sequence of operations aimed at 'adding':
- First, if appropriate, modifying the state
Then
- the physiology and
- internal sensory repre-sentations (modalities and sub-modalities)

One can further think 'as if' ("What if...?") and add elements from these operations into each part of the TOTE by starting with the goal

'As if' can also be used independent of the contrastive analysis

SECTION 5.4 / MAP C

Key Points

The goal of the T.O.T.E. transfer is not to find the "right map" but rather to enrich one's map through the process of thinking "as if" and "what if."

By enriching our maps we have more perceptions about what can be done.

Activities

Act "as if" you could apply some of the same goals, evidences, operations, resources and assumptions that you used in the effective example in the difficult situation. What new choices of action or response do you have?

There are sometimes 'either... or' assumptions implied in limiting TOTEs. Alternatively, complementary 'both...and' aspects should be identified in an experience

|

This allows choices to be added rather than replaced

Assumptions can be added to, or substituted for, those implicitly adopted in the limiting situation, whether derived from the resource situation, or 'constructed' in order to expand the perceptual space (viewpoint, time frames, the 'why of the whys')

In general: Exploring the different levels of an experience is important for the enrichment of the map

---

Creativity principles should be applied as guides to identify what/where to add in the 3 TOTE areas

---

Creativity principles can be used as a test to identify the limiting aspects of a TOTE

SECTION 5.4 / MAP D

Key Points

Applying principles of creativity and well-formedness conditions helps find holes and missing links in ineffective creativity strategies.

Coaching itself involves a significant amount of creativity. It is important for coaches to apply the principles of creativity as a guide for his or her own interaction.

Activities

Apply the principles and well-formedness conditions of creativity to your difficult situation. In what ways could you meet these principles and conditions more fully in that situation?

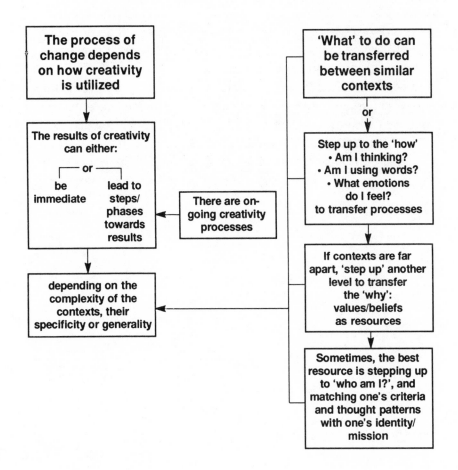

Section 5.4 / map E

Key Points

Contrasting specific situations gives information about micro level patterns. Contrasting general classes of situations gives information about macro level patterns.

Activities

Think of two situations which were similar in almost every respect except that the results with respect to successful creativity were different. For example, a successful delegation to a specific person and an unsuccessful delegation to the same person.

What kind of perceptual or behavioral influences accounted for the difference in creative results? (Think in terms of micro behavioral and cognitive patterns.)

Think of two situations in which the result was different (i.e., one was positive and one was negative) and the contexts were also very different. What could be learned from the successful context that could be transferred to enrich the ineffective context? (Think in terms of general attitude, beliefs, values, etc.)

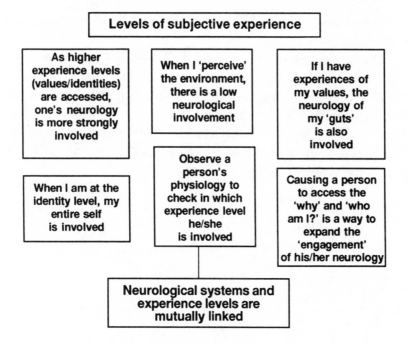

SECTION 5.4 / MAP F

Key Points
Different types and intensities of behavioral cues are
associated to different levels of process.
In general, higher levels of process mobilize a deeper
commitment of the nervous system; i.e., 'thinking' uses deeper
neurological processes than routine action; beliefs and values
are experienced and processed at a deeper level than thinking,
etc.

Activities
Explore how different levels of processes within yourself
engage different physical and neurological 'circuitry.'
(a) Passively look at and listen to your immediate external
environment for a moment.
(b) Make a simple behavioral action like opening and closing
your hand.

(c) Try to recall one of the diagrams from a previous Section of the book.

(d) Think of something you really believe or value about your job.

(e) Think of something you could do but do not do because it doesn't fit with who you are as a person.

Notice how each of these different levels of activities requires that you engage different kinds of cognitive space and effect your experience in different ways.

Section 5.5
Transferring an
Effective Creativity
Strategy Across Contexts

While it is possible to transfer elements of creative processes across widely different contexts, this adds a dimension of challenge that may not be appropriate when you are first practicing this kind of coaching process. It is a good idea to start with a kind of context that is not going to allow for too much variation between contextual influences. For instance, you may want to choose two situations involving face-to-face communication: one in which you are able to be effective and one in which you are not so effective. This way, the potential influences introduced by widely different contexts will be minimized. This will also allow you to concentrate more on some of the micro level patterns that we have been exploring up to this point.

Obviously, the space of a problem gets wider as more individuals are involved in it. The kinds of beliefs, capabilities, and behavior that you mobilize when you are by yourself are different than what you would need to mobilize as a parent, a spouse or with respect to your colleagues, subordinates or boss. Each relationship rearranges your priorities of values and the cluster of required capabilities and skills. One challenge in creatively managing different relationships comes in terms of coordinating the different cluster of values and skills required by the different contexts. With respect to your family, one set of values has priority. With respect to your boss, other values have priority. And, of course, where life becomes challenging, is when you are put into situations having multiple relational reference points.

According to NLP, however, regardless of whether you are by yourself or with a hundred people, your ability to respond creatively is a function of your map, your physiology and your ability to utilize your 'neuro-linguistic programs' to address the problem space of the situation. That is a key presupposition behind transferring process elements. You are not transferring the content of a previously effective solution, but rather process elements related to the use of your senses, physiology, beliefs, values, etc. These processes can help to produce more potential alternatives independent of context.

Different kinds of strategies and T.O.T.E.s are effective to cover different kinds of problem spaces. The purpose of the T.O.T.E. transfer process is to identify and apply mental processes that are useful to widen perceptions of a problem space.

In terms of the problem space relevant to the solution of a specific problem, context is very important. In terms of creativity, however, the creative process is still the same and still valuable regardless of context because it's expressed through us personally. In terms of solutions, you have to consider context. In terms of creativity, on the other hand, you are accessing a process that has relevance in many contexts and might still be useful even though two problem contexts are different. When you initially try this, however, try to minimize the contextual issues. Keep the contexts to be contrasted similar so you are not having to account for influences introduced by wide variation in context.

Relevant mental processes are found by contrasting T.O.T.E. elements of effective and ineffective examples of creativity. The overall process is to find two situations (such as face-to-face communication), one in which you are able to be creative and one in which you find yourself more limited than you would like to be. Phase one of the process involves defining the key elements of the two T.O.T.E.s. In phase one you are not trying to change anything, you are just eliciting the structure of the explorer's own current map of the situation. Phase two involves identifying and transferring relevant elements from the effective T.O.T.E. to the ineffective one.

It is often helpful for coaches to use spatial sorting to make the contrast clearer and easier. For example you might use two different chairs to sort the two different states. One chair can be for the resourceful reference experience and one for the more problematic context. This makes it easier to associate all the cues and elements associated with the context to be enriched in one location. Then, when you are transferring, it is as if you are taking them from one chair to the other.

Use the chart provided in the book to help you to identify and compare the different elements of the T.O.T.E.s for the two situations. Coaches should also pay attention to physiology differences because, as we have explored before, physiology is a powerful tool for leveraging cognitive processes. Also pay attention to differences in representational channels. These are the three basic tools that we've been working with so far.

As you are engaging in this process there are several points that might be useful to keep in mind.

Goals

Goals are tangible expressions of values. Values related to goals may be a relevant element to identify and transfer.

There are often clusters of goals associated with particular situations. In a communication situation, for example, if you don't define your goals with respect to relationship as well as task, you will be less likely to enact any kind of creativity with respect to the relationship. The fact that task and relational goals may be different doesn't change the problem; it just points to the need for a different kind of creativity.

Some goals are not initially conscious. Situations often imply goals that are not stated. But because they have not been made explicit, a person is not effectively able to purposefully operate toward them. Thus, it is sometimes useful for coaches to probe for goals that may be presupposed or unstated.

Evidences

Evidences relate to types of goals. Sometimes a person has shifted goals but is still trying to use the same evidence and operations that worked effectively for a different goal. The evidence and operations will thus not be adequate to accomplish the goal.

There are different types of evidences for different levels of goals. Some evidences may be inappropriate for certain types of goals. There are ongoing evidences and evidences of completion that operate in different time frames.

Sometimes people only look for how a situation is not meeting their evidences; they are always looking for how empty the glass is rather than how full it is.

Operations and Responses to Problems

Different operations relate to different goals and should be sorted out. Responses to problems are often a key factor in creativity. Different levels of operations serve as resources for different kinds of problems and interferences.

It is important for the coach to observe aspects of the physical state and even ask questions about other aspects of the state, such as his or her emotional responses. Sometimes the biggest difference is simply in the states associated with the two situations. As a successful leader once said, "When I enter a challenging situation, I think about what state I want to be in, not what I want to say or do. Because if I am in the right state the inspiration will come."

Assumptions

Assumptions related to particular situations and general contexts are also part of a problem space creating issues involving motivation and permission for creative thinking. The transfer of positive beliefs and assumptions can often make the greatest impact.

Applying principles of creativity

Applying principles of creativity and well-formedness conditions helps find holes and missing links in ineffective creativity strategies.

1. *Outcome frame*
   There needs to be an outcome.

2. *Feedback versus failure*
   Evidence procedure has to provide feedback that leads in the direction of the goal.

3. *Flexibility*

   If what you're doing isn't working, anything is a better choice. The three principles apply to goals, evidences and operations respectively.

Remember you are not trying to find the one 'right map'—especially in the area of creativity. According to NLP, there can never be one right map anyway. The map isn't the territory. The best solution is to have a rich map with many choices and alternatives.

Coaching itself involves a significant amount of creativity. It is important for coaches to apply the principles of creativity as a guide for their own interactions. One of the basic tools of NLP is acting 'as if.' Acting 'as if' simply means putting something into your map; not necessarily into the territory.

The whole purpose of NLP is to be able to transfer and to add new resources into a situation. By enriching our maps we have more perceptions about what can be done. The goal of the T.O.T.E. transfer is not to find the "right map" but rather to enrich one's map through the process of thinking "as if" and "what if." The belief behind this is that if you enrich your map, your response to reality will automatically start to change.

Structure of the Exercise

This exercise is best done in a format in which one person is the explorer and the other is a coach. The explorer picks two situations to contrast (such as face-to-face communication). The coach helps the explorer to find the key micro elements of the T.O.T.E.s—asking the questions and watching for patterns of physiology and clues about thinking styles.

The first step is to elicit the T.O.T.E. elements of the resourceful reference experience. Then, elicit the state and thinking style associated with the positive reference example. Define the physical state and any behavior cues and thinking styles associated with the positive reference situation.

Step two is to elicit the T.O.T.E. elements of the problematic situation. And then to define the physical state and thinking style associated with that situation.

Step three involves comparing the two examples and find what levels of resources might be transferred from one situation to the other. The purpose is to widen the perception of the problem space. Through the process of the comparison, new insights about the problem space will emerge along with the contributions from the coach. Coaches will often ask questions that bring out new distinctions in relations to the problem space.

Another operation of step three is to apply the principles of creativity to see what might be added or transferred to the problematic situation.

Step four involves transferring resources, starting with the physiology, state and thinking style. Its purpose is to start to open up solution space by adding elements from the effective process to the ineffective one.

You may then explore higher levels of problem space and solution space in terms of assumptions, values and beliefs. Identifying and confronting limiting presuppositions can open up more potential solution space.

In summary, the T.O.T.E. transfer exercise is in itself a T.O.T.E. The goal is to enrich the explorer's perceptions of a problem space. The evidence for success involves changes in the explorer's state and micro level cognitive and behavioral patterns related to the problem, and the explorer's awareness of other choices and alternatives. The operations involve the contrasting of the T.O.T.E. related to a difficult situation with an example of effective creative problem solving in order to find cognitive and behavioral elements that can be added to enrich the explorer's approach and choices with respect to the problem situation.

T.O.T.E. Elicitation Checklist			
Context:			
Goals	**Representational Channel**	**Behavioral Patterns**	**Levels**
What are your goals?	Visual Verbal Emotional Imagination Memory External	Body Posture Gestures Voice Tone Eye Position Language Pattern	What How Why Who
Evidence			
How do you know whether you are achieving your goals?	Visual Verbal Emotional Imagination Memory External	Body Posture Gestures Voice Tone Eye Position Language Pattern	What How Why Who
Operations			
What do you do to achieve your goals?	Visual Verbal Emotional Imagination Memory External	Body Posture Gestures Voice Tone Eye Position Language Pattern	What How Why Who
Response to Problems			
How do you respond to problems or interferences to reaching your goals?	Visual Verbal Emotional Imagination Memory External	Body Posture Gestures Voice Tone Eye Position Language Pattern	What How Why Who

Demonstration of T.O.T.E. Utilization Process

(From *Tools for Dreamers*, pp. 156-161)

RBD: So, C., what is a context in which you are able to be effectively creative?

C: Making a presentation—in a training program for instance.

RBD: What is the context in which you would like to improve your creative abilities?

C: Selling my presentations.

RBD: OK. Selling your presentations. This sounds like it ought to be interesting!

What I want you to do first is step into what it is like when you are presenting and imagine you are there doing it. What are your goals?

C: To improve people's know-how. That is basically it.

RBD: All right, step out of that.

Come over here and step into the "trying to sell" process. What are your goals?

C: To sell and make them pay!

RBD: OK. Here we have an interesting difference in goals! One of the interventions you might already begin to think about is to imagine approaching selling as just being about increasing people's knowledge of your product. Who says that selling has to be about making people pay? Selling could be just giving them the know-how to make the decision.

Let's return to effective presentations for a moment. How do you know that you are increasing people's knowledge in a presentation? Do you see things in their faces, do you hear things in their voices?

C: Yes, there are all these things you have said, and perhaps some more concrete tests like doing exercises.

RBD: So, you have an activity; then what do you do? During the activity, how do you tell?

C: Afterwards, by the looks on their faces as I'm talking. And they make richer propositions and have better questions.

RBD: So one is the look on their faces and the other is somehow in the content of what they are saying. You do an exercise and that you listen for enriched questions and propositions.

Let's go back to the ineffective selling process. How do you know that you are going to successfully make people pay?

C: That may be where I have a problem. When they pay, I guess.

RBD: Here the only evidence is from the result after it is all over; whereas with the effectively creative process the evidence is going on during the process.

Now let's explore some of your operations. What do you do in order to increase people's knowledge, and get the kind of looks on their faces, and the kind of enriched propositions and questions?

C: I pay a lot of attention to their language, to their representational systems. I start by gathering as much information as possible about who they are, then I try to make my actions fit with their image of the world.

RBD:What do you do if you are running into trouble during a presentation when it doesn't seem that it is going well?

C: I think then that I made a wrong analysis and I try to recycle the analysis of their image of the world.

RBD: We have some basic simple things.

I pay attention to their language.

Find out about who they are and what their world view is.

Try to make actions that fit with their world models.

If I am having trouble I recycle to gather more information, to recheck my understanding of their models.

What do you do when you try to sell a presentation to somebody?

C: The same thing, but maybe I have the belief that I can't spend so much time.

RBD: So you do listen to their language?

C: Yes.

RBD: And you do find out who they are and try to make your actions fit with their models of the world, and if you have trouble you just recycle and say, "Oh, I probably misunderstood their model of the world?" Or do you go, "Oh, no!"?

C: That's it. Maybe I don't think that I have enough time and I shouldn't be using up their time

RBD: So you don't recycle?

C: Not as well as I should.

	Effective Context	Ineffective Context
What are your goals?	Improve people's know-how.	Sell people and make them pay.
How do you know you are achieving your goals?	Look on their faces. Enriched propositions and questions.	When they pay.
What do you do in order to reach your goals?	Pay attention to language. Find out about their world view.	Pay attention to language. Find out about their world view.
	Make actions that fit their model of the. world	Make actions that fit their model of the world.
What do you if you are not satisfactorily reaching your goals?	Recycle to gather more information about their world view.	Feel that I shouldn't be using up their time.

Figure 5.4
Comparison of C's Effective and Ineffective T.O.T.E.s

RBD: So when you don't reach the goal you just quit. Your basic operational steps are the same but your response to resistance is different. You mentioned that there is a kind of belief that popped up here which is probably one of the reasons why you are not as effective as in the presentation context.

But there are also other differences between the two T.O.T.E.s. In the ineffective T.O.T.E. you use essentially the same operation, but have no ongoing evidence and a different goal. It's sort of like saying, "Hey, this process works so well for presentations that I will just use it for this other situation where I have no evidence and a completely different goal. Why isn't it working?"

My point is that the fact that you do the same thing is irrelevant if you don't have the appropriate guidance at the upper level of the T.O.T.E. Doing the same behavior for a different set of values will make a completely different result.

There is a difference between listening to someone's language with the intention of showing friendship and to create rapport *versus* listening to their language for the purpose of manipulating him to do something. An effective strategy is not only a function of the *what* and *how* but also of the *why*.

One of the other things that seems significant to me is that while you say that you believe you don't have enough time, you do your whole sales presentation before you check whether you are being effective or not. That seems like a terrible waste of the little time you have. When you are improving people's know-how you are checking constantly. If you only check once every hour it might take three hours to get better. Whereas, if you checked once a minute you might be able to pack a lot more into the time you have. When you delay your feedback as long as you do in your sales presentations you can only be a dreamer or a critic, not a realist.

Let's now explore how we can utilize the elements of your effective T.O.T.E. to enrich your own know-how in selling your presentations.

If you took the goal you have when you make presentations and brought it into the selling context, what would happen? You are not going to get rid of the other goal, by the way. You are just going to add the goal of increasing their know-how to the process of selling. It is not a matter of either having to increase these people's knowledge or make money. Some people think that.

How would you do that same thing in selling your trainings? Maybe you don't have to make the sale right away anyhow. So you don't have to worry about time. You don't want to manipulate people. You want them to make an advised, appropriate decision. And if they make that decision without the knowledge, it could be a lot worse for you because they will be disappointed.

C: I know. I've had cases like that.

RBD: I think it is to your benefit to add in that goal. Put yourself back into one of those selling situations, and just imagine that you are not only trying to sell something, you are giving them important know-how.

OK. Let's also take the evidence procedure that you use when you make a presentation into this selling situation. How would you act and engage them in activities in which you could stimulate enriching propositions and questions? They might be a lot more apt to come to a program if they know they will be enriched by it.

Take the same group of people that you are having trouble selling to, and imagine looking at their faces *while* you are in the process of selling them.

C: Their questions are about the content of what we are exploring. It's completely different. It's even fun!

RBD: And now you have an opportunity to recycle instead of quitting. In other words, you can tell a lot sooner if you are fitting their model of the world.

So that is how you are going to double sales in the next five years!

C: Thank you!

RBD: All communication is just communication. This is one belief that I found in creative managers. They say there is no difference between delegating or negotiating or persuading or teaching. It is all communication. The difference between persuasion and teaching is only in your inner map, not in how you interact. The principles that make you effective in both are the same. The same goals, evidences, and operations are effective for both.

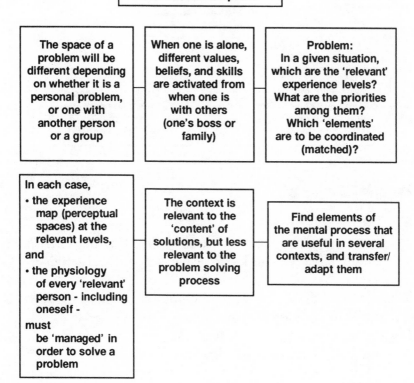

The Problem Space

| The space of a problem will be different depending on whether it is a personal problem, or one with another person or a group | When one is alone, different values, beliefs, and skills are activated from when one is with others (one's boss or family) | Problem: In a given situation, which are the 'relevant' experience levels? What are the priorities among them? Which 'elements' are to be coordinated (matched)? |

| In each case,
• the experience map (perceptual spaces) at the relevant levels,
and
• the physiology of every 'relevant' person - including oneself -
must
be 'managed' in order to solve a problem | The context is relevant to the 'content' of solutions, but less relevant to the problem solving process | Find elements of the mental process that are useful in several contexts, and transfer/ adapt them |

SECTION 5.5 / MAP A

Key Points

Different kinds of strategies and T.O.T.E.s are effective to cover different kinds of problem spaces.

The purpose of the T.O.T.E. transfer process is to identify and apply mental processes that are useful to widen perceptions of a problem space.

Activities

Identify some different strategies you have for approaching a problem. What kinds of 'space' do the different strategies cover?

In what ways do the Dreamer, Realist and Critic processes cover different spaces?

```
┌─────────────────────────────────┐
│   TOTE elicitation sequence in   │
│        contrastive analysis      │
└─────────────────────────────────┘
```

```
┌──────────────────────┐      ┌──────────────────────┐
│          1.          │      │          2.          │
│  First elicit goals, then   │  Begin by eliciting all │
│ evidences and operations,   │    the element of the   │
│   and finally responses     │      'resource' TOTE     │
│       to problems           │    (effective context)   │
└──────────────────────┘      └──────────────────────┘
```

SECTION 5.5 / MAP B

Key Points

Relevant mental processes are found by contrasting T.O.T.E. elements of effective and ineffective examples of creativity.

Activities

Think of a situation involving communication in which you would like to be more creative but find it difficult.

Identify another situation in which you are able to communicate creatively and flexibly

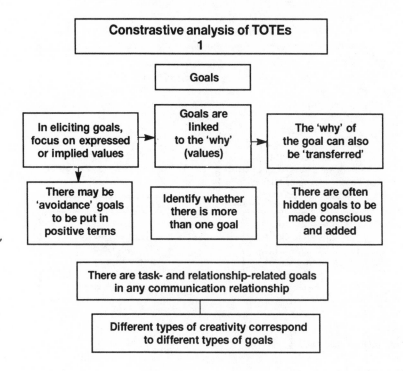

SECTION 5.5 / MAP C

Key Points
Goals are tangible expressions of values. Values related to goals may be a relevant element to identify and transfer. There are often clusters of goals associated with particular situations; e.g., there are task and relational goals associated with managing people.
Some goals are not initially conscious.
Different types of goals stimulate different types of creativity.
Activities
Identify the goals you have for the two communication situations you have identified in relation to both task and relationship.
What values are implied by the goals in the effective situation? What are the differences between the goals and implied values in the two situations?

```
┌─────────────────────────────────────┐
│     Constrastive analysis of TOTEs   │
│                  2                    │
└─────────────────────────────────────┘
              ┌──────────────┐
              │  Evidences   │
              └──────────────┘
```

```
┌──────────────────────────┐      ┌──────────────────────────┐
│      Many types of        │      │   Evidences for each goal │
│   evidences can be used:  │      │    and evidences for both │
│    e.g., for reaching the │      │      hidden goals and     │
│ 'outcome' of the task or for│    │    criteria/values should be│
│ achieving 'consensus' within│    │        available          │
│     the relationship      │      │                           │
└──────────────────────────┘      └──────────────────────────┘
        ┌──────────────────────┐      ┌──────────────────────┐
        │   Time constraints    │      │      The same         │
        │   influence both      │      │  type of evidences    │
        │    the type of        │      │    can be used        │
        │   evidences and       │      │ and observe what is   │
        │     evidence          │      │  similar or what is   │
        │    procedures         │      │     different         │
        └──────────────────────┘      └──────────────────────┘
```

Section 5.5 / map D

Key Points

Evidences also relate to types of goals.

Some evidences may be inappropriate for certain types of goals.

There are ongoing evidences and evidences of completion that operate in different time frames.

There are different types of evidences for different levels of goals.

Activities

What kinds of evidences do you use to evaluate your progress toward your goals in the two situations?

Do you have evidences that indicate ongoing progress as well as the ultimate achievement of the goal?

Do you have different types of evidences for different levels of goals?

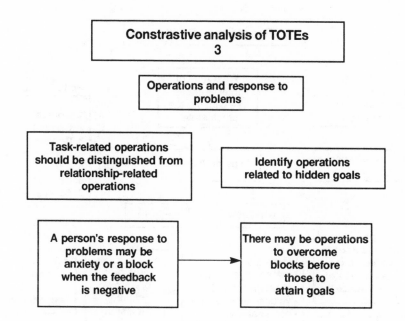

Constrastive analysis of TOTEs
3

Operations and response to problems

Task-related operations should be distinguished from relationship-related operations

Identify operations related to hidden goals

A person's response to problems may be anxiety or a block when the feedback is negative

There may be operations to overcome blocks before those to attain goals

SECTION 5.5 / MAP E

Key Points
Different operations relate to different goals and should be sorted out.
Responses to problems are often a key factor in creativity.

Activities
What sorts of operations do you use for achieving task *versus* relational goals in the two situations?

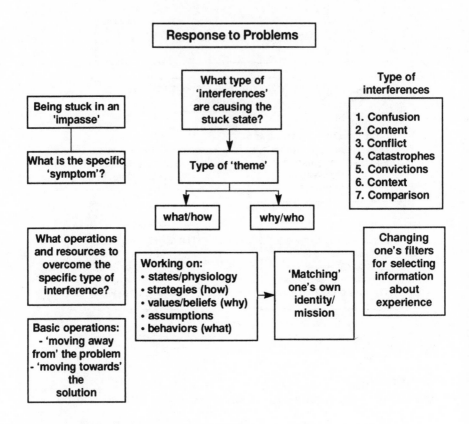

SECTION 5.5 / MAP F

Key Points
Problems arise as interference or 'symptoms.'
There are different classes of interferences related to different causes.
Different levels of operations serve as resources for different kinds of interferences.

Activities
What kinds of problems or interferences arose in the two situations? How did you perceive and respond to these interferences?
What kinds of resources and alternatives do you have available in the two situations?
At what levels were your responses in the different situation

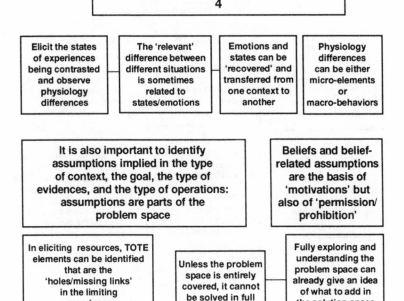

SECTION 5.5 / MAP G

Key Points

Assumptions related to particular situations and general contexts are also part of a problem space creating issues involving motivation and permission for creative thinking.

Activities

What were your assumptions about the contexts of the two situations? How did those assumptions promote or inhibit your ability to be creative?

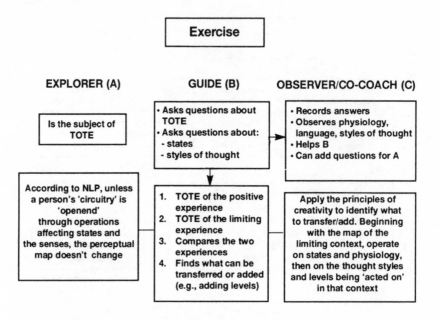

SECTION 5.5 / MAP H

Key Points

The T.O.T.E. transfer exercise is itself a T.O.T.E.

The goal is to enrich the explorer's perceptions of a problem space.

The evidence for success involves changes in the explorer's state and micro level cognitive and behavioral patterns related to the problem, and the explorer's awareness of other choices and alternatives.

The operations involve the contrasting of the T.O.T.E. related to a difficult situation with an example of effective creative problem solving in order to find cognitive and behavioral elements that can be added to enrich the explorer's approach and choices with respect to the problem situation.

Activities

To what degree are you being a Dreamer, Realist or Critic in the effective example and problem situations? What thinking style is being used by the other person? How could you make the different thinking styles more balanced?

How could you adapt the T.O.T.E. transfer process to your own working reality in order to improve your own personal creative problem solving ability? As a coach to help others be more creative?

Section 5.6
Assessing Improvement
in Creativity

Assessing improvement in creativity is a function of evaluating the degree to which a person has been able to widen their perception of the problem space. In assessing improvement in creativity with respect to problem solving it is important to remember that creative ability can improve even if a specific solution to the problem has not yet been found. Just the increased awareness of problem space elements, or more meta cognition of the creative process itself can be an important indicator and result of creativity.

One general way to assess improvement in creativity that we have already discussed is to apply the three principles of creativity to the three major elements of the T.O.T.E. being used for creative problem solving:

1. Are the goals oriented toward a positive outcome?
2. Does the evidence procedure provide effective feedback?
3. Is there enough flexibility and variety in the operations to manage the problem space?

In essence, effective problem solving involves:

1. 'Wanting to';
2. Knowing 'how to,' and,
3. Getting the 'chance to' identify and enact an adequate solution.

According to Yeager (1985) one needs the motivation, the means and the opportunity in order to effectively approach and solve the problem. Each of these factors relates to a different level in the problem solving process. 'Wanting to' relates to beliefs and values with respect a particular problem. Knowing 'how to' relates the development and mobilization of the capabilities and behaviors necessary to identify and implement solutions. Getting the 'chance to' relates to the perception of constraints or opportunities in the problem environment or context.

On an individual level, then, improvement in creativity may be assessed in terms of positive changes with respect to either of these three factors:

1. The degree of motivation and permission one feels with respect to creativity in the problem situation;

2. The subjective experience of the degree of resourcefulness of one's state or physiology with respect to the situation, and

3. The richness of one's own map of the situation and the quantity of potential opportunities and alternatives.

In later Sections we will be exploring ways of stimulating creativity in a group. In assessing the enhancement of creativity in a group it is important to bear in mind that a person is a system of elements and is also part of larger systems. In a group, improvement in creativity may be assessed in relationship to:

1. The degree to which goals, evidences and assumptions are shared by group members;

2. The acceptance, encouragement and coordination of different thinking styles and creative processes within the group, and

3. The range of capabilities being expressed and utilized by group members.

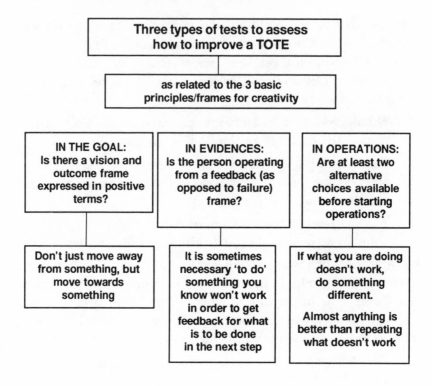

SECTION 5.6 / MAP A

Key Points
One general way to assess improvement in creativity is by
applying the principles of creativity to the three major
elements of the T.O.T.E. being used for creative problem
solving:
(a) Are the goals oriented toward a positive outcome?
(b) Does the evidence procedure provide effective feedback?
(c) Is there enough flexibility and variety in the operations to
manage the problem space?
Activities
Review your experience during the previous Section.
In what ways do you think you have broadened or improved
your creative capacity in the specific situations you were
exploring? In general?

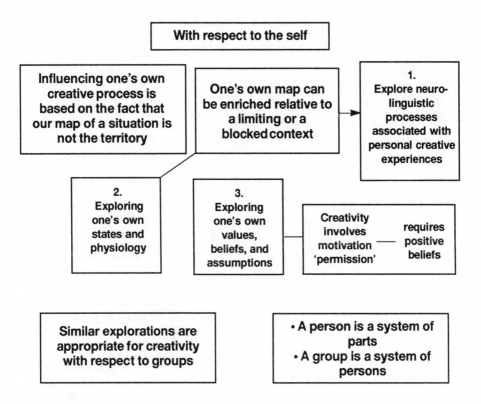

SECTION 5.6 / MAP B

Key Points

With respect to oneself, creativity may also be assessed in relationship to (1) one's subjective experience of the richness of one's own map of the situation, (2) changes in one's state or physiology with respect to the situation and (3) the degree of motivation and permission one feels with respect to creativity in that situation.

Activities

What changed most about your experience of the difficult situation: your map of the situation? your state? your sense of motivation or permission to be creative?

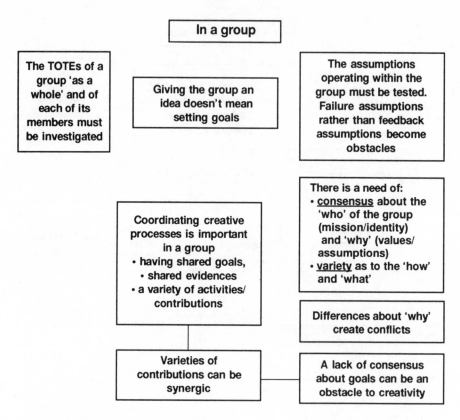

The TOTEs of a group 'as a whole' and of each of its members must be investigated

In a group

Giving the group an idea doesn't mean setting goals

The assumptions operating within the group must be tested. Failure assumptions rather than feedback assumptions become obstacles

Coordinating creative processes is important in a group
• having shared goals,
• shared evidences
• a variety of activities/ contributions

There is a need of:
• consensus about the 'who' of the group (mission/identity) and 'why' (values/ assumptions)
• variety as to the 'how' and 'what'

Differences about 'why' create conflicts

Varieties of contributions can be synergic

A lack of consensus about goals can be an obstacle to creativity

SECTION 5.6 / MAP C

Key Points

In a group, improvement in creativity may be assessed by (1) the degree to which goals, evidences and assumptions are shared by group members, (2) the acceptance, encouragement and coordination of different thinking styles and creative processes within the group and (3) and the range of capabilities being expressed and utilized by group members.

Activities

Think of some groups that you have been in that were able to be effectively creative. Contrast them with groups that have not been creative.

What is your evidence that one group was effectively creative and the other was not?

What would need to have changed in order for the ineffective group to have improved?

Chapter 6

Developing
Multiple
Perspectives

Overview of Chapter 6

General objectives for Chapter 6

1. Discuss different ways of representing and mapping 'problem space' and the impact of assumptions in relation to interpreting a problem.

2. Present and discuss general processes for enhancing creative thinking ability through different modalities of representation.

3. Assist readers in a 'co-creative' activity to create multiple representations of a problem space and to understand the benefits of having multiple representations for effective problem solving.

4. Discuss the influence of different kinds of representations and assumptions on identifying problems.

Sections and goals of each Section

Section 6.1 Representing Problem Space

Present different ways of representing and mapping 'problem spaces.'

Section 6.2 Uncovering Assumptions About a Problem Space

Describe the influence of assumptions on problem solving and their relationship to representational maps.

Section 6.3 'Intervision'—Multiple Perspectives of a Problem Space

Present the co-creative process of creating multiple maps of a problem space.

Section 6.4 Influence of Assumptions and Kind of Representations on Problem Solving

Define and discuss the influence of different kinds of representations and assumptions on the perception of a problem space.

Section 6.1
Representing
Problem Space

The way in which we represent a problem will greatly influence how we perceive the problem and seek solutions. As a simple example, the problem, "what is 2/3 of 1/2" seems more difficult than "what is 1/2 of 2/3" even though the answer (2/6 or 1/3), and the process for arriving at the answer, are the same. In this Section we will be exploring some strategies for representing problems and problem space.

There are several general processes which can be used to represent problem space, and to improve and enhance creative thinking ability. Each of them involves the process of representing something in a different way:

1. Using metaphorical or symbolic representations.

2. Changing representational systems.

3. Creating multi sensory maps.

One of the most basic creative processes is that of representing one thing as something else, either in symbolic representation or as a metaphor.

Another process for representing problem spaces in different ways is changing the representational channel through which you are perceiving or mapping it—such as changing from a verbal channel to a visual channel by drawing, or from visual to kinesthetic by acting something out, etc.

Another very basic creative process, that was used by Disney, is *synesthesia*, which has to do with a synthesis of sensory representations. Mozart, for instance, claimed that he heard and saw music at the same time; not music as notes but like abstract imagery. He also felt the music. So, he had a multi-sensory representation of sounds. He even implied that music had a kind of taste, claiming that one of his strategies for composing music was similar to making a meal. Different kinds of music had to be balanced together as one would mix different flavors. Some phrases might go more with dessert, others made a good *hors d'oeuvre*.

In summary, there are three basic ways to enrich a representation of a problem space:

1. Metaphor and symbolism.

2. Changing representational channels.

3. Synthesizing channels of representation.

In general, the more richly a person is able to use his or her representational systems, the greater the number of possibilities will be stimulated or perceived.

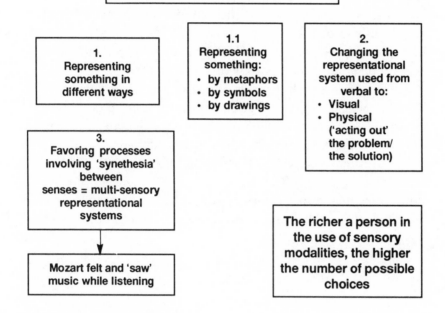

SECTION 6.1 / MAP A

Key Points

There are several general processes which can be used to improve and enhance creative problem solving ability. Each of them involves the process of representing problems and goals in different ways.

(1) Metaphorical or symbolic diagrams.

(2) Changing representational systems.

(3) Creating multi sensory maps.

In general, the more richly a person is able to use his or her representational systems, the greater the number of possibilities that will be perceived.

Activities

How well are you able to use all of your sensory modalities?
Which is your strongest modality? Which one is most familiar?
Which do you use the least?

Identify some situations in which you already use metaphors
or symbolic diagrams in problem solving.

Practice making multi-sensory maps of your experiences.
Recall a pleasant or relaxing experience and map out what
you saw, heard, felt, smelled and tasted in that experience.

Think of some situations in which you switched
representational channels. How did it effect your thinking
process?

Practice representing experiences in different channels by
describing them, drawing them and acting them out.

Section 6.2
Uncovering Assumptions
About a Problem Space

One of the dangers in problem solving is being too abstract or "reductionistic"—that is, getting so caught up in the model or theory itself that one loses contact and feedback with concrete experience. This leads to the problems caused by generalization, deletion and distortion. As Albert Einstein so elegantly advised:

> *"Everything should be made as simple as possible, but not simpler."*

If it is made too simple, it becomes *simplistic*.

In order to conduct our lives and solve problems, we are all constantly making models of our experiences. The question is how to determine when to simplify those models versus when they are too simple. Einstein, for instance, constantly sought to find the limiting assumptions that either made our thinking too simplistic or not simple enough. As he was fond of saying:

> *"Our thinking creates problems that the same type of thinking will not solve."*

When we think about something we often make tacit assumptions about things that we come to take for granted. While these assumptions generally help to provide short cuts for our thinking, they can limit us if we forget that they are there. For instance, consider the following problem:

> *A boy and his father were in an automobile accident. The boy's father sustained only minor injuries and sat anxiously in the waiting room while the boy was taken into the emergency room at the hospital. The emergency room doctor came rushing in to assist the boy but stopped abruptly and exclaimed, "I can't operate on this boy. He's my son!" Who was the emergency room doctor?*

Many people in Western culture still have the unconscious assumption that doctors are primarily men. This causes quite a few individuals to hesitate for a moment before arriving at the most obvious answer that the emergency room doctor is the boy's mother. Some even become baffled, or venture guesses such as the boy has a step father, etc.

In companies, problems generally relate to patterns and causes within an entire system of events. Sometimes some of the systems in the "totality of systems" have been left out of the description or model being used. When persons or other factors are not included in the representational map of a problem space, their actions influence the ones included in the map in a way that appears random or only statistical. As an analogy, consider the following problem:

Which of the following numbers is most different from the others?

> 1. One   2. Thirteen   3. Thirty-One

If we only consider the system of written numbers, we will be forced to make up answers in an attempt to arbitrarily argue why 'one,' 'thirteen,' or 'thirty-one' is special or unique in some way. If, on the other hand, we realize that the 1, 2 and 3 are also numbers, the number 2 becomes an obvious solution, because it is the only even number and refers to neither a one nor a three as do all of the other numbers.

Strategies for Finding Unconscious Assumptions

To adequately define a problem space we must uncover our assumptions. One way to find unconscious assumptions is to apply several different modalities of representation. Albert Einstein's strategy is a good example. Instead of words or mathematical formulas, Einstein claimed to think primarily in terms of visual images and feelings. In a letter to cognitive psychologist Jacques Hadamard, Einstein explained:

"The words or the language, as they are written or spoken, do not seem to play any role in my mechanism of thought. The psychical entities which seem to serve as elements in thought are certain signs and more or less clear images which can be 'voluntarily' reproduced and combined."

"I very rarely think in words at all. A thought comes, and I may try to express it in words afterward."

We all know that words are often ambiguous and 'slippery.' And yet we take language so much for granted that we often forget that 'the map is not the territory' and are not conscious of where we are making key assumptions. Einstein described the problem with language quite elegantly when he said:

"In an early stage the words may correspond directly to impressions. At a later stage this direct connection is lost insofar as some words convey relations to perceptions only if used in connection with other words (for instance such words as: "is", "or," "thing"). Then word-groups rather than single words refer to perceptions. When language becomes thus partially independent from the background of impressions a greater inner coherence is gained.

"Only at this further development where frequent use is made of so-called abstract concepts, language becomes an instrument of reasoning in the true sense of the word.

"But it is also this development which turns language into a dangerous source of error and deception. Everything depends on the degree to which words and word-combinations correspond to the world of impression."

The potential of language to be a *"dangerous source of error and deception"* is probably the reason Einstein choose imagery and feelings rather than words during his thinking process. These were a way to keep the concepts and relationships encoded by *"words and word-combinations"* closer to the *"world of impression."* As an illustration of Einstein's point, consider for a moment the following problem:

A police officer on traffic duty saw a bus driver going the wrong way down a one way street, yet the police officer did not issue the bus driver a ticket. Why?

Because the problem has been defined verbally, we must make many unconscious assumptions about the problem. In this case, the key to the seeming anomaly revolves around presuppositions related to the 'words' and 'word-combinations' "bus driver" and "going." Most people assume that the "bus driver" is inside of a bus and that "going" means 'driving the bus.' If we realize that the bus driver could be walking down the street, the seeming anomaly is resolved.

Einstein's approach to this problem would have been to find the words that are most visually ambiguous, such as *going*, and then try to form a symbolic but clear cognitive map of the interaction defined by the problem forming an imaginary visual construction and putting himself in the perceptual positions of both the bus driver and the police officer. To construct a clear picture of the problem that is being described (such as a symbolic drawing) you would have to at some point consciously put the bus driver into a bus. This would create much more of a chance to discover the assumption than simply considering the problem verbally.

Exercise: Using Symbolic Metaphors to Find and Challenge Basic Assumptions

Consider the following problem and how you would approach it.

You are the person in charge of factory "B." The chief of your Maintenance Department manages 6 eight-man teams, working under 6 foremen. You are worried because these teams don't work efficiently. As a matter of fact, the workers in the teams tend to do just what strictly concerns their specific tasks. As a result, work and programs of this Department are slowed down. Only in cases of emergency is this routine overcome. You also know, on the other hand, that the capabilities and competence of the workers are higher and allow for more effective utilization.

How would you approach solving this problem?

Draw a picture representing your understanding of the problem space described in the scenario and write a short description of your approach to reaching a solution. The picture may be a sketch, a metaphor, or symbolic representation.

When you have finished, go back over the scenario, your picture and your approach to the problem and find out what you have assumed or presupposed by your representation of the problem space.

> What did you assume about the *where, when, what, how, why* and *who* of the problem situation?
>
> Did you assume it was a "how to" problem or a "want to" problem"?
>
> Did you assume it was a problem of motivation? Of organization? Of communication? Of leadership?
>
> From who's perspective did you form your map? The person in charge of the factory? The chief of maintenance? The foremen? The workers?
>
> What did you assume about the perspective and values of the person in charge of the factory? The chief of maintenance? The foremen? The workers?
>
> What did you assume was the cause of the problem? The person in charge of the factory? The chief of maintenance? The foremen? The workers? Factors coming from parts of the organization other than the ones described in the problem statement?
>
> What kind of visualization of the system and the problem did you make?
>
> Did you mentally simulate any scenarios or interactions?

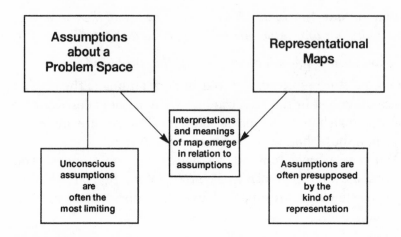

Key Points

In addition to the way we represent a problem space, the creativity of our approach to a problem is influenced by the assumptions we have about a problem space.

Generally the most limiting assumptions are the ones we are unaware of.

The meaning of a situation arises out of the connection of a representational map to a set of assumptions.

Representations themselves will reflect assumptions.

One way to identify assumptions is by examining the presuppositions of our representational map of a situation.

Activities

Think of a situation in which you limited your ability to be creative because of an assumption you made.

Think of a situation in which you were able to find or enact a solution that others did not because they had different assumptions than you.

Think of some examples of assumptions that promote creativity. That inhibit creativity.

Think of a common road map. What assumptions do you have to make in order to interpret it and give it meaning?

Find an example of a map that you were not able to interpret because you did not know what to assume.

Section 6.3
Multiple Perspectives
of a Problem Space

One powerful form of co-creativity arises out of the fact that people have different maps of the world. The way that somebody else represents a particular individual's problem can automatically provide a way of thinking which is different than the type of thinking which is creating the problem.

The next exercise is designed to take advantage of this natural process of co-creativity. It is called "inter-vision." In "supervision" there is an implied hierarchical relationship between people; the supervisor provides the 'right map' to the other person. In "inter-vision" it is assumed that people are peers and that there is no one right map. There is also an important implication in the term "vision." One of the goals of the exercise is to apply visual and symbolic thinking strategies in a group context.

The exercise has to do with the influence of the way we represent and conceptualize a problem space on our ability to find potential solution space. It is best done in a group of four in order to get enough of a range of diversity.

One of the group members, the 'explorer,' describes a problem that he or she is dealing with to the other group members. When the explorer has finished describing the problem, all four people draw a symbolic or metaphoric picture of the problem. It can be any kind of a diagram or a sketch. For example, somebody might draw a dog chained up; another person may just draw a group of symbols like rectangles, circles and stars and connect them with lines and arrows. What is certain is that the other members will not represent the explorer's problem in the same way. Everyone will have a different map of the problem.

Each person is to make his or her own representational map individually without looking at the other drawings. So, each draws his or her own individual picture of what this problem space is, including the explorer, making a total of four pictorial maps of the problem space. Then group members share their pictures and discuss the assumptions behind the various drawings and interpretations. Some guidelines about types of assumptions that you might want to check are presented later in this Section. Contrasting different peoples' maps and assumptions about a problem space is a way to enrich perceptions about that space and uncover other assumptions.

This is an exercise on representing and widening the perception of a problem space. "Intervisors" are to explain their drawings without trying to give a solution to the problem. They are simply explaining their representation and what assumptions they made. In other words, the goal of an "intervisor" is not to solve the explorer's problem, but rather to widen his or her perception of the problem space. The group is not yet attempting to find specific solutions to the explorer's problem. Finding solution space will be explored in a separate exercise. So, in this exercise, intervisors don't try to tell the explorer how to solve his or her problem; they simply show and explain the way they represented the "problem space" of the problem. Of course, the fact that they've represented the explorer's problem differently may already start to change his or her perception of it.

At the end, the explorer is to give feedback to the group in terms of how his or her own map of the problem space has been enriched. The explorer restates the problem and describes in what ways his or her map has been enriched.

To summarize:

1. The explorer describes (in 5 minutes or less) a problem he or she is dealing with.

2. Each person, including the explorer, draws a picture (in 5 minutes or less), or a visual map of the problem space.

3. Group members compare the pictures, explain them and discuss the assumptions behind them. The discussion should also be kept within a time limit of approximately 5 minutes per person.

The presupposition of the exercise is that making external maps in the form of drawings is an effective method to:

1. Acknowledge the diversity of maps between people, and

2. Develop multiple perspectives of a problem space.

'Intervision' Exercise

1. Explorer describes a problem or goal to the other group members. Make a concise description or statement defining the problem you are confronting. You may want to write it down and look for any key words that might seem especially ambiguous or problematic.

2. Each person in the group (including explorer) individually draws a picture representing his or her own understanding of the problem space. The picture may be a sketch, a metaphor, or symbolic representation.

3. All group members share, compare and explain their pictures. Explore the beliefs, values and assumptions presupposed by each person about their representation of the problem space.

For each key element (visualizing symbol) in the picture, ask "What are the assumptions behind your choice of that representation?"

Explore assumptions about the problem space in relationship to some of the following areas:

What did you assume about the where, when, what, how, why and who of the problem situation?

What elements of the problem did you assume were the most priorital?

Did you assume it was a "how to" problem or a "want to" problem"?

Did you assume it was a problem of motivation? Of organization? Of communication? Of leadership?

From who's perspective did you form your imaginary construction?

What did you assume about the perspective and values of the persons involved in the problem?

What did you assume was the cause of the problem?

What did you assume were the symptoms of the problem?

What did you assume was the outcome of the problem?

What did you assume were the anticipated effects of reaching the outcome?

What kind of visualization of the system and the problem did you make?

Did you simulate any scenarios or interactions?

At what levels did you assume there were constraints or limitations:

Environment (where, when)?

Behavior (what)?

Capabilities (how)?

Beliefs and Values (why)?

Identity (who)?

```
┌─────────────────────────────────┐
│       Intervision exercise      │
└─────────────────────────────────┘

┌─────────────────────────────────┐
│  Groups of 4 define the reference │
│     (work or other) contexts    │
└─────────────────────────────────┘
```

1.	2.	3.
'A' describes a problem or project on which he/she is working to the other members of the group	Each member (individually, including 'A') makes a symbolic or metaphoric drawing representing the idea according to his/her own perceptual space/ map	The members, all together, compare and explain their drawings in the group (intervision), and suggest what different perceptual spaces have emerged

SECTION 6.3 / MAP A

Key Points

One powerful form of co-creativity arises out of the fact that people have different maps of the world.

Making external maps in the form of drawings is an effective method to (1) acknowledge the diversity of maps between people and (2) develop multiple perspectives of a problem space.

The way that somebody else represents a particular individual's problem can automatically provide a way of thinking which is different than the type of thinking which is creating the problem.

Contrasting different people's maps and assumptions about a problem space is a way to enrich perceptions about that space and uncover other assumptions.

Activities

Think of some examples of situations in which you benefited from the fact that other people had a different perspective than you.

Think of a situation in which assuming that someone else had the same map of the situation as you did created problems.

Think of an example in which making a symbolic diagram or metaphor helped you to more creatively approach a problem.

Recall an experience in which you contributed significantly because you had a different map than everyone else.

Section 6.4
Influence of Assumptions and Kind of Representations on Problem Solving

A problem space is defined by the parts of a system one considers to be relevant to the problem. The way you represent a problem space will determine what kind of problem states and desired states you look for and how you define them. Different kinds of representations 'punctuate' a problem space in different ways and highlight different factors and relationships in that space. Different types of representations and representational channels also encourage different types of thinking processes. For instance, a critic is more likely to emerge in response to words than symbolic images.

Different forms of maps are more effective for representing information on different levels:

What ----------------- >	words
How ----------------- >	diagrams
Why ----------------- >	symbolic representations
Who ----------------- >	metaphors

Figure 6.1   Forms of Maps

In order to give meaning to a particular problem situation you must make *assumptions* about the problem space in which you are operating. Different assumptions influence the priority and relevance we give to elements of the problem space.

One's representation of and assumptions about a problem space will influence and will be influenced by a number of key elements of problem solving:

1. *Interpretation of the meaning of an input or event.*
   Interpretations in the form of inferences or conclusions involve connecting and fitting a particular input or event into other frameworks. Most often, inferences are based

upon assumptions about cultural habits and attitudes and knowledge about context. The difficulty with this is that assumptions may be valid only within a narrow social or historical scope. This can make interpreting the meaning of clues and events subject to a lot of potential variation.

2. *Completeness/thoroughness of coverage of the problem space.*

   Since everyone must make assumptions in order to give something meaning, we might ask, 'How does one minimize problems brought about by inappropriate assumptions or mistaken interpretations?' One answer relates to how thoroughly one covers the total possible problem space. For instance, there are multiple perspectives which can be taken. Perspective is one key element of problem space. Time frames are another. Perceiving events from different time frames can change the implications that they have.

3. *Order in which problem features/elements are attended to.*

   The sequence in which one makes observations and inferences can also influence the conclusion one draws—especially when inferences are being drawn from one another. Some inferences are not possible to make unless others have already been made.

4. *Priority given to problem elements/features.*

   In addition to sequence, the priority or emphasis given to various clues or elements determines their influence in shaping an inference or conclusion. The importance of different clues vary depending on the perception of their relevance to the problem space. For instance, certain clues might give more indications about the character of a person, others give more information about the state of a person, others are more priorital in determining environmental influences.

5. *Additional knowledge about the problem from sources outside the problem space.*

The assumptions used to give meaning to clues and features are often derived from information that comes from knowledge brought to bear on a particular problem from frameworks or sources not directly related to the problem space.

6. *Degree of involvement of fantasy and imagination*
Another source of knowledge that originates outside of a particular problem space is *imagination*. Albert Einstein, who claimed that "Imagination is more important than knowledge," maintained:

> *"[K]nowledge of what is does not open the door directly to what should be. One can have the clearest and most complete knowledge of what is, and yet not be able to deduct from that what should be the goal of our human aspirations... [O]ur existence and our activity acquire meaning only by the setting up of such a goal and of corresponding values."*

Problem solving based on imagination generally involves imagining possible paths and then using deduction and observations to select and confirm possible scenarios.

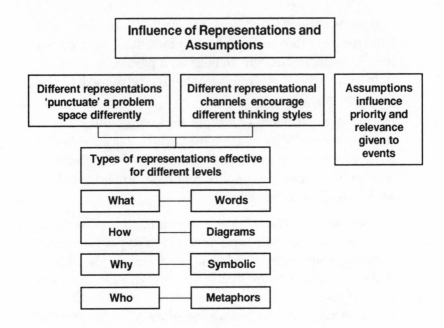

SECTION 6.4 / MAP A

Key Points

Different kinds of representations 'punctuate' a problem space in different ways and highlite different factors and relationships in that space.

Different assumptions influence the priority and relevance we give to elements of the problem space.

Different types of representations and representational channels encourage different types of thinking processes (e.g., a critic is more likely to emerge in response to words than symbolic images).

Different forms of maps are more effective for representing information on different levels:

What	words
How	diagrams
Why	symbolic
Who	metaphors

Activities

Think of a problem you are currently working on. Draw a
picture of it and explain your drawing to someone else or a
group of others. Have them also draw their own map.

Think about your own drawing. Were there any elements that
you drew in your drawing but didn't realize their significance
until you started to explain it?

Compare the different kinds of drawings that emerged during
the exercise. How did they each 'punctuate' the problem space
differently?

How did different kinds of drawings put emphasis on certain
relationships and not on others?

How do drawings and symbols imply priorities?

How did the different assumptions of group members lead to
different interpretations of the problem?

What kinds of drawings and assumptions seemed to allow for
the richest coverage of the problem space?

Which kinds of representations seemed to draw out more of
the Dreamer? Realist? Critic?

What surprised you or impressed you the most about other
people's maps?

In what way did you benefit the most from the maps of
others?

What types of maps most effectively represented different
levels? (i.e., environment, behaviors, capabilities, beliefs,
values and identity)

Chapter 7

Promoting Lateral Thinking

Overview of Chapter 7

General objectives for Chapter 7

1. Present and discuss how to use metaphors and other lateral thinking methods to discover and create potential 'solution space.'

2. Present and discuss procedures by which lateral thinking skills may be applied as an individual or group process to find or open up solution space to a particular problem.

3. Assist readers in a 'co-creative' activity to applying lateral thinking processes to enrich maps of a problem space an open up solution space.

4. Help readers to understand and experience the concrete benefits of metaphor and lateral thinking strategies for effective problem solving and discuss how lateral thinking processes effect representational maps and assumptions about a problem space.

Sections and goals of each Section

Section 7.1 Opening Up Solution Space
Present different ways of opening up 'solution spaces' through metaphors and other lateral thinking methods.

Section 7.2 Processes that Facilitate Creativity
Define several processes by which lateral thinking skills may be applied to a particular problem to find or open up solution space.

Section 7.3 Exploring Different Assumptions and Modes of Representations
Describe the co-creative process of applying lateral thinking processes to enrich maps of a problem space and open up solution space. Discuss how they effect representational maps and assumptions about a problem space.

Section 7.4 Defining States and Paths Within a Problem Space (The S.O.A.R. Model)
Present the basic conceptual elements of the general problem solving approach defined by the SOAR Model.

Section 7.5 Defining a Path
Expand the notion of 'transition states' and how they form a 'path' through various aspects of a problem space.

Section 7.1
Opening Up
Solution Space

Opening up solution space is essentially achieved by shifting our point of view and thinking in a way that is different from the type of thinking that is creating the problem. The basic dictum for finding solution space is Einstein's statement that, "You cannot solve a problem with the same thinking that created it." If what you are doing or how you are thinking isn't working, then try something else! This is why developing lateral thinking skills is an important way to enrich perceptions and find solution space.

Metaphor is probably the most fundamental form of lateral thinking. We often think of metaphors as being simply 'illustrations' of reality, but in many ways our perceptions of reality are influenced by the deeper metaphors we 'live by.' That is, we often organize reality according to metaphors instead of the other way around. Metaphors offer simple but very highly encoded representations of fundamental relationships. They are often the most effective way of representing deeper level issues relating to values and identity.

Our perceptions of problems and potential solutions are also greatly effected by the point of view or perspective from which we consider a problem. NLP identifies three basic "perceptual positions" from which a problem space may be viewed. Perceptual positions refer to the fundamental points of view one can take concerning the relationship between oneself and another person:

> *1st Position:* Associated in your own point of view, beliefs and assumptions, seeing the external world through your own eyes.

> *2nd Position:* Associated in another person's point of view, beliefs and assumptions, seeing the external world through the eyes of others.

3rd Position: Associated in a point of view outside of the relationship between yourself and the other person—an 'observer perspective.'

Another way to facilitate changing a point of view is shifting either:

1. Internal thinking styles, or

2. External channels of representation.

When someone is speaking out loud he or she is using a verbal channel of external representation. A more visual or symbolic form of external representation would involve drawing or displaying symbols and diagrams.

An internal 'style' of representation might involve engaging the process of visualization instead of using verbal logic or emotions. Different modalities of representation have different strengths. The verbal mode of internal representation, for instance, has a lot of strengths in terms of how information is sequenced with respect to logical dependencies. The visual channel is often the best way to synthesize information into a whole or 'gestalt.' Acting out a problem physically brings out its concrete aspects.

Creativity can be enhanced by either strengthening somebody's weakness or utilizing their strengths. If somebody does not typically use visualization, encouraging them to think in terms of pictures could be very useful for them. If somebody is good at visualizing, emphasizing and enriching the use of that capability can also increase creative abilities in certain situations.

Other ways to change your mode of representation involve:

1. Changing your state;

2. Changing focus to different levels;

3. Changing the time frame in which you are considering the problem.

Purposefully shifting perceptual levels, perspectives and time frames is an effective method to trigger creativity and find new solution space.

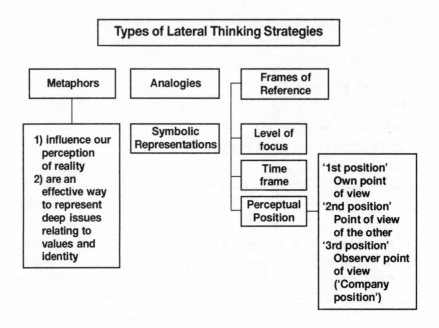

SECTION 7.1 / MAP A

Key Points

Developing lateral thinking skills is an important way to
enrich perceptions and find solution space.

Metaphor is a fundamental form of lateral thinking.

Our perceptions of reality are influenced by the deeper
metaphors we 'live by' (as opposed to the other way around).

Metaphors are often the most effective way of representing
deeper level issues relating to values and identity.

Changing focus to different levels effects perceptions of which
problem space elements are significant.

Perceptions of problems are influenced by the time frame in
which we consider them.

Our perceptions of problems are greatly effected by the point
of view or perspective from which we consider the problem.

Perceptual positions refer to the fundamental points of view
you can take concerning a relationship between yourself and
another person.

1st Position: Associated in your own point of view, beliefs and assumptions, seeing the external world through your own eyes.

2nd Position: Associated in another person's point of view, beliefs and assumptions, seeing the external world through his or her eyes.

3rd Position: Associated in a point of view outside of the relationship between yourself and the other person as an observer.

Purposefully shifting perceptual levels, perspectives and time frames is another effective method to find new solution space.

Activities

Think of some examples of the ways in which you use 'lateral thinking' already.

Think of some metaphors that are personally significant for you? your work? the way you approach a problem?

What do you think is a deep metaphor for your company?

What are some of the metaphors that are most often used in your company?

Think of some things that are difficult to express directly but are more easily expressed through metaphor.

Think of examples of how metaphors and lateral thinking processes have been used by significant historical figures (e.g., Jesus, Einstein, etc.)

Think of some examples in which changing your perception of time frame opened up new choices that you had not previously been aware of.

Identify some examples in which changing your perceptual position opened up new choices that you had not previously been aware of.

Think of some examples in which changing the level you were focusing on opened up new choices that you had not previously been aware of.

Section 7.2
Processes that
Facilitate Creativity

Once a problem space has been defined, solution space can be explored by adding new elements to the existing map of a problem space or by changing that map in some way. Adding new perspectives, by 'being in someone else shoes,' or taking the perceptual position of some historical figure or personal mentor can create new insights into a potential solution space. Focusing on a different level (who, why, how, what, where, when) can change the implications of a particular situation. Just shifting representational channels and modalities can stimulate new perspectives.

Metaphorical representation is a very common and powerful way of engaging creativity with respect to problem representation and problem solving. It is also a useful tool to transfer resources between different contexts. It stimulates a type of thinking that might lead to the level of abstraction necessary to transfer or apply resources between contexts.

Making analogies between very different types of problem solving contexts can indicate new areas of solution space. For example, you might find that, although skiing is something you do by yourself and an office context has lots of other people, there still might be a kind of a metaphorical or analogical relevance between skiing and working in an office. You might make the analogy that avoiding trees and potholes while skiing is like dealing with the potential interferences created by people in your office.

Listening for micro metaphors within the idiomatic language used by a person (or common to a culture) can also serve to identify limiting assumptions or presuppositions and point the direction for new metaphors. For example, a person might talk about a communication problem in terms of an overly aggressive micro metaphor such as a "battle." If such a metaphor is shifted to something less aggressive like 'stepping on each other's toes," new solution spaces might be more easily found. Similarly, a leadership metaphor such as "holding the stick" could be shifted to something like "passing the baton."

It is by metaphor that language grows.

The lexicon of language... is a finite set of terms that by metaphor is able to stretch out over an infinite set of circumstances, even to creating new circumstances thereby.

A theory is... a metaphor between a model and data. And understanding in science is the feeling of similarity between complicated data and a familiar model... understanding a thing is arriving at a familiarizing metaphor for it...

—Julian Jaynes
*The Origin of Consciousness
in the Breakdown of the Bicameral Mind*

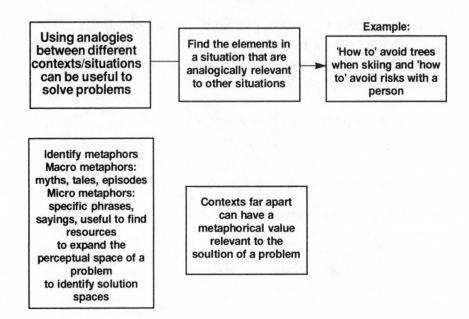

SECTION 7.2 / MAP A

Key Points

Once a problem space has been defined, solution space can be
explored by adding new elements to the existing map of a
problem space or by changing that map in some way.
Making analogies between very different types of problem
solving contexts can indicate new areas of solution space.
Adding new perspectives, by 'being in someone else shoes', or
taking the perceptual position of some historical figure or
personal mentor can create new insights into a potential
solution space.
Focusing on a different level (who, why, how, what , where,
when) can change the implications of a particular situation.
Even offering a purely metaphorical solution can be effective
to open up solution space.

Activities

Think of a problem situation that you have been working on. Make an analogy between that situation and something else that is completely different. (For example, how would a marketing problem be similar to cooking?)

Think of what kind of sport would be most metaphorically relevant to the problem situation.

Take different points of view (first position, second position, third position) in relation to the problem situation.

Identify someone that you know who has been a mentor to you and who you really respect, or someone who you think is a very capable creative person.

Imagine you could be in the shoes of the person you identified and fully take on his or her perspective, beliefs, values, assumptions and cognitive maps. How would you experience the problem and potential solutions differently?

Focus on the problem "as if" it were something purely environmental.

Focus on the problem "as if" it were something purely behavioral.

Focus on the problem "as if" it were something purely a matter of capabilities.

Focus on the problem "as if" it were something purely related to beliefs and values.

Focus on the problem "as if" it were something purely an issue of identity.

What do you learn from these different levels?

Change the time frame through which you are perceiving the problem. Make it a very long time frame — even beyond the scope of your own life. Make it an immediate time frame.

How do the different time frames effect your perception of the problem and potential solutions?

Section 7.3
Exercise: Exploring Different Assumptions and Modes of Representation

Return to the group you were in during the previous activity. For this exercise, refer to representational maps that were made during that activity.

Phase 1: Widening Perception of the Solution Space

Each of the three "intervisors" is to assist the explorer to find potential solution space through a different process:

Person 1

Person 1's goal is to assist the explorer to find a time frame in which he or she is able to perceive other alternatives or in which the issues are perceived as less of a problem.

a. Find the time frame that is being assumed or presupposed by the explorer.

What time frames are you assuming / presupposing?

b. Assist the explorer to change the time frame from which he or she is operating—change from short term to long term, from present to past, or from short term future to long term future, etc.

What would happen if you lengthened / shortened it?

What would happen if you included more / less of the past / future?

Person 2

Person 2's goal is to assist the explorer to find a perceptual position or point of view from which the explorer is able to perceive other alternatives or from which the issues are perceived as less of a problem.

a. Find the set of perceptual positions which are being used or presupposed by the explorer.

Which perceptual position(s) are you assuming / presupposing?

b. Assist the explorer to find a completely new point of view from which to consider the problem. This can involve the identification of personal mentors or individuals who the explorer perceives as having exceptional creative problem solving ability.

What would happen if you changed / added / reduced the perspective(s) from which you were viewing the problem?

Person 3

Person 3's goal is to assist the explorer to focus on a different level such that the explorer is able to perceive other alternatives or such that the issues are perceived as less of a problem.

a. Find the level or levels at which the explorer is most focused.

Which level(s) is the primary focus of your map (where, when, what, how, why, who)?

b. Assist the explorer to shift the logical level from which he or she is considering the problem—i.e., look at the intention or presuppositions behind the action instead of the action, think about values or motivation for which you have developed a capability instead of the capability itself, etc.

What would happen if you shifted the level of focus?

This should assist the explorer to move to a different level of thinking than the one which created the problem.

Phase 2:   Representing New Solution Space

1. As a group, discuss and identify the assumptions, beliefs or values that could be added or changed in the cluster of beliefs and values that currently underlie the explorer's

approach to the problem. Explore how making these changes or additions to the explorer's assumptions and beliefs would alter or enrich his or her perception of the problem.

2. Each group member, including the explorer who is to go last, makes a representation of the solution space he or she thinks would be most valuable to the explorer.

To make their individual representations, group members may either:

a. Make a new map.

b. Add directly to their previous map of the problem space.

c. Add directly to the explorer's map of the problem space.

d. Present a metaphor or analogy.

Exercise:
Applying Symbolic Metaphors and Lateral Thinking in Creative Problem Solving

I once consulted with a man who was in a situation somewhat similar to the problem in the factory. He was a project leader in charge of a group of engineers working to develop products in a technology company. His problem, as he described it, was that at the beginning of a project he would call a meeting of the team members in which he would communicate very clearly and precisely to his project team the type of product they were to make; how it was to look and operate. He would then clearly specify the roles, and responsibilities of each team member. He then checked with all the group members to make sure their understanding was clear. When he was satisfied that they understood his instructions he would send them out to work on the project. Invariably, however, as time went on the team members and thus the project would become progressively more inefficient, slowing the project down and producing errors that the team leader would have to correct.

I asked him to create a symbolic metaphor of the problem. The image he made depicted himself as a kind of source of light, like a lighthouse. He imagined a bright reddish light emanating from his head to his team members, whom he imagined as being like ships floating in the ocean. While the ships were nearby, his light could guide them to see their way to their destination and avoid the rocks near the shoreline. But as they got farther away, the ships lost sight of the guiding light and began to flounder at sea.

We then began to seek out the assumptions that were presupposed by his problem description and his symbolic construction. One important assumption was that the light was sufficient for navigation. He realized that the purpose of a lighthouse was only to provide a reference point and help people avoid shipwrecks while they were in the locality. Another assumption was that the ships did not have their own sources of light and that they were always sailing in the dark.

I asked him to take the perceptual position of the team members and imagine how they would perceive him as a leader and his communications. His sense was that, while they respected and understood him, his clarity about the design and responsibilities related to the project made it clear that it was his project and not theirs; so they lacked the feeling of enthusiasm that comes with ownership—they did not identify with the project. Further, while they understood his instructions to them clearly as individuals, they did not have a map of the whole project. While they understood on an information level, they did not really know how their individual actions were coordinating with the actions of the other team members in an ongoing way.

As a result of this, I invited him to change some of his assumptions and alter his imaginary construction to create a different approach. He visualized himself still as a kind of lighthouse. But instead of sending out a bright red light for short periods of time, he saw himself emanating a soft but constant pinkish light. After a period of time, little pink and reddish lights would begin to flicker on aboard some of the ships. If he kept the pinkish light shining long enough, all of the ships would have their own flames burning. By his maintaining the pinkish light, the flames on board the ships would begin to burn brighter and brighter, casting light and providing guidance for one another as well.

He then implemented this symbolic plan. applying some of the techniques we have explored in this Section. Rather than describe the project clearly and precisely, he would start by giving only a general overview or outline of the project. He would then have the team members individually draw their own pictures in the form of imaginary constructs or symbolic metaphors of what they thought he meant. He would then have everyone compare and explain their pictures and explore the assumptions they each had about the project and their various roles and responsibilities. Since the project leader had already thought the project through thoroughly and already had a clear idea of the issues involved in the project, he could be more of a guide or coach to help all the different members discover key assumptions or beliefs. Not only did this solve many of the motivational and conceptual problems that had been making the team inefficient, the team members adopted it as a general problem solving process among themselves.

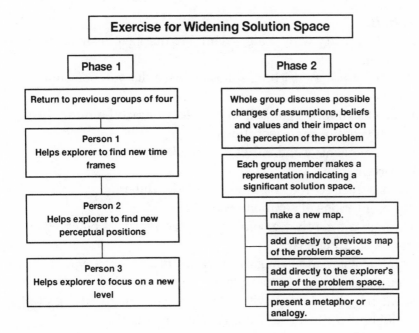

Exercise for Widening Solution Space

Phase 1

- Return to previous groups of four
- Person 1
  Helps explorer to find new time frames
- Person 2
  Helps explorer to find new perceptual positions
- Person 3
  Helps explorer to focus on a new level

Phase 2

- Whole group discusses possible changes of assumptions, beliefs and values and their impact on the perception of the problem
- Each group member makes a representation indicating a significant solution space.
  - make a new map.
  - add directly to previous map of the problem space.
  - add directly to the explorer's map of the problem space.
  - present a metaphor or analogy.

SECTION 7.3 / MAP A

Key Points

Different types of metaphors, time frame, levels and perspectives are associated with and expressed through different assumptions and representations.

The purpose of enriching a map through lateral thinking processes is not to produce a specific solution but rather to open up new solution space.

In reality, solutions arise naturally from the connection of the elements of the problem space (symptoms, causes, outcomes, anticipation of effects) to the solution space.

Humor is a state that is often associated with finding new and unexpected solution spaces.

Humor also promotes non-traditional thinking and can be useful for creative problem solving.

Activities

Do this activity with the problem you mapped in the last Chapter.

Which modes of enriching solution space did you personally find most useful?

Which assumptions or beliefs seemed to have the most effect? Which types of representations?

Which element of the S.C.O.R.E. model played the most important role?

What surprised you the most about the different representations of solution space?

Think of a time that a solution you didn't expect emerged from a solution space.

Think of some problem solving situations in which you have been involved that humor played a positive role in.

What role does humor with respect to changing state? getting a different perspective? finding solution space?

Think of ways you can you adapt some of the lateral thinking processes you have been exploring to your own working reality.

Section 7.4
SUMMARY: Defining States and Paths Within a ProblemSpace
The S.O.A.R. Model

The SOAR Model is a general information processing and problem solving structure developed by artificial intelligence experts. It was developed as a computer programming model whose purpose was to teach computers how to master something by learning heuristically through experience. An 'expert system,' in the terms of the SOAR Model, is a system that is continuously learning, updating and enriching its map of a problem space. A true 'expert' doesn't just know one right way to do something. In accordance with the law of requisite variety, the expert is constantly varying, changing and updating his or her capabilities.

The SOAR structure was designed to allow computers to learn complex problem solving tasks such as how to play chess. The computers were not programmed in how to play chess, but rather in how to learn to play chess through receiving feedback from the activity of playing chess. Each time it plays a new game, the computer learns something new. Thus, it continually keeps getting smarter and smarter. This has important implications for managers and organizations—success and expertise are a function of the ability to constantly learn, add to and expand one's range of choices.

According to the SOAR Model, the process of goal directed change in an organization or system involves moving from a present state to a desired state through a path of transition states that cover different areas of problem space. The 'problem space' relates to all of the physical and non-physical elements that effect the state of the company or individual.

SOAR stands for State-Operator-And-Result, which defines the basic feedback loop for navigating a path through a problem space. In essence, the SOAR model is the integration of the

TOTE model with the notion of 'problem space' involving a wider system. The application of an operator changes the present state in a direction that is either toward or away from the desired state. The results of applying operators become stored as a set of 'condition-action' rules which is composed of (a) evidences for identifying key states within the problem space, and (b) clusters of operators with which to change those states in the desired direction.

In the game of chess, for example, the problem space is defined by the chess board, the various chess pieces and the role of 'opponents.' The starting state is defined by the positions of the various pieces on the board. The goal state is to corner the opponent's King creating a 'checkmate.' The operations are the legal moves assigned to each of the pieces. The computer manages it's path to the desired state by accessing and storing 'control' information in the form of priorities given to various possible moves based on the current state of arrangement of the various pieces on the board. Priorities are assigned as a probability of success given the current state of the board, the number of moves the computer is allowed to anticipate and the level of value assigned to particular chess pieces.

Overview of the S.O.A.R. Model

The ability to set and achieve a wide range of goals is one of the principal hallmarks of intelligence. The SOAR model is an Artificial Intelligence (AI) programming model for general problem solving. SOAR (which stands for State, Operator, And Result) was developed by Allen Newell, Herbert Simon, and Clifford Shaw in the 1950's and was used to create the computer chess playing programs by teaching the computer how to become a chess expert by learning from its experience through remembering how it solved problems. These expert chess programs have been the most successful application of AI to date.

"According to the model, all the mental activity being devoted to a given task takes place within a cognitive arena called the problem space. A problem space in turn

consists of a set of states, which describe the situation at any given moment, and a set of operators, which describe how the problem solver can change the situation from one state to another. In chess, for example, the problem space would be [the set of parameters which define] "a chess game" [such as the two opponents, the chess board, etc.], a state would consist of a specific configuration of pieces on the chess board, and an operator would consist of a legal move, such as "Knight to King-4." The task of the problem solver is to search for the sequence of operators that will take it from a given initial state (say, with the pieces lined up for the start of the chess game) to a given solution state (the opponent's king in a checkmate)." (Waldrop, 1988)

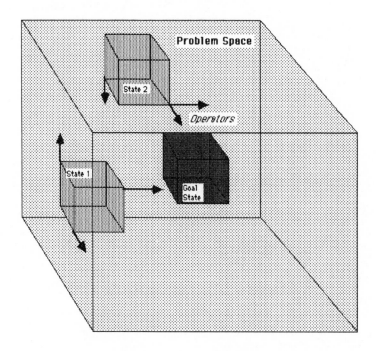

Figure 7.1   Problem Space

Once these parameters have been defined the problem solver must formulate a guidance strategy in order to find the sequence of operators that will lead from the starting state to the goal state. This takes place through a set of prioritized condition-action rules in the form of "**IF** you perceive a certain state, **THEN** apply a certain sequence of operators."

If an impasse is reached, sub-goals and sub-operations (i.e., sub-T.O.T.E.s) are triggered, which are then remembered as new condition-action rules. Following this course, the problem solver moves from a Trial-and-Error guidance strategy (novice), through Hill Climbing (doing what seems best at the time) to one involving Means-Ends analysis (expert).

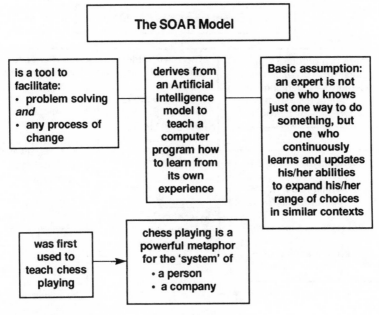

The SOAR Model

is a tool to facilitate:
• problem solving *and*
• any process of change

derives from an Artificial Intelligence model to teach a computer program how to learn from its own experience

Basic assumption: an expert is not one who knows just one way to do something, but one who continuously learns and updates his/her abilities to expand his/her range of choices in similar contexts

was first used to teach chess playing

chess playing is a powerful metaphor for the 'system' of
• a person
• a company

SECTION 7.4 / MAP A

Key Points

The SOAR Model is a general problem solving structure developed by artificial intelligence experts.

The SOAR Model was developed as a computer programming model whose purpose was to teach computers how to learn heuristically through experience.

An 'expert system,' in the terms of the SOAR Model, is a system that is continuously learning, updating and enriching its map of a problem space.

Activities

Recall some examples of skills that you have learned through experience (as opposed to instruction).

Intuitively think about the kinds of learning processes and creative processes that are necessary in order to learn through experience.

What are some things that you think are best acquired through experience rather than other methods?

Think about something in which you have developed expertise.

Think about the ways in which you continually update and enrich the capabilities required to maintain that expertise.

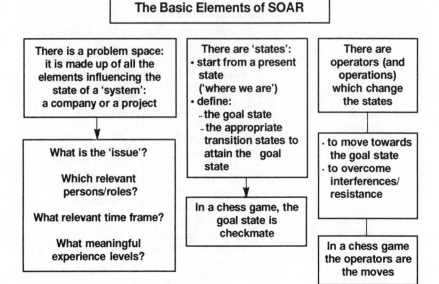

The Basic Elements of SOAR

There is a problem space: it is made up of all the elements influencing the state of a 'system': a company or a project

↓

What is the 'issue'?

Which relevant persons/roles?

What relevant time frame?

What meaningful experience levels?

There are 'states':
• start from a present state
  ('where we are')
• define:
  .. the goal state
  .. the appropriate transition states to attain the goal state

↓

In a chess game, the goal state is checkmate

There are operators (and operations) which change the states

│

• to move towards the goal state
• to overcome interferences/ resistance

│

In a chess game the operators are the moves

SECTION 7.4 / MAP **B**

Key Points

According to the SOAR Model, the process of goal directed change in an organization or system involves moving from a present state to a desired through a path of transition states that cover different areas of problem space.

SOAR stands for State-Operator-And-Result, which defines the basic feedback loop for navigating a path through a problem space.

In the SOAR Model, a path is essentially a set of 'condition-action' rules which is composed of (a) evidences for identifying key states within the problem space and (b) clusters of operators with which to change those states in the desired direction.

In an organization, a 'state' can be defined in terms of (a) the relevant persons, perspectives and roles involved, (b) the relevant time frame(s) and (c) the relevant levels of interaction and change (environment, behavior, capabilities, beliefs and values, identity).

Activities

Recall an example in which you participated in solving an organizational problem. Reconstruct the starting state, target state, the path of transition states, and the operators that were involved in identifying and solving the problem.

Think about a current problem state in your organization. What persons/roles, time frame(s) and levels of process are involved in creating the problem state.

Section 7.5
SUMMARY: Defining a Path

A good example of the application of the SOAR model to individual problem solving is the T.O.T.E. transfer process. The starting state is defined by the situation in which you would like to be more creative. The goal state is defined in terms of the positive reference experience. The transfer process involves the application of operators in the form of physiology, thinking style changes, internal thinking techniques, additions to operations and evidences, etc., in order to move toward the goal state inside of the problem space related to the difficult situation.

The NLP models of T.O.T.E. and S.C.O.R.E. are frameworks with which to define states and paths of transition states. The NLP distinctions relating to cognitive strategies, physiology, metaphor and meta programs are operators with which to change states. The process of 'chunking'—the movement between macro level and micro level elements—is the basic problem solving and learning mechanism of the SOAR Model. A pathway, in terms of personal creativity, would be defined in terms of the sequence and level of operators that would most effectively lead to the creative state given the starting state and context.

The pathway to a creative state in one context is often different than in another context because the problem spaces are different. Even for the same goal state, paths might be different because of variations in the context and the system.

The SOAR Model also applies to group and organizational creativity. In group creativity, the problem space dealt with by individuals must be linked to the problem space that needs to be addressed by the group or project through the synthesis and coordination of micro maps and macro maps. A project team, for example, has to work inside of a particular organizational problem space.

With respect to creativity, a manager must move the group from its starting state to the goal state of manifesting a productive creative process in the context of the problem space associated with both task and relationship. In a group, the manager applies operators in terms of contextual constraints, timeframes, rules, etc. To move the group to the goal state, creativity is required by the leader of a group or team for defining and navigating a path of transition states.

The NLP distinctions of levels, perceptual positions and time frame are parameters with which to define states within an organizational system. In an organization, a 'state' can be defined in terms of:

1. The relevant persons, perspectives and roles involved;

2. The relevant time frame(s), and

3. The relevant levels of interaction and change (environment, behavior, capabilities, beliefs and values, identity).

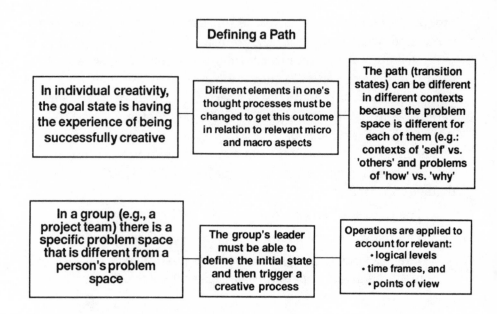

SECTION 7.5 / MAP A

Key Points

In group creativity the problem space dealt with by
individuals must be linked to the problem space that needs to
be dealt with the group or project by the synthesis and
coordination of micro maps and macro maps.

The process of 'chunking'—the movement between macro level
and micro level elements—is the basic problem solving and
learning mechanism of the SOAR Model.

Even for the same goal state, paths might be different because
of variations in the context and the system.

Creativity is required by the leader of a group or team for
defining and navigating a path of transition states.

The NLP models of T.O.T.E. and S.C.O.R.E. are frameworks
with which to define states and paths of transition states.

The NLP distinctions of levels, perceptual positions and time
frame are parameters with which to define states within an
organizational system.

The NLP models of R.O.L.E., B.A.G.E.L., metaphor and meta
programs are operators with which to change states.

Activities

Recall a situation in which you participated in solving an organizational problem.

*How were the problem spaces dealt with by the individuals involved in solving the problem coordinated and linked in order to effectively deal with the the overall organizational problem space to be addressed?

*Relate the NLP models of T.O.T.E. and S.C.O.R.E. to how the states and paths of transition states were defined. Which of the S.C.O.R.E. elements were most emphasized?

*Relate the NLP distinctions of levels, perceptual positions and time frame to the structure of states that made up the problem state, goal state and path of transitions states. Which of these distinctions changed the most in order to reach the goal state.

*Relate the NLP models of R.O.L.E., B.A.G.E.L. and metaphor with some of the specific operations that were enacted in order to change people's perceptions or behaviors to reach the goal. Which distinctions were most relevant?

*Identify a goal or objective that is important for you to reach on a recurring basis.

*Think of how the problem space changes in relation to changes and variations within the system in which you must attain the goal.

*How does creativity play a role in consistently reaching this goal?

Managing Group Creativity

Dynamics of Creativity in
Problem Solving in Organizations

Stimulating and
Managing Innovative
Thinking in Groups and Teams

Overview of Part Three
Managing Group Creativity

The purpose of Part Three is to:

1. Define the creative process within the dynamic system of a group or team within an organization.

2. Identify and explore the skills necessary to manage the interactions of others in situations requiring creative and innovative thinking.

Part Three is made up two chapters:

Chapter 8   **Dynamics of Creativity in Problem Solving in Organizations**

Provides a set of distinctions and tools to define the creative process within the context of an organization and organizational goals and problems.

Chapter 9   **Stimulating and Managing Innovative Thinking in Groups and Teams**

Identifies and explores communication skills necessary to convey innovative ideas to others and inspire creative thinking in a group or team.

Defines and illustrates the leadership skills necessary to manage the creative cycle of a group or team within an organization.

Overview of Part Three
Managing Group Creativity

The material to be covered in Part Three is based on a set of assumptions about creativity, problem solving and group process.

Assumptions

Groups, team and organizations are natural systems and follow certain self-organizing principles.

There is a natural cycle to the creative process.

The key element in effective organizational creativity is managing the transitions states along a path or cycle.

There are a number of different levels of processes which influence the creativity of a group or team.

There are different modes of problem solving and creative strategies that are required for different types of problems or goals.

The key to stimulating and managing the process of creativity in a group or team is in managing the process of communication between group members.

There are a number of different levels of messages sent and received during the communication between people, both verbally and non-verbally.

Managing the creative process of a group is most effectively done through an incremental process of acknowledging and adding to the contributions of team members.

The core criteria for effectively managing the creative process of a group or team are (1) thoroughness of coverage of the problem space, (2) relevance of the issues addressed by the team given the problem space, and (3) balance of contribution of people in different roles and wit different thinking styles.

302

Chapter 8

Dynamics of Creativity in Problem Solving in Organizations

Overview of Chapter 8

General objectives for Chapter 8

1. Define basic types of problems that arise in relation to organizational change.

2. Establish the relationship between managing the pathway of transitions states in organizational change to the stages of the creative cycle.

3. Define and discuss issues related to organizing and coordinating the creative process of a group.

4. Define basic macro patterns and thinking styles that are relevant to group process.

5. Present and discuss ways of stimulating creativity and managing the cycle of creativity in a group.

Sections and goals for each Section

Section 8.1 Types of Problems in
Groups and Organizations

Distinguish between recurring problems and 'virgin' problems and the different kinds of operations and evidences required to manage them effectively.

Section 8.2 Identifying and Coordinating
the Thinking Styles of Others

Define some of the key elements and issues which make up the 'problem space' of identifying and coordinating the different thinking styles of individuals who make up a group.

Section 8.3 Basic Attitudes and Filters of Experience
(Meta Program Patterns)

Introduce and define basic meta program patterns and their role and influence within the process of a group or team. Establish the relationship between managing the pathway of transitions states in organizational change to the stages of the creative cycle.

Section 8.4 Coordinating Goals, Evidences
and Operations in Co-Creativity

Explain how the T.O.T.E. process operates in a group and define the key issues related to coordinating the different elements of the T.O.T.E. in the creative process of a group or team.

Section 8.5 Managing The Creative Cycle of a Group

Define and discuss some of the key issues involved in managing the creative cycle of a group.

Section 8.6 Developing a Common goal in a Group

Set up an experience of applying NLP models and distinctions to a leadership situation involving managing different thinking styles and attitudes of group members to create a common group goal.

Section 8.1
Types of Problems in
Groups and Organizations

There is a distinction between recurrent problems and 'virgin' problems in an organization. These different types of problems involve different types of problem spaces.

Recurrent problems are ongoing situations in which the issues and potential variances that are related to the problem are not particularly wide. Recurring problems generally involve less complexity and smaller increments of change or adjustment. With respect to the law of requisite variety, the amount of variation or flexibility required is relatively minimal.

In 'virgin' problems many aspects of the problem space are uncertain or volatile because the problem is either new or there is a big change in some dimension of the broader system such as the market, the political climate, etc. 'Virgin' problems involve a greater degree of uncertainty and require a greater need for interaction, communication and a shared understanding of the problem space among the individuals addressing the problem.

There are different kinds of group evidences and operations required to effectively approach these different types of problems. Evidences for the resolution of recurrent problems are generally defined in terms of specific outcomes to be achieved in successive times and stages. Evidences for 'virgin' problems are generally defined in terms of the level of consensus and integration of different individuals and perspectives in the successive stages.

Recurring problems generally require operations relating to the breakdown of problem elements and the delegation of specific actions. 'Virgin' problems generally require operations relating to forming a team, synthesizing information about problem elements and generating new perspectives and multiple descriptions of the problem space.

Creativity is involved in different ways in the two types of situations, but is especially relevant with respect to new problems in highly uncertain situations. Since managing creativity with respect to 'virgin' problems involves dealing with uncertainty, the goals and evidences tend to revolve around creating shared understandings and consensus involved in defining problems, determining outcomes, and sharing common competence and knowledge. On the one hand, the group is sharing experiences and understandings. On the other hand, the group is attempting to generate new perspectives, draw out individual strengths and utilize individual competence.

The degree and the type of interaction necessary to address a 'virgin' problem is more intense than in the typical approach for dealing with recurrent problems. This introduces special relational issues related to communicating and responding to members of the group because of the complexity of interactions. In the coming modules we will be exploring the operations that might be effective to manage this kind of interaction with respect to the duel T.O.T.E.s of task and relationship; that is, creating and promoting understanding, and at the same time effectively solving the problem.

Summary:
Problem Solving in Organizations

To recap, in order for a leader to do effective problem solving with others he or she needs a typology of both problems and approaches that can be linked together in an operational way.

'Ongoing' problems are those encountered during the execution of standard procedures employed to achieve specific company results (eg., efficiency). 'Ongoing' problems may be further divided into:

1. Problems in overall approach,

   versus

2. Mistakes or variances in procedures.

Their effects on company results may be divided into those which are:

1. Measurable or quantitative and can be chunked into a number of pieces

   versus those which are

2. Not measurable and are more qualitative; such as quality of service.

'Virgin' problems are those which have no precedent in the company and are associated with a high degree of uncertainty in relation to both procedures and results. 'Virgin' problems tend to be precipitated by changes in the environment or organizational system. To successfully deal with this type of problem the leader needs to gather together the appropriate number of perspectives and overcome the uncertainties by creating a shared understanding of the problem.

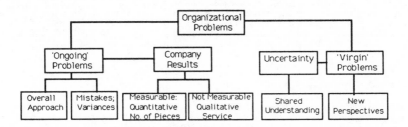

Figure 8.1   Organizational Problems

'Ongoing' institutional problems tend to be more linear and structured. Operations primarily consisted of chunking and analyzing the problem into its components and delegating responsibilities to the appropriate functions. Evidence procedures relate to the completion of specific steps, timing and deadlines.

'Virgin' problems are more systemic in nature. Operations involve a more interactive, lateral approach such as partnering or team building. Evidence for progress is measured in terms of the consensus of the group.

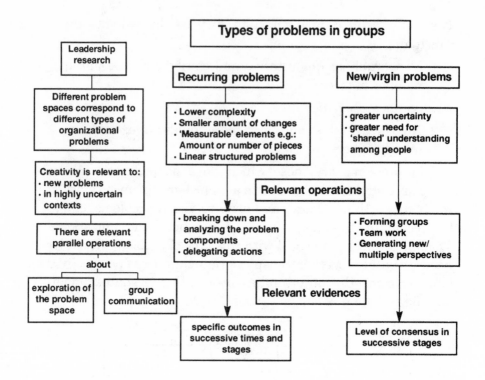

SECTION 8.1 / MAP A

Key Points

There is a distinction between recurrent and 'virgin' problems in an organization.

The different types of problems involve different types of problem spaces.

Recurring problems generally involve less complexity and smaller increments of change or adjustment.

'Virgin' problems involve a greater degree of uncertainty and require a greater need for interaction, communication and a shared understanding of the problem space among the individuals addressing the problem.

Evidences for the resolution of recurrent problems are generally defined in terms of specific outcomes to be achieved in successive times and stages.

Evidences for 'virgin' problems are generally defined in terms of the level of consensus and integration of different individuals and perspectives in the successive stages.

Activities

Think of an example of an ongoing or recurring problem within your organization and contrast it with a new or 'virgin' problem.

How are the two types of problems different with respect to complexity, uncertainty and the integration of different perspectives?

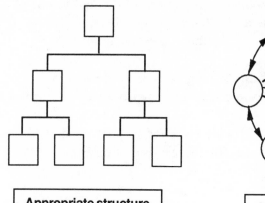 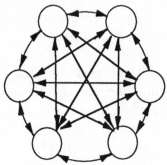

Appropriate structure to deal with recurring problems associated with specific business outcomes

Appropriate structure to deal with new problems associated with changes and uncertainty

SECTION 8.1 / MAP **B**

Key Points

Recurring problems generally require operations relating to the breakdown of problem elements and the delegation of specific actions.

'Virgin' problems generally require operations relating to forming a team, synthesizing information about problem elements and generating new perspectives and multiple descriptions of the problem space.

Creativity is involved in different ways in the two types of situations, but is especially relevant with respect to new problems in highly uncertain situations.

Activities

Identify a situation in which you successfully managed a group or team to achieve a solution to recurrent problem. What kinds of evidences and operations did you use to correct the problem? How did you manage the group or team?

Identify a situation in which you successfully managed a group or team to achieve a solution to a new unprecedented problem.

What kinds of evidences and operations did you use to correct the problem? How did you manage the group or team?

What kinds of creativity were required by the different situations? Which situation do you think required more creativity?

Section 8.2
Identifying and Coordinating the Thinking Styles of Others

Effective group process is organized around the T.O.T.E. The operations of a team are directed toward the goals that define the purpose of that team and the performance of the group is evaluated with respect to evidence indicating its progress toward its goal. To function effectively, it is important that group members share goals and evidence procedures. In order to creatively accomplish common goals, however, a team T.O.T.E. needs a range and diversity of operations and operators in the same way that an individual needs flexibility.

Different kinds of capabilities and thinking styles among group members are necessary to fulfill the various functions and roles required to reach goals. In an effective group there is an awareness of the value of different capabilities and thinking styles. Managing the creative process of a group involves the ability to identify and coordinate the different thinking styles of group members in order to most effectively achieve the group's goals.

Managing the creative process of a group also involves the alignment of different levels of experience: i.e., actions, plans, beliefs, values and roles. Creativity in a group is a multi-level process. In an effective group, the *what* is connected to the *how*, *why* and *who*. That is, the behavior of the group take place within the context of a plan, a set of values and a sense of role identity or 'group spirit.' A behavior that is not connected to values is just an empty 'technique.' This is an especially important issue with respect to creativity and creative problem solving.

People sometimes make the mistake of focusing on the behavioral aspect of a process that somebody has applied successfully. But when that behavior becomes separated from the inspiration, values and beliefs that were all the part of the system that made the process work to begin with, then people are just 'going through the motions.' The techniques become trivial or simply rote reactions. Assuming a creative physiology, for example, is just an act if you are not also accessing the *how* and the *why* of that behavior.

The process of managing creativity can be likened to cooking. A manager is like a chef. Typical techniques for creativity tend to focus on the *what* and are like a particular recipe. Strategies for creativity and managing creativity require addressing the *how* and the *why* and are more like learning how to cook.

A lot of creativity naturally arises from the interaction between different levels of process. The creativity of a group is influenced by both micro and macro level processes. Cognitive strategies and behavioral patterns will influence individual group members on a micro level. But groups are also guided by more general process—such as the 'outcome frame.'

A group often has dynamics that transcend the specific styles and proclivities of the people who make it up. For example, regardless of any particular individual physiology, certain general cognitive patterns are related to different phases of the creative cycle. An important part of managing a group on a macro level, relates to the general attitude of the group and its members. One important challenge in managing the creative process of a group is how to maintain structure and a common attitude among all group members without interrupting or discounting their individual creative abilities.

NLP provides ways to identify and calibrate the micro processes of individuals, but at the same time it also provides distinctions related to the more general patterns of people's interaction and attitude in a group. These patterns are called 'meta programs.' 'Meta program' patterns are general classes of attitudes that are associated with how people sort information on a macro level.

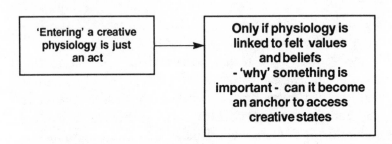

SECTION 8.2 / MAP A

Key Points
Different kinds of capabilities and thinking styles support different contexts, functions and roles.
The most effective way to activate and lead group creativity is to create positive and active states amongst group members without interrupting their individual creative abilities.
Managing a group's creativity is a multi-level process.
In an effective group the 'what' is connected to the 'how,' 'why' and 'who.' That is, the behavior of the group take place within the context of a plan, a set of values and a sense of role identity.

Activities
Think of a time you were involved in a group in which the actions of the group were not connected to any particular plan or strategy. What kinds of problems did you encounter?

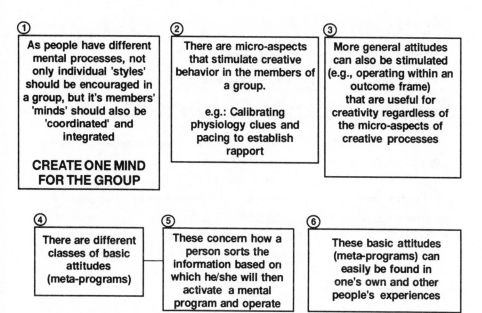

① As people have different mental processes, not only individual 'styles' should be encouraged in a group, but it's members' 'minds' should also be 'coordinated' and integrated

CREATE ONE MIND FOR THE GROUP

② There are micro-aspects that stimulate creative behavior in the members of a group.

e.g.: Calibrating physiology clues and pacing to establish rapport

③ More general attitudes can also be stimulated (e.g., operating within an outcome frame) that are useful for creativity regardless of the micro-aspects of creative processes

④ There are different classes of basic attitudes (meta-programs)

⑤ These concern how a person sorts the information based on which he/she will then activate a mental program and operate

⑥ These basic attitudes (meta-programs) can easily be found in one's own and other people's experiences

Section 8.2 / map B

Key Points

There are micro and macro aspects involved in managing a groups creative process.

Cognitive strategies and behavioral patterns will influence individual group members on a micro level.

'Meta programs' are general classes of attitudes that are associated with how people sort information on a macro level.

Activities

Think of a time you were involved in a group in which the actions and/or strategy of the group were not connected to any clear values or purpose. What kinds of problems did you encounter?

Think of a time you were involved in a group in which the identity and roles of the group were not clear. What kinds of problems did you encounter?

Section 8.3
Basic Attitudes and Filters of Experience: Meta Program Patterns

In many ways, the NLP meta program distinctions are more general versions of many of the process we have already been exploring in this book. Meta program patterns are descriptions of the different ways in which a problem space, or elements of a problem space, may be approached.

As with the other NLP distinctions, a person can apply the same meta program pattern regardless of content and context. Also, they are not "all or nothing" distinctions and may occur together in varying proportions.

Meta Program Patterns

In approaching a problem one can emphasize moving *toward* something or *away from* something, or some ratio of both. In a group, a problem may be approached in varying degrees of 'proactivity' and 'reactivity.'

Chunk-size relates to the level of specificity or generality with which a person or group is analyzing a problem or problem space. Situations may be analyzed in terms varying degrees of detail (micro chunks of information) and generalities (macro chunks of information).

Problem situations may be examined with reference to long term, medium term or short term time frames; and within the context of the past, present or future. The *timeframe* within which a problem or outcome is considered can greatly influence the way in which it is interpreted and approached. There might be both long term and short term solutions.

Some people tend to look at history for solutions more so than the future. A good example is the difference between former Soviet leader Michail Gorbachev and the people who attempted to overthrow him before the break up of the Soviet Union. One was trying to prepare for the future, the others were trying to preserve the past.

Problems and outcomes may be considered in relation to the achievement of the *task*, or in relation to issues involving *relationship*, such as 'power' and 'affiliation.' The question of balance of focus with respect to task and relationship is obviously a key one with respect to problem solving for managers. In the achievement of the task, either goals, procedures or choices may be emphasized. Issues involving relationship may be approached with an emphasis on the point of view of oneself, others or the context ('the company,' 'the market,' etc.) to varying degrees.

A problem may be examined by comparing for similarities (*matching*) or differences (*mismatching*) of problem elements. At the level of a group this relates to whether they are trying to reach consensus or encourage diversity.

Strategies for approaching problems may emphasize various combinations of vision, action, logic or emotion. Micro cognitive patterns on an individual level may be expressed in terms of a general *thinking style* on the macro level or group level. Vision, action, logic and emotion are more general expressions of visualization, movement, verbalization and feeling.

Different problem solving styles and approaches are characterized by different clusters and sequences of meta program patterns in various ratios. One person's approach might involve an 80% focus on relationship and 20% focus on task, and 70% emphasis on long-term versus 30% short-term considerations. Someone else may emphasize the task as 90% of the focus and think mostly in terms of short term considerations.

The different clusters of meta program patterns clearly cover different areas of problem space. In this respect, there are no 'right' or 'wrong' meta programs. Rather, their effectiveness in connection with problem solving relates to the ability to apply them to cover the space necessary to adequately deal with a problem.

Different kinds of activities require different sorts of attitudes and approaches. Some activities require or emphasize the ability to focus on the micro chunks and details. Others require the ability to see the big picture. Different phases in the creative cycle of a group or team may call upon different thinking styles. Therefore, particular attitudes or clusters of meta program patterns might be more or less beneficial at different stages in a group's process. An emphasis on results more than procedures might either be a help or a constraint to creativity at different times. Some phases might require achieving consensus and other phases it is important to encourage differences in perspectives.

Managing Transition States

The process of solving problems in an organization or group involves defining and managing a series of transition states via a macro feedback loop that is composed of a series of micro feedback loops. Managing transition states effectively involves the application of the creative cycle on both a macro and micro level.

On a macro level, the Dreamer, Realist and Critic cycle can be used to identify basic elements of the path of transition states to reach the desired state.

> *The Dreamer stage is involved in generating and choosing the goal state.*

> *The Realist stage is involved in defining and implementing the path of transition states to reach the goals state.*

> *The Critic stage is involved in evaluating and providing feedback in relation to progress toward the goal state according to organizational and personal criteria.*

In general, the Dreamer phase tends to be oriented towards the longer term future. It involves thinking in terms of the bigger picture and the larger chunks in order to generate new alternatives and choices.

The Realist phase is more action oriented in moving towards the future, operating with respect to a shorter term time frame than the Dreamer. The realist is often more focused on procedures or operations.

The Critic phase involves the logical analysis of the path in order to find out what could go wrong and what should be avoided. The Critic phase needs to consider both long and short-term issues, searching for potential sources of problems in both the past and the future.

Different problem solving styles and approaches will have different values at different stages in the creative cycle. In the Dreamer phase, for example, it may be beneficial to direct thinking in terms of the big picture and a longer timeframe. At the Realist phase it may be more useful to be focused on short term actions. At the Critic phase it may be more appropriate to logically consider details with respect to the task, etc.

In this view, managing the creative process of a group essentially involves the pacing and leading of the different meta program patterns of the group members to fill in 'missing links' and widen the perception of the problem space.

SUMMARY:
Problem Solving
and Meta Programs

To recap, meta program patterns are a useful way to think/talk about different ways of 'punctuating' and perceiving a problem space.

Meta Program Patterns Related
to Problem Solving in Organizations

1. Approach to Problems
a. Towards the Positive - Proactive
b. Away From the Negative - Reactive

2. Chunk Size
   a. Large Chunks - Generalities
   b. Small Chunks - Details
3. Time Frame
   a. Short Term - Long Term
   b. Past - Present - Future
4. Approach to Problem Solving
   a. Task (Achievement)
      1. Choices - Goals
      2. Procedures - Operations
   b. Relationship (Power; Affiliation)
      1. Self - *My, I, Me*
      2. Other - *You, His, Their*
      3. Context - *We, The Company, The Market*
5. Mode of Comparison
   a. Match (*Similarities*) - Consensus
   b. Mismatch (*Differences*) - Confrontation
6. Thinking Style
   a. Vision   c Logic
   b. Action   d. Emotion

```
                    ┌─────────────────────────────┐
                    │        Metaprograms          │
                    └─────────────────────────────┘
```

1.	2.	3.
In approaching a problem one can: • move 'away from', or 'towards', something, (or both) • be 'proactive' or 'reactive'	When a situation is being analyzed, it can be dealt with in terms of: • details - small information chunks • generalities - large information chunks	Anything can be examined: • within 'short-term' or 'long-term' time frames • in relation to Past-Present-Future and combinations thereof

4.	5.
In problem solving, aspects can be considered in relation to: • 'Task' (the 'value' of the 'outcome') • Choices - Goals • Procedures - Operations • Relationship (the 'value' of 'power' or 'affiliation') • The points of view of: •• Self (I, Me) •• Other (You) •• Context (We, The Company, The Market)	Situations can be compared by: • Mismatching for Differences (Confrontation) • Matching for Similarities (Consensus)

6.
One can think in terms of: • Vision • Action • Logic • Emotion

SECTION 8.3 / MAP A

Key Points

In approaching a problem one can emphasize moving "toward" something or "away from" something, or some ratio of both—that is, a problem may be approached in varying degrees of proactivity and reactivity.

A problem situation may be analyzed in terms varying degrees of detail (small chunks of information) and generalities (large chunks of information).

Problem situations may be examined with reference to long term, medium term or short term time frames; and within the context of the past, present or future.

Problems may be considered in relation to elements related to the achievement of the task, or issues involving relationship, such as power and affiliation.

In the achievement of the task, either goals, procedures or choices may be emphasized.

Issues involving relationship may be approached with an
emphasis on the point of view of oneself, others or the context
('the company,' 'the market,' etc.).

A problem may be examined by comparing for similarities
(matching) or differences (mismatching) of problem elements.

Activities

Think of examples of how you have approached solving a
problem by either moving toward a desired goal or away from
difficulties.

Think of examples of how you have approached analyzing a
problem by focusing on details (small chunks of information)
or generalities (large chunks of information).

Think of examples of how you have examined a problem
situation with reference to long term, medium term or short
term time frames; and within the context of the past, present
or future.

Think of examples of how you have approached a problem by
focusing on the achievement of the task. Think of other
examples in which you have focused on relationship.

Think of the differences between accomplishing a task by
focusing on goals versus emphasizing procedures.

Think of what it is like to view a problem from the point of
view of oneself? Others? The context ('the company', 'the
market', etc.)?

Think of examples of approaching a problem by comparing
elements for similarities (matching) or differences
(mismatching).

Think of what it is like to approach a problem by emphasizing
vision; action; logic; emotion. What is the difference? What are
the advantages of the different approaches?

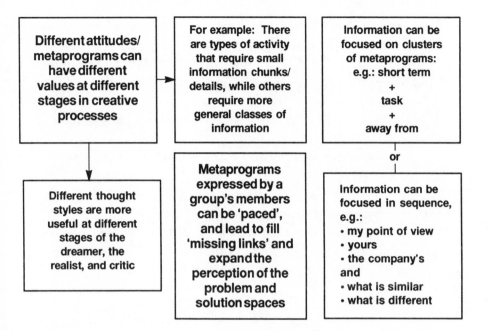

SECTION 8.3 / MAP B

Key Points
Strategies for approaching problems may emphasize various combinations of vision, action, logic or emotion.

Different meta program patterns cover different areas of problem space.

Different problem solving styles and approaches may be characterized by different clusters and sequences of meta program patterns in various ratios.

Different problem solving styles and approaches have different values at different stages in the creative cycle.

Managing the creative process of a group involves pacing and leading of the different meta program patterns of the group members to fill in 'missing links' and widen the perception of the problem space.

Activities

Think of examples of how meta program patterns are reflected in the emphasis of different organizational functions and roles.

Find examples of meta program patterns in the styles of different cultures.

Think of what kind of space is covered by the different meta program patterns.

Think of the effects of combining different clusters of meta program patterns.

Which clusters of meta program patterns would you associate with the different stages in the creative cycle.

Which clusters of meta programs do you think would be most effective for defining symptoms? finding causes? establishing outcomes? anticipating effects? identifying resources?

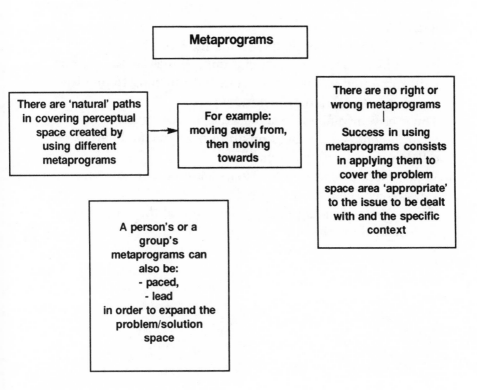

SECTION 8.3 / MAP C

Key Points

Meta program patterns are descriptions of the different ways in which a problem space, or elements of a problem space, may be approached.

Meta program distinctions are not "all or nothing," they may occur together in varying proportions.

There are no 'right' or 'wrong' meta programs, rather, their effectiveness in connection with problem solving relates to the ability to apply them to cover the space necessary to adequately deal with a problem.

Activities

Think of examples of problems you have been involved in solving by yourself and with a group. Which meta program patterns would you most associate with helping to find the solution in the different instances?

Think of your different collaborators in your work environment. Which meta program patterns do different collaborators seem to emphasize.

Which meta program patterns are most clear and familiar for you? Which seem most foreign?

Which kinds of meta programs do you find the most difficult to deal with in others?

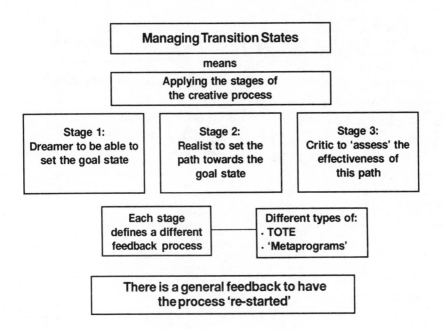

SECTION 8.3 / MAP D

Key Points

The process of solving problems in an organization or group involves defining and managing a series of transitions states via a macro feedback loop that is composed of a series of micro feedback loops.

Managing transition states effectively involves the application of the creative cycle on both a macro and micro level.

On a macro level, the Dreamer, Realist and Critic cycle can be used to identify basic elements of the path of transition states to reach and desired state.

The Dreamer stage is involved in generating and choosing the goal state.

The Realist stage is involved in defining and implementing the path of transition states to reach the goals state.

The Critic stage is involved in evaluating and providing feedback in relation to progress toward the goal state.

Activities

Recall a situation in which you participated in solving an organizational problem.

Identify how the Dreamer-Realist-Critic cycle was applied on both a macro and micro level.

Think of the different kinds of processes involved in (a) forming and selecting a goals state, (b) establishing and navigating a path to the goal state and (c) evaluating progress toward the goal.

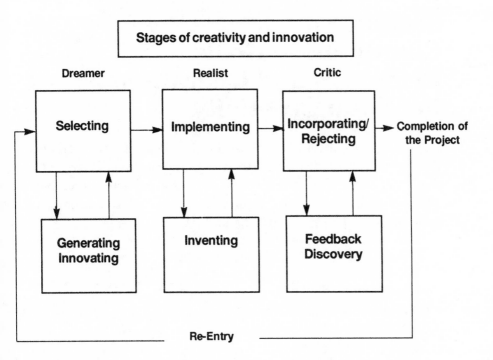

SECTION 8.3 / MAP E

Key Points
On a micro level the Dreamer, Realist and Critic cycle can be applied—in terms of the T.O.T.E. elements and clusters of meta programs—to address the specific issues and individuals involved in moving from one transition state to the next.

Activities
Think of some of the specific issues involved in moving through various transition states involved in achieving organizational goals.

How does the Dreamer-Realist-Critic cycle apply to movement from one transition state to another?

Section 8.4
Coordinating Goals,
Evidences and Operations
in Group Creativity

Meta program patterns relate to the way in which the various T.O.T.E. functions are established and approached. These patterns will influence the scope and style of a particular creative effort. The figure below summarizes some of the relations between meta program patterns and T.O.T.E. elements.

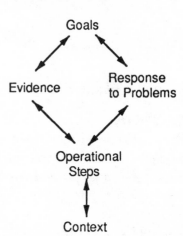

Meta Program Patterns	**T.O.T.E. Elements**

Toward Positive - Away From Negative
Approach - Avoid

Task - Relationship

Internal Reference - External Reference
Self - Others - Environment

Match - Mismatch
Similarities - Differences

Long Term - Short Term
Past - Present - Future

Representational Preference
Vision - Logic - Action - Emotion

Large Chunks - Small Chunks
Generalities - Details

Figure 8.2   Meta Program Patterns/TOTE Elements

Goals may be established in relation to task or relationship and in terms of either something to be approached or avoided. Effective group process generally operates as a set of parallel T.O.T.E.s involving the task of the group and the relationship between its members. Evidences and operations with respect to relationships are generally geared toward consensus. Evidences and operations with respect to tasks are generally geared toward results.

Evidences may be established in reference to oneself, the perceptions of others or in terms of environmental consequences. The evaluation of an evidence may be made in terms of how much something matches the evidences or does not match it. Evidences and operations may be either geared toward long or short term results and involve different degrees of vision, action, logic and emotion.

There are different levels of specificity of goals, evidences and operations in group T.O.T.E.s. Thus, a group might have both macro goals and micro goals. There are different levels of evidences corresponding to different levels of outcomes. An evidence may be as broad as 'convergence of ideas' or as specific as the use of particular kinds of words being used by group members.

It is possible to have T.O.T.E.s within T.O.T.E.s within T.O.T.E.s. These are called 'nested' T.O.T.E.s in NLP. For a macro level T.O.T.E., the operations might be defined in terms of another set of more micro level T.O.T.E.s. Sometimes what is an operation for one goal serves as an evidence for some other goal. One interesting thing about managing a system of creativity is things might serve a function as a goal, evidence or operation based on how a particular interaction is being punctuated. The achievement of micro objectives might be evidences for macro objectives.

There are also sequential T.O.T.E.s in a group's process—such as the movement from conceptual to operational activities. There are evidences related to both ongoing and final results; talking about something versus doing something, for instance. (During the conceptual phase, for example, there is often an inverse relationship between the amount that a goal is talked about and the amount that it is understood or shared.)

It is important to keep in mind that there is a distinction between evidences and 'evidence procedures.' Evidence procedures will often determine the quality of evidence that is possible to gather and the types of responses to problems that are perceived as available. For instance, establishing 'round table' discussions as a frame for feedback at set time intervals is a procedure for gathering evidence that is different than a 'suggestion box.' Evidence and evidence procedures often imply certain beliefs and values. For example, preestablishing times for round table discussion is a statement about the role of feedback within the group process. It symbolicly implies both the value of feedback and the permission to give it.

Clusters of task and relational goals may be established at different 'chunk' sizes and different levels. For example, 'producing more ideas' is a goal defined on a *what* level; 'forming a plan to manifest those ideas' is a goal on the *how* level; 'defining expectations related to outcomes' is on the *why* level.

The degree to which different levels and chunk sizes of goals, evidences and operations are matched and aligned between group members is an important factor in the effectiveness of a group.

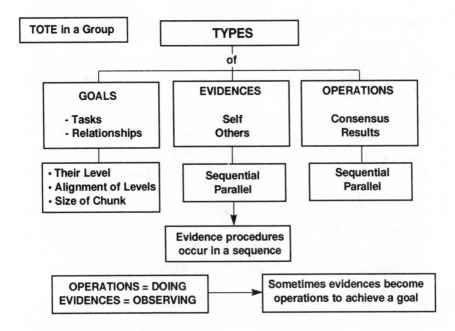

SECTION 8.4 / MAP A

Key Points
Effective group process operates as a set of parallel T.O.T.E.s involving the task of the group and the relationship between its members.
Task and relational goals may be established at different levels and different 'chunk' sizes.
The degree to which these goals are matched and aligned between group members is an important factor in the effectiveness of a group.
There are also sequential T.O.T.E.s in a group's process—such as the movement from conceptual to operational activities.
Evidences for task related goals are often established in reference to an individual's own perceptions while relational evidences are referenced to the perceptions of others in the group.
There are evidences related to both ongoing and final results. Operations with respect to relationships are generally geared toward consensus. Operations with respect to tasks are generally geared toward results.

Activities

Think of groups that you have been in that have both a balance and imbalance of task and relational goals. What kinds of problems arise out of an imbalanced focus on task? on relationship?

What is it like to be in a group that is aligned toward similar goals? What is it like to be in a group that is not aligned toward similar task oriented goals? relational goals?

Think of the typical sequence of phases you follow in a work group. Can you identify the T.O.T.E.s for the sequence?

What are the differences in evidences for task versus relational goals?

What are the differences in evidences related to the ongoing progress toward a group goal versus those related to the final results?

At what times do you feel it is more important to focus on your own point of view in a group?

At what times do you feel it is more important to focus on the point of view of others?

At what times is it more important to focus on consensus in a group?

At what times is it more important to focus on results?

Section 8.5
Managing the Creative
Cycle of a Group

Creativity can be stimulated in relationship to each element of the T.O.T.E. Goals can be widened and enriched with respect to the different meta program patterns expressed by them (e.g., short term —> long term; task —> relationship; logic —> vision, etc.).

Creativity with respect to evidences can be stimulated by shifting levels of perception—i.e., what people do or say versus how they think or what values they express. Evidence procedures may also be widened with respect to meta programs (i.e., self, other, company points of view; past precedents versus future projections; people's emotional response as well as actions; matching versus mismatching criteria, etc.).

Operations are also expressed at different levels (behavioral, cognitive, beliefs and values, identity) and through different meta programs which may be expanded and enriched.

It is important to consider the creative cycle of the group when managing their creative process. There are both macro and micro level T.O.T.E.s in the management of the creative process of a group. Macro T.O.T.E.s relate to the feedback cycle of the group's process to accomplish its task; micro T.O.T.E.s relate to the activities of the manager to direct the behavior of the group members.

The creative cycle in a group often involves the movement between large chunks (the big picture or 'vision') and small chunks (the establishment of micro objectives to reach the larger goal). A key part of managing a group's creativity involves the ability to break down the general roles of group or team members into the specific cognitive and interactive processes required to implement or fulfill that role. Similarly it is important to define evidences of a general type (such as 'consensus') in terms of observable behavioral cues within the interaction of group members. For example, goals that stimulate creativity are usually set towards something in the future. In the Dreamer phase, they are more long term. At the Realist phase, they are more short term.

In the processes of evolving, encouraging and drawing out the creativity of others it is important to be able to identify and adapt to both physical and psychological constraints. Managing the creative cycle of a group involves establishing physical and psychological constraints which direct the group's process in relation to the phase of the creative cycle they are in.

Different stages of the creative cycle involve constraints relating to different types of evidences. An evidence for dreaming might be the number of ideas generated. But, for the critic, having a lot of ideas is perceived as a problem.

Meta program patterns often relate to one another in natural clusters (e.g., shortening a time frame for a project tends to focus people on the task instead of the relationship). As we pointed out earlier, there are clusters of meta program patterns that can be associated with the Dreamer, Realist and Critic. Knowing about these clusters can allow you to recoginize them in people or, to draw them out of people intentionally. The flexibility of a group can even be enhanced by assigning or encouraging different clusters of meta program patterns to individual group members.

For effective group creativity it is important to incorporate:

1. All three of the stages of the creative cycle (Dreamer, Realist, Critic)

   and

2. To incorporate the different points of view of the group members in all three stages

One of the problems that can often happen during a meeting is that the Dreamer says something that is perceived as outrageous to which the Critic responds negatively. In reaction to the Critic, the Dreamer polarizes and starts defending the dream even more. The Critic complains and they go around and around in a vicious circle. Finally the Realist says, "We are running out of time. Let's get down to work." But it ends up as a chaotic mix of polarities. The cycle doesn't progress because the Dreamer is constantly being interrupted by the critic and so on.

In an effective group, each would support or complement each other's strengths by having the dreamer output a number of ideas to a realist who outputs a prototype to the critic, who evaluates the specific prototype, etc.

An important criterion for stimulating creativity in a group is to maintain balance. On the one hand, a manager needs to draw out as full a range of potential as possible in group members. On the other hand, it is also important to draw out and utilize individual strengths.

Disney's strategy acknowledges that there are different kinds of potentials within people. Some people have strengths as a Dreamer or Realist or Critic. One way to stimulate creativity is to try to develop the flexibility of everybody to cover the different phases. Another strategy is to identify and then utilize the particular strengths of certain individuals, but avoiding categorizing them in a way that 'pigeon holes' them.

Different processes are effective to stimulate creativity at the different stages of the creative cycle. Disney, as you recall, had different rooms for Dreamer, Realist and Critic. He had one room that was a dreamer room which had pictures and inspirational drawings and sayings all over the walls. Everything was chaotic and colorful in this room, and criticisms were not allowed—only dreams! For their Realist space, the animators had their own drawing tables, stocked with all kinds of modern equipment, tools and instruments that they would need to manifest the dreams. The tables were arranged in a large room in which all of the animators could see and talk to other animators. For the Critic, Disney had a little room that was underneath the stairs where they would look at the prototype pencil sketches and evaluate them. The room always seemed cramped and hot, so they called it the 'sweatbox.'

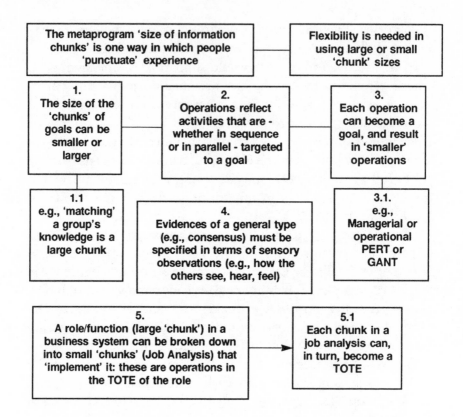

The metaprogram 'size of information chunks' is one way in which people 'punctuate' experience

Flexibility is needed in using large or small 'chunk' sizes

1.
The size of the 'chunks' of goals can be smaller or larger

2.
Operations reflect activities that are - whether in sequence or in parallel - targeted to a goal

3.
Each operation can become a goal, and result in 'smaller' operations

1.1
e.g., 'matching' a group's knowledge is a large chunk

4.
Evidences of a general type (e.g., consensus) must be specified in terms of sensory observations (e.g., how the others see, hear, feel)

3.1.
e.g., Managerial or operational PERT or GANT

5.
A role/function (large 'chunk') in a business system can be broken down into small 'chunks' (Job Analysis) that 'implement' it: these are operations in the TOTE of the role

5.1
Each chunk in a job analysis can, in turn, become a TOTE

SECTION 8.5 / MAP A

Key Points

There are macro T.O.T.E.s and micro T.O.T.E.s in the management of the creative process of a group.

The creative cycle in a group often involves the movement between large chunks (the big picture or 'vision') and small chunks (the establishment of micro objectives to reach the larger goal).

There are both parallel and sequential operations in the creative cycle of a group.

Meta program patterns often relate to one another in natural clusters (e.g., shortening a time frame for a project tends to focus people on the task instead of the relationship).

Activities

Think of work groups you have been in that were effectively creative. In what ways did you move back and forth between large and small chunks during the creative process?

Take a task or job that you are involved in and break it down into the parallel, sequential and embedded T.O.T.E.s that are necessary to implement it.

How does setting time constraints influences a group's creativity in terms of meta program patterns?

What types of creativity might be stimulated by setting time constraints? What types of creativity might be inhibited?

How does setting geographical constraints influence a group's creativity in terms of meta program patterns?

There are clusters of metaprograms 'naturally' associated with the dreamer, realist, and critic

Dreamer	Realist	Critic
What	How	Why
Vision 'towards' • long term • Future	Action 'towards' • short term • Present	Logic 'away from' • long/short term • Past/Future

If different types of metaprogram constraints are imposed, the individual is led to different styles of thought

Metaprograms can become important tools:
• to widen a group's perceptual space
and
• to develop the range of flexibility of the group's members
• to move towards the solution space

e.g.: Set a time limit (5"): people become realists

SECTION 8.5 / MAP **B**

Key Points

Specific clusters of meta program patterns can be associated with each of the stages of Dreamer, Realist and Critic.
The flexibility of a group can be enhanced by assigning different clusters of meta program patterns.
Meta program distinctions provide a non-judgmental way of describing and discovering differences of individual styles and approaches.

Activities

Think about the natural connection between some of the meta program patterns. Identify some that seem to be naturally associated (such as vision <—> long term; action <—> task; logic <—> small chunks, etc.).
What other contextual elements might influence the meta programs of a group?
Think of some ways in which you could apply meta program distinctions in your own professional reality.

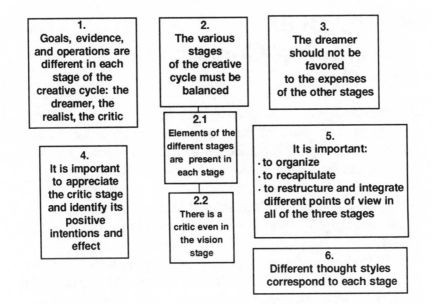

1.
Goals, evidence, and operations are different in each stage of the creative cycle: the dreamer, the realist, the critic

2.
The various stages of the creative cycle must be balanced

3.
The dreamer should not be favored to the expenses of the other stages

2.1
Elements of the different stages are present in each stage

5.
It is important:
· to organize
· to recapitulate
· to restructure and integrate different points of view in all of the three stages

4.
It is important to appreciate the critic stage and identify its positive intentions and effect

2.2
There is a critic even in the vision stage

6.
Different thought styles correspond to each stage

SECTION 8.5 / MAP C

Key Points

Balance is a core criterion in managing the dynamics of group creativity. No one stage or type of creativity should favored at the expense of the others.

The effective management of creativity in a group involves the continual recapitulation and incorporation of the different perspectives of all group members.

Activities

What kinds of problems can arise if the Dreamer is favored over the Realist? The Critic?

Section 8.6
Developing Consensus
in a Group

Systems and groups intuitively seek balance and equilibrium with respect to different processes and functions. The roles of Dreamer, Realist or Critic are not so much personality types as they are an expression of the tendency of an individual to enact or express a certain attitude or meta program in a group or team. This tendency is often shaped and influenced by dynamic influences coming from other team members and the team leader.

It is important for managers (especially those in leadership roles) to develop the capability to assume all three of the different roles of Dreamer, Realist and Critic in order to be able to understand and direct the creative process of group members. The fundamental principles for effectively directing the creativity of a group toward a common goal are 'pacing and leading' and 'acknowledging and adding.'

The next exercise is designed to explore the application of the skills you have been developing to the management of the different meta program patterns associated with the different roles within the creative cycle. The focus of the activity is to explore how to apply some of the NLP models and distinctions to managing the Dreamer phase of the group's process. Instead of trying to solve a problem, the group leader is going to propose an idea or a dream and attempt to lead the group to a consensus about a common goal. The objective for the leader is to acknowledge and draw out each role in a way that it contributes constructively to the creative cycle. A leadership position in a group is also often a meta position.

After the interaction each individual group member is to draw a picture representing his or her understanding of the problem from the perspective of his or her role as Dreamer, Realist, Critic of Leader. The group will then compare and explain their pictures. Instead of trying to look for the differences, the leader is to try to find the common elements of the pictures and to attempt to pace and lead the group to a common picture or vision that incorporates the elements of the group member's individual perspectives.   The objective is to synthesize the individual perspectives of the Dreamer, Realist, Critic and Leader into a common diagram or image that incorporates common elements of different thinking styles. This process is similar to the one used by the manager described in the example given in Section 7.3 to coordinate his development team.

The group is then to go to a meta position with respect to their own process. In a sense, the group members will become fish bowl observers to their own process. A group's ability to be aware of and self correct patterns of its own process as well as its task is important in developing an effective team. Meta cognition of a groups process is facilitated by taking a physical 'meta position' to their own group interaction.

Each group member is to acknowledge two or three things he or she really appreciated about the Leader's skills and suggests something the leader might add or do more of in terms of messages, encouraging meta programs, pacing and leading, etc.

The total time frame for the presentation of the project and the discussion should be about 20 minutes. The time frame for the final meta position is 10 minutes.

When you are finished, compare the dynamics of this exercise, which involves complementary relationships, to the 'intervision' exercise of the previous Chapter, which presupposed symmetrical relationships. This exercise is often more challenging in several respects. In the intervision exercise, it is often easier to focus on the solution rather than the problem because the interaction has already started with a problem. It's easier for the critic to come out in this exercise than in the intervision exercise because the Critic tends to be more apt to find problems with the new idea; whereas the first exercise has already defined a problem. They are starting from a different part of the creative cycle.

Exercise: Developing Consensus in a Group

1. Get into a group of four: a 'Leader,' a 'Dreamer,' a 'Realist' and a 'Critic.' The Dreamer, Realist and Critic assume a role based on the meta program guidelines below.

	Dreamer	**Realist**	**Critic**
	What	*How*	*Why*
Representational Preference	Vision	Action	Logic
Approach	Toward	Toward	Away
Time Frame	Long Term	Short Term	Long/ Short Term
Time Orientation	Future	Present	Past/Future
Reference	Internal - Self	External - Environment	External - Others
Mode of Comparison	Match	Match	Mismatch

2. The Leader describes a general project or idea to the group and interacts with them (for 10-15 minutes) to refine it.

   a. The leader is to attempt to pace and lead each of the group members to reach a consensus.

   b. The basic strategy of the leader should be to acknowledge contributions of group members and then add to it in order to widen or direct the focus in the direction of a common goal.

3. After the interaction, the Leader, Dreamer, Realist and Critic each independently draw a picture representing his or her own understanding of the project or idea and compare their pictures to see how similar they are.

4. As group members share and explain their pictures, the Leader acknowledges which aspects of the drawing matches his or her image and suggests additions to the picture which would bring it more in line with the Leader's own perceptions.

5. When the leader has finished, the group members leave their roles and move to a physical meta position. Each group member acknowledges two or three things he or she really appreciated about the Leader's skills and suggests something the leader might add or do more of.

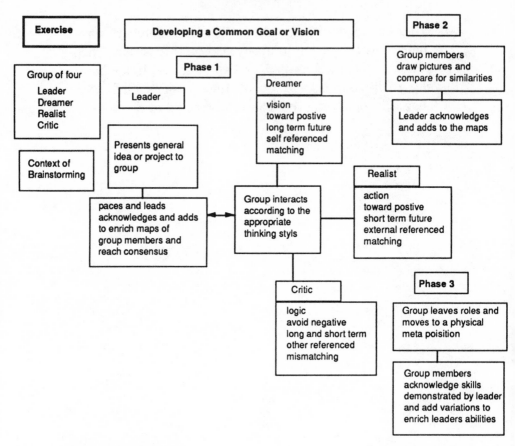

SECTION 8.6 / MAP A

Key Points

The focus of the activity is to explore how to apply some of the models and distinctions presented in this book to manage the Dreamer phase of the group's process.

There is no one right way to lead a group. Different group leaders have different styles that can be equally effective. The fundamental principles for effectively directing the creativity of a group toward a common goal are 'pacing and leading' and 'acknowledging and adding.'

A group's ability to be aware of and self correct patterns of its own process as well as its task is important in developing an effective team.

Meta cognition of a group's process is facilitated by taking a physical 'meta position' to their own group interaction.

Activities

Think of examples in which you have successfully managed the creative process of a group.

How did you use 'pacing and leading' or 'acknowledging and adding' to lead the group toward a common goal, vision or mission?

How important do you think a group's awareness of its own process is in order for it to be successful?

What elements of its own process should a group be aware of?

Chapter 9

Stimulating and Managing Innovative Thinking in Groups and Teams

Overview of Chapter 9

General objectives for Chapter 9

1. Present and discuss types of communication strategies relating to creativity, emphasizing issues related to leadership.

2. Define the role of non-verbal communication in stimulating and managing the creativity of a group.

3. Define and set up a role play synthesizing the different dynamics and skills involved in effectively managing group creativity.

Sections and goals of each Section

Section 9.1 Dynamics of Group Creativity
Review and summarize (a) the different phases of the creative cycle, (b) basic strategies for stimulating creativity in each phase and (c) the relationship of different types of creativity to achieving organizational goals and solving problems.

Section 9.2 Types of Communication Strategies
Define the influence of different levels, relationships and communication channels on a groups creative process and the communication strategies utilized by the group or team leader.

Section 9.3 Managing Creativity in Complementary versus Symmetrical Roles
Describe and discuss the issues that arise as a result of leader-collaborator relationships in group creativity and discuss differences in communication strategies and approaches necessary to stimulate and facilitate group creativity within the context of complementary as opposed to peer roles.

Section 9.4 Messages and Meta Messages
Describe and provide examples of the influence of non-verbal communication on the management of a group's process through 'meta messages' and 'psychogeography.'

Section 9.5 Stimulating and Enriching the Maps of Others
Define and discuss ways in which a leader can shape contexts, attitudes, states, cognitive processes, communication channels and rules of interaction to draw out more creativity from a group or team.

Section 9.6 Team Roles and the Creative Cycle
Define a role play to be conducted within the context of a 'fish bowl' and explain the different roles. Review the influence of thinking styles and representational channels with respect to (a) an individual's perceptions on a micro level, (b) the process of pacing and leading individuals to be more creative and (c) their general application in managing the creative process of a group.

Section 9.7 Making Observations in a Group

Explain the perceptual filters to be used by the observers of the role play, the relevant patterns to be attended to and define the purpose and rules for making observations. Provide an example of a role play pointing out the influence of the style and skill of the leader in managing the creative process of a group.

Section 9.1
Dynamics of Group Creativity

The effective management of creativity in a group involves the continual recapitulation and incorporation the different perspectives of all group members. Thus, when leading a group, it is important to maintain a balance between:

1. Encouraging different perspectives,

   and

2. Sharing an understanding of the goal or problem.

Further, here are two basic possible uses for creativity in an organization:

1. To solve problems,

   or

2. To establish or implement ideas.

Implementing ideas and solving problems are interrelated processes that can be managed and balanced in a complementary manner. Generally, if the context is problem solving, the manager's emphasis is on finding new perspectives. If the context is proposing and exploring a new idea, the emphasis is on synthesizing. That is, if the group is solving a problem, the manager is seeking differences in perspectives. If the group is implementing a new idea, the manger is seeking commonalities and consensus.

Balance is a core criterion in managing the dynamics of group creativity. No one stage or type of creativity should favored at the expense of the others. The phases of creativity apply differently in achieving and implementing ideas versus solving problems. Dreamer, Realist and Critic are not rigid personality types, but rather are tendencies within every person. On a group level there are general purposes for each phase of the creative cycle:

The Dreamer phase is to widen perceptual space.

The Realist phase is to define actions.

The Critic phase is to evaluate payoffs and drawbacks.

The tendency to Dreamer, Realist or Critic can be drawn out by contextual circumstances and also by relational interactions with others. One important thing about systems is that they attempt to balance. For instance, even if you are typically a dreamer, if you get around a bunch of dreamers, you might find yourself thinking "Wait a minute! We've got to be a little realistic here." When someone else is dreaming for you, your focus is no longer the dream or the representation of the dream. It becomes a matter of progressing toward the dream. This begins to automatically trigger aspects of the realist and critic. In other words, if somebody starts dreaming your dream with you, you are free to start being a realist.

There is a kind of dynamic balancing of processes that occurs in a group that can either be managed such that different thinking styles complement one another or produce a conflict. And the question is, "Does it balance itself in a cycle that is productive or by polarizing the different thinking styles in a kind of 'Mexican standoff.' " These different functions and capabilities can either support each other or be destructive. A basic issue in managing a group is how you go about managing this dynamic balance within the group.

For instance, there are some ways to help keep the critic from being destructive. Very often when a critic is destructive, it is because the critic is criticizing the Dreamer or the Realist as opposed to the plan that the dreamer and realist have formulated. So, the critic is criticizing the *who* and not the *how* or *what*. There is a big difference between the Critic criticizing the dream and the Critic criticizing the Dreamer. That one shift in focus might make the difference of whether a Critic is perceived as constructive or destructive. This can be managed by focusing the Critic on the level of the 'how.'

In this Chapter we will explore how to synthesize together all of the models, skills and tools we have been developing throughout the book to practically manage the dynamic process of group creativity.

One phase 'pulls another': both phases can be handled in a complementary balanced way

In a process that starts from an idea:

- 'widening' the map is easier
- finding the solution / the path is easier

In a process that starts from a problem:

- 'narrowing' the map is more difficult
- finding the goal is easier
- eliciting the critic is easier, and
- the realist also emerges more easily

Addressing the 'how' of the problem often leads to all the creative levels

- The 'what'
- The 'how' of 'what'
- The 'why' of 'how' and 'what'
- The 'where' and 'when' can be faced in sequence

SECTION 9.1 / MAP A

Key Points
The phases of creativity apply differently in achieving and implementing ideas versus solving problems.
Implementing ideas and solving problems are interrelated processes that can be managed and balanced in a complementary manner.
Managing the creative process of a group is a multi level process that is often most expediently addressed by focusing on the level of the 'how.'

Activities
Think of the differences in how creativity is applied to implement an idea *versus* solve a problem.
In what ways are the two processes complementary?
What is the basic way in which a Dreamer contributes to implementing an idea? A Realist? A Critic?
What is the basic way in which a Dreamer contributes to solving a problem? A Realist? A Critic?

In the dreamer phase, use the 'differences' (mismatching) metaprogram to widen the space	In the realist phase, use the 'similarities' (matching) metaprogram to define actions	In the critic phase, use differences to establish payoffs and drawbacks

SECTION 9.1 / MAP B

Key Points
There are general strategies and purposes for each phase of the creative cycle:

The Dreamer phase is to widen perceptual space.

The Realist phase is to define actions.

The Critic phase is to evaluate payoffs and drawbacks.

Activities
Review what you have learned so far in the book about the creative cycle of Dreamer, Realist and Critic.

What are the cognitive processes associated with each phase?

Which meta program patterns and thinking styles are associated with each phases?

What kinds of problem space are addressed by each phase?

What type of creativity is associated with each phase?

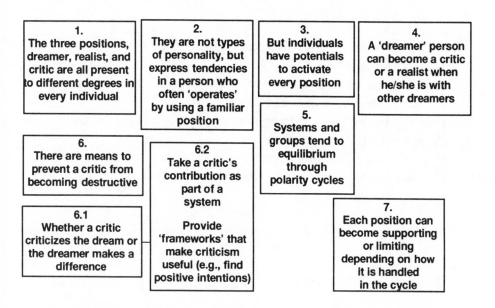

1.
The three positions, dreamer, realist, and critic are all present to different degrees in every individual

2.
They are not types of personality, but express tendencies in a person who often 'operates' by using a familiar position

3.
But individuals have potentials to activate every position

4.
A 'dreamer' person can become a critic or a realist when he/she is with other dreamers

5.
Systems and groups tend to equilibrium through polarity cycles

6.
There are means to prevent a critic from becoming destructive

6.2
Take a critic's contribution as part of a system

Provide 'frameworks' that make criticism useful (e.g., find positive intentions)

6.1
Whether a critic criticizes the dream or the dreamer makes a difference

7.
Each position can become supporting or limiting depending on how it is handled in the cycle

SECTION 9.1 / MAP C

Key Points
The role of Dreamer, Realist or Critic is not so much a personality type as it is an expression of the tendency of an individual to enact or express a certain attitude or meta program in a group or team.

Systems and groups intuitively seek balance and equilibrium with respect to different processes and functions.

It is important for managers (especially those in leadership roles) to develop the capability to assume all three of the different roles of Dreamer, Realist and Critic. A leadership position in a group is also often a meta position.

The goal of the exercise is for the leader is to acknowledge and draw out each role in a way that it contributes constructively to the creative cycle.

Activities

Recall some examples of effective and ineffective teams you have participated in.

Identify how individuals in the group naturally took on the role of Dreamer, Realist and Critic.

How did the effective management and coordination of the three roles influence the effectiveness of the group?

What degree of flexibility did the members of the different groups have with respect to the different roles?

Section 9.2
Types of Communication Strategies

A key aspect in managing the creativity of a group is the communication strategy adopted by the manager or leader of the group. In the previous Sections of this book we have explored the creative process with respect to personal creativity and co-creativity. Our most fundamental definition of creativity has been that it involves a widening of the map from which a person or group is working. Stimulating creativity involves doing something with the map to open up new spaces; either in terms of defining problem space or finding solution space. We have explored some of the neuro-linguistic processes associated with widening perceptual maps, including:

1. The physiology of the individual or group;
2. The cognitive maps and perceptual channels used by the individual or group,
3. Meta program patterns which direct attention to different areas of perceptual space;
4. Beliefs, values and assumptions related to the motivation, and also the permission to be creative.

All of these influences contribute to the creativity of groups as well as individuals. The communication strategy of a manager involves the way in which he or she defines and directs these four key elements of creativity.

Levels of Communication

In forming a communication strategy it is important to remember that there are different types of group goals related to different levels of group process (*who, why, how, what, where* and *when*). The different levels of *what, how* and *why* are a particularly significant aspect of group creativity in the same way that they are for personal and co-creativity. In managing others, it is important to consider the values, beliefs and the kinds of T.O.T.E.s that the group is operating from. Often, the situations that people perceive as limiting or constraining have to do with the assumptions or beliefs concerning which contexts it is considered appropriate or permissible to be creative. For instance, the beliefs and values shared by group members will effect their sense of motivation and permission. If you give a group the ownership of an idea, but then impose evidences that lead them to perceiving unprofitable ideas as failures instead of feedback, the group might be more stressed.

There are different levels of operations to stimulate and manage creativity. Some operations could be on the level of environment and behavior—establishing the *where*, the *when* and the *what* in terms of timeframes, constraints and actions. Other operations involve establishing plans, thinking styles and meta programs to draw out individual competencies—the *how*. Clearly operations on the level of the *why*—beliefs and values— are particularly significant for group creativity. There are also operations on the level of the *who*. Creating a team spirit involves the establishment of the identity of the group. Thus, there are different types of strategies that may be used by a manager for addressing issues of 'want to,' 'how to,' 'chance to' and 'who to.' For instance, consensus at certain levels might inhibit creative thinking. Instead of encouraging differences it encourages a more homogeneous view. This is where the different levels of process become important. When a team is first forming, a manager might not define goals in terms of specific objectives, but rather in terms of values or the desired effect to be manifested by the group. It might be important to initially maintain flexibility with respect to the *what*, but consensus with respect to the *why*. A communication strategy might encourage consensus about *who* and *why*, but differences and diversities of perspectives with respect to *how* and *what* . If there are too many different opinions relating to *why* and *who*, the differences are more likely to produce conflict rather than being productive.

Relational Considerations

Managing the relationship and rapport between group members is a crucial element in the kind of communication strategy a manger uses to guide the creative process of a group. In fact, in some cases, the effort of managing a group's creativity might be 80% in terms of relationship and 20% in terms of task. Stimulating innovation in organizations and in groups often involves working more with the relationships between people than the tools that they are working with. Consider some of the highly creative environments you've been in yourself. How important were the relationships with people in addition to the tools that you had with which to be creative? Many of the most important creative developments have come from the co-creative efforts of partners or teams of people. The synergy that is created by the interactions between people is often more responsible for innovative thinking than the tools they are working with.

Relationship creates the space for creativity. It may come out of two or three core people or it may come out of groups. You might find a higher intensity between a few people, but it depends then on the type of creativity you are considering. The influence of relationship is different depending on the type of creativity required from the group. For example, unlike America, Japanese companies don't tend to encourage the situation in which two or three key creative people are driving a project. They tend to work within the context of a general ongoing, creative contribution by all group members. The type of creativity produced by this relational context is incremental as opposed to the more inspirational or breakthrough type of creativity that comes from relationships built around product champions. The result is different depending on the relational set up and communication strategy. This does not de-emphasize the individual contribution of a person. It simply acknowledges that their sense of themselves, in relation to the whole group, plays an important role.

In forming a strategy for managing creativity, it is important to realize that the role of an individual as a team member may be different from the role of that person in the larger organization. Sometimes when you are putting together a new team, you might need to let roles develop. And, in a team, roles with respect to the creative process may not necessarily be related to function and role within the larger company or organization. A person might have a realist role with respect to the organization and a critic role with respect to the group.

The Influence of Representational Channels

Representational channels are another important dimension of a manager's communication strategy. Different representational channels and verbal patterns direct the cognitive processes of group members in different ways and influence the perceptions of a group role relations. For instance, writing is a simple way of encouraging consensus, because once something is out on a board the person who proposed it is not so intimately associated with the idea anymore. Externalizing an idea allows you to separate the *what* from the *who*. When somebody has to continually verbalize his or her own idea in order to bring it into the group process, it is as if that person's identity becomes associated with the suggestion or the proposal. And those kinds of confusions create a kind of conflict. An effective communication strategy matches the channels and modes of communication to accomplish different levels of goals and maintain rapport between group members.

Different channels of communication and representation have different uses and strengths. Representational channels may be enhanced to increase creativity in a number of ways:

1. Enriching the channel that is most used and valued (enhancing a strength);

2. Using a channel that is not often used to find a new way of thinking or perceiving (strengthening a weakness);

3. Emphasizing the representational channel most appropriate or most suited to a particular cognitive process or type of creativity;

4. Enhancing overlaps or 'synesthesia' between different representational channels.

It is dangerous to automatically assume that others have the same thinking style as our own. Sometimes a person is not used to visualizing even though people are talking about things that require the ability to remember or fantasize visually. At other times a person might tend to focus too much on a particular image that has become imprinted in his or her mind. It stands out because it's unique or it's the only one that person has been exposed to. In challenging or stressful situations, people often revert to their most familiar representational channel.

Thinking Styles

We often make assumptions that others have the same cognitive capabilities that we do. But this most often not the case. In communicating with others, matching their channel of represen- tation is an important method of establishing rapport.

Thinking styles are expressed through different kinds of physiology. From the NLP point of view, the physiological cues associated with a particular representational channel is a very useful tool to direct or focus attention. At the level of a whole group, patterns of macro physiology, language and representa- tional channels my be used to 'pace' and 'lead' the general thinking style whole group.

On a macro level, the 'state' of a person in a particular role is determined by that person's outcome plus his or her attitude. Attitude may be represented in terms of the cluster of meta program patterns the person manifests in relation to his or her goal.

One of the principles of creativity we have been exploring involves the importance of widening the coverage of a problem space. In that sense, no one meta program or meta program pattern or thinking style is right or wrong. The success of a group will be based on its ability to cover the appropriate issues within the problem space. In some way the manger must eventually get to all of these spaces: short-term to long-term, future, past, task relationship, etc.

Systems attempt to balance themselves. Given the general state of a system and the increment of change attempted in the systemic meta program, the pattern may either:

1. Escalate   2. Flip polarity
3. Become neutralized/balanced   4. Shift to something else

The S.C.O.R.E. Model

The key is to find the appropriate incremental variation with which to pace and lead the meta program to a new area of problem space. The S.C.O.R.E. Model distinctions plus clusters of Meta Program operations may be used as a guide to widen the perception of problem space and solution space in order to tackle a problem in the most comprehensive manner. Different clusters of meta program patterns are more suited to cover the different areas of problem space associated with the S.C.O.R.E. distinctions. For example:

S. Symptom	**C.** Cause	**O.** Outcome	**R.** Resource	**E.** Effect
Away From	Away From	Toward	Toward	Toward
Past/Present	Past	Future	Present	Future
Short Term	Long Term	Short Term	Short Term	Long Term
Action	Emotion	Vision	Action	Vision
Other	Other/Self	Self	Self	Context

The essential goal of the manager's communication strategy for working with the group is the coordination of different types of creative processes. Generally, the most creative group will have shared goals and shared evidences, but will acknowledge and encourage individual differences with respect to capabilities and actions.

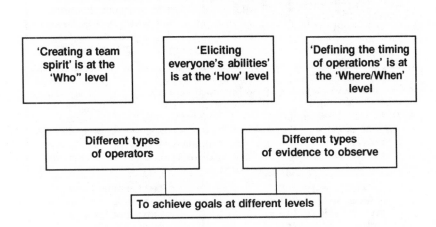

SECTION 9.2 / MAP A

Key Points
There are different types of group goals related to different
levels of group process (*who, why, how, what, where* and
when).
There are different types of strategies (operators and
evidences) for addressing issues of 'want to,' 'how to,' 'chance
to' and 'who to.'

Activities
Recall an example of a team or group you have been involved
with.
Think about how different levels of goals were communicated
and dealt with. How were issues such as purpose, roles, task,
timing and constraints communicated and established?
What kinds of problems can arise in a group when there is no
sense of identity or 'team spirit'?
What kinds of problems can arise in a group when there is no
sense of purpose or values?
What kinds of problems can arise in a group when there is no
clear sense of direction or rules of interaction?
What kinds of problems can arise in a group when there is no
sense of timing or constraints?

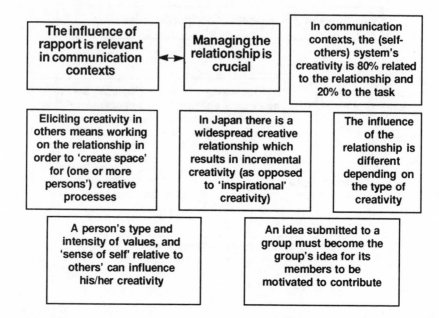

SECTION 9.2 / MAP **B**

Key Points

Managing the relationship and rapport between group
members is a crucial element in the effective creative process
of a group.

The influence of relationship is different depending on the type
of creativity required from the group.

Activities

What kinds of problems can arise in a group when there is no
sense of roles and role relations?

Think of the different roles that the relationship and rapport
between different group members plays in different kinds of
contexts requiring creativity.

In which kinds of contexts is the relationship between group
members less important? more important?

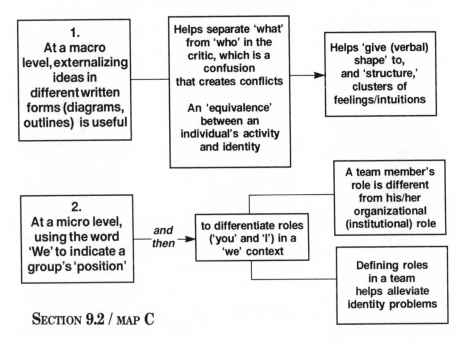

SECTION 9.2 / MAP C

Key Points

The role of an individual as a team member is different from the role of that person in the larger organization.

Different representational channels and verbal patterns direct the cognitive processes of group members in different ways and influence the perceptions of group role relations.

An effective communication strategy matches the channels and modes of communication to accomplish different levels of goals and maintain rapport between group members.

Activities

Think about a group or team you have been a member of in which your role as a team member was very different from your role in the organization.

What kinds of interferences to creativity can the lack of rapport between group members create?

Think about which kinds of channels of communication are more effective for communicating different levels of information to the members of a group (i.e., *what, how, why,* etc.).

Explore the influence of thinking of a group in terms of 'we' *versus* 'I' and 'you.'

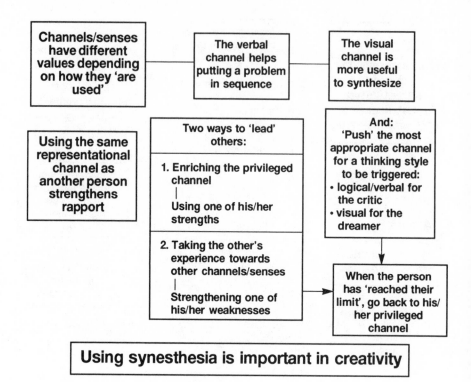

Channels/senses have different values depending on how they 'are used'	**The verbal channel helps putting a problem in sequence**	**The visual channel is more useful to synthesize**

Using the same representational channel as another person strengthens rapport

Two ways to 'lead' others:

1. Enriching the privileged channel
|
Using one of his/her strengths

2. Taking the other's experience towards other channels/senses
|
Strengthening one of his/her weaknesses

**And:
'Push' the most appropriate channel for a thinking style to be triggered:**
• **logical/verbal for the critic**
• **visual for the dreamer**

When the person has 'reached their limit', go back to his/her privileged channel

Using synesthesia is important in creativity

SECTION 9.2 / MAP D

Key Points

Different channels of communication and representation have different uses and strengths.

In challenging or stressful situations, people often rely on their most familiar representational channel.

In communicating with others, matching the channel of representation is an important method of establishing rapport. Representational channels may be used to enhance creativity in a number of ways: (1) enrich the channel that is most used and valued (enhancing a strength); (2) use a channel that is not often used to find a new way of thinking or perceiving (strengthening a weakness) (3) emphasize the representational channel most appropriate or most suited to a particular cognitive process or type of creativity, (4) enhance overlaps or 'synesthesia' between different representational channels.

Activities

Think about which representational channels you prefer to use in relationship to different kinds of tasks with respect to a group.

What do you think are the strengths of pictures and images? Written words? Spoken words? Feelings?

In challenging or stressful situations, which representational channel do you rely on the most?

Think of some specific individuals you feel a lot of rapport with. In what ways do you share similar ways of representing and thinking about things?

Think of some ways you have enhanced your creativity or the creativity of others by: (1) enriching the channel that is most used and valued (enhancing a strength); (2) using a channel that is not often used to find a new way of thinking or perceiving (strengthening a weakness); (3) emphasizing the representational most appropriate or most suited to a particular cognitive process or type of creativity; (4) enhancing overlaps or 'synesthesia' between different representational channels.

Thinking styles/representational channels in group process

During group interactions, thought styles change: from vision to logic to emotion to action	Observe the associated • language • physiological cues and their sequence — in order to	1. 'Pace' group members 2. Focus/lead others on to a desired though style

'Pacing' the sequence of all the senses in mental process that are used by a person is effective for communication	If not paced, the person perceives that 'something is missing' in the others' communication	A person can be lead towards a type of representation that he/she does not usually use	People sometimes focus on a 'vision' which is the result of an imprint from far back in time

Never assume that others have the same thinking style as one's own

SECTION 9.2 / MAP E

Key Points

At the level of a whole group, patterns of macro physiology, language and representational channels my be used to 'pace' and 'lead' the general thinking style of the whole group. Often people who share a similar culture, function or background also share similar strategies for approaching various issues and problems. Matching that strategy enhances rapport and strengthens credibility with that group. Failing to match the strategy leaves group members with the sense that something is missing.

It is dangerous to automatically assume that others have the same thinking style as our own.

Activities

Recall some examples in which you have been able to direct or sway the thinking styles of people in a group. What did you do to accomplish it? In what way did you pace and lead language or behavioral patterns?

Think of examples of situations in which you have matched or unintentionally mismatched the collective thinking strategy or expectations of a group. How did mismatching the groups' strategy effect your rapport and credibility with the group?

Think of some examples in which you assumed that others had the same thinking style you did. What kinds of problems resulted from that assumption?

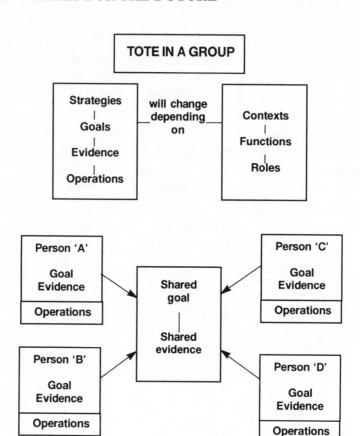

SECTION 9.2 / MAP F

Key Points

Effective group process is also organized around the T.O.T.E. In an effective group, group members share goals and evidence procedures with which to evaluate performance and progress toward goals. There is also an awareness of the value of different capabilities and thinking styles and an acceptance and encouragement of the full range of capabilities latent in group members.

Activities

Think about an effective group or team you were a member of.
To what degree did you share goals?
Did you agree upon evidences and evidence procedures?
How were the differences in capabilities and thinking styles of the group members acknowledged a utilized?

Section 9.3
Managing Creativity
in Complementary
versus Symmetrical Roles

There are differences between the process of facilitating group creativity as a leader versus as a peer or collaborator. For example, it makes a different impact on a group if a boss is a Critic than if a peer or subordinate is a Critic.

In complementary relations, such as 'leader-collaborator,' types of creativity are often specified to different roles. For example the leader might be responsible for innovative and evaluative processes whereas collaborators are creative with respect to implementation.

There are different issues of 'want to,' 'how to' and 'chance to' in complementary versus symmetrical relationships. People will employ different values and attitudes in 'being creative for me' versus 'being creative for you' or 'being creative for us.' For instance, there is a difference between 'consensus' and 'owner-ship'. The fact that a group 'owns' a problem or idea does not insure that there will be consensus among group members about how to approach it. Likewise, the fact that group members agree about a particular approach does not insure that they will feel personally involved. In fact, sometimes it is easier to for a group to reach consensus about something that they are not personally involve in. The difference has to do with the *who* versus the *what*—who's idea versus what is the expression of that idea.

Consensus itself might interfere with the kinds of interactions which could produce different perspectives about the idea. Further, people don't tend to invest a lot of time trying to find new perspectives if they're not somehow personally involved with an idea or a problem. People are more motivated to search for solutions when a problem touches everybody at a deep level. Motivation for creativity is related to how deeply you feel for the problem and the ownership of the answer to the problem. If you feel connected to it personally you tend to mobilize more of your neurology.

Issues of relationship and rapport are often even more crucial to the creative process of a group in situations involving complementary relationships. There is a significant difference between saying, "*You* write this down and *you* do that," and, "Are *we* all writing or is one of us going to take responsibility?" It is often a useful strategy to start from a *we* position and differentiate a person's role in the group from function in the organization.

The fact that the role someone has in the team is different than the role they formally have in the company often confuses people—especially in relation to complementary roles. Group members might have complementary roles with respect to the organization but symmetrical roles in the team. Explicitly defining or establishing the two frames of reference (organization and team) in relation to roles can do a lot to promote clarity and alleviate tension.

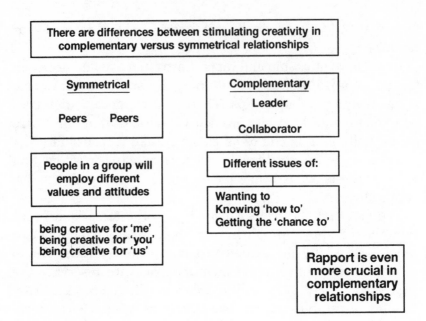

SECTION 9.3 / MAP A

Key Points

There are differences between the process of facilitating group creativity as a leader versus as a peer or collaborator—i.e., there is a different impact on a group if a boss is a Dreamer than if a peer or subordinate is a Dreamer.

There are different issues of 'want to,' 'how to' and 'chance to' in complementary versus symmetrical relationships.

People will employ different values and attitudes in 'being creative for me' versus 'being creative for you' or 'being creative for us.'

Issues of relationship and rapport are often even more crucial to the creative process of a group in situations involving complementary relationships.

In complementary relations, such as 'leader-collaborator,' types of creativity—innovation of new ides, implementation, evaluation—are often specified to different roles (e.g., boss = innovator, evaluator; collaborators = implementors).

Activities

Recall examples in which you have been involved in a team in which (a) you were a peer of all of the team members, (b) you were the formal leader of the team, (c) you were a formal subordinate of one or more of the team members.

How did the different relationships effect your (1) motivation, (2) ability and (3) opportunities to be creative in the different situations? Think of the different kinds of relational and rapport issues that came into focus in the three different situations.

When there were problems or interferences to the effectiveness or creativity of the group, did your role relation in the group effect your perception of the source of the interference?

Think of which types of creativity are more naturally manifested in the role of a leader? peer? collaborator?

Section 9.4
Messages and Meta Messages

The effectiveness of people to work as a group is dependent on their ability to communicate with one another. Communication between the individual members of a group happens both verbally and non-verbally, and there are both verbal and non-verbal influences on the behavior of the group as a whole.

There are ways in which a manager can nonverbally recognize and encourage moments of creativity that come up spontaneously in a group. One method is called "shaping." Shaping has to do with encouraging something in a physiological way. For example, there is a story about a psychology professor who conducted an experiment with a group of university students. He instructed the students in his class to complement or express approval for women who wore red sweaters. They were not to comment on the sweater itself but just to say something like, "Oh, you look nice today," or to smile at them. Supposedly, after a week he walked into the dining hall and it was filled with women in red sweaters.

Apparently the students also decided to try the process on the professor himself. If the professor went to one side of the room when he was teaching, the students all agreed among each other to yawn and act bored. If he went to the other side of the room, they all sat up, nodded their heads and acted very interested. After a while the professor found himself doing all of his teaching from one side of the room!

Managers often do similar things, but generally they are unaware of what they are doing. For example, a top manager at IBM unconsciously used this process of shaping to direct people to 'discover' that they agreed with his approach. When he was talking with somebody that was thinking along similar lines as he was, he was a wonderful and very active listener, constantly making eye contact, nodding his head and saying things like, "Oh really?" "That's interesting." "Tell me more about your idea." If somebody started to go off in a direction he didn't like, he would stare blankly and mumble "Uh huh...Uh huh." It was like talking to a brick wall. As soon as the other person began to shift directions, the manager would come back to life and become very interested in the other person's direction of thinking. People found themselves eventually coming around to his way of thinking without understanding why.

It is also possible to non-verbally anchor processes in a group by associating certain cues with the state of a group. For example, when a group is in a particularly productive state of creativity, a manager can give some kind of stimulus like clapping his or her hands or giving an encouraging gesture. Pretty soon, if he or she claps or makes the encouraging gesture it begins to be like a trigger for the creative state.

In the language of NLP these non-verbal cues are considered 'meta messages.' The basic process of communication involves the transmission of both messages, which carry the content of a communication, and 'meta-messages', which are higher level messages about the content. Meta messages are messages *about* other messages. Meta messages are typically about:

1. The type or level of message being sent;

2. A person's state, or

3. About the status or relationship between group members.

People also send meta messages about the messages that they have received, like the IBM manager.

Meta messages are essential for the interpretation of a message. There is a difference between what a person 'says' and what he or she 'means' or intends. The message received is not always the message that was intended or sent. And in practical reality, the meaning of a communication to another person is what that person received regardless of what was intended.

In face-to-face communication meta messages are most often transmitted non-verbally. People are constantly sending meta messages, even when they themselves are not talking. Linguists call this the 'grunts and groans' phenomenon of communication. When people are listening they are often making noises like

"Ah," "Uh huh," "Hhmmm," etc. As it turns out, these noises are not just random. If somebody is rapidly going "Ah ha, ah ha, ah ha," it indicates he or she is receiving the message differently than if that person sort of slowly says, "Ahhh haaaa."

Somebody even experimented with the influence of meta messages in relationship to the computer. One of the problems with a computer is that it doesn't give meta messages. So, they decided to program the computer to give meta messages to the people who were using it. The computer would constantly print responses like, "Oh yes." "I see." "Very good." It turned out that people really liked using this computer! They were actually more productive with the computer because they somehow felt more rapport with the computer, even though they couldn't tell you why.

Different kinds of meta messages are used in different ways in different cultures. For example, someone once did a study on the interactions between people in English pubs and in French bistros. They found that the French touched each other on the average about 110 times per hour. The English touched each other only an average of three times per hour.

The geographical relationship between group members is another non-verbal influence on group process. It often has both a physical and symbolic influence on shaping the interaction between group members. For example, sitting in a circle, as in a round table, encourages certain kinds of feedback and interactions between group members than sitting at rectangular table or in a 'theater style' arrangement. A round table also conveys a different kind of symbolic relationship between group members. In NLP this is influence is called 'psychogeography.' For an outline of some key dimensions affecting communication, see Appendix A.

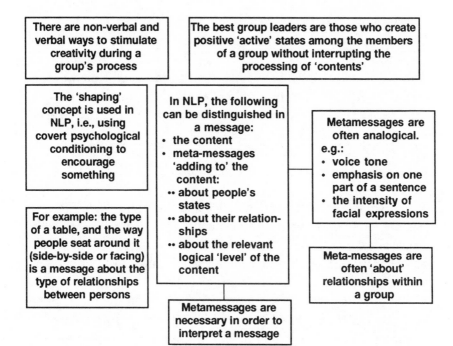

There are non-verbal and verbal ways to stimulate creativity during a group's process

The best group leaders are those who create positive 'active' states among the members of a group without interrupting the processing of 'contents'

The 'shaping' concept is used in NLP, i.e., using covert psychological conditioning to encourage something

In NLP, the following can be distinguished in a message:
• the content
• meta-messages 'adding to' the content:
•• about people's states
•• about their relation- ships
•• about the relevant logical 'level' of the content

Metamessages are often analogical. e.g.:
• voice tone
• emphasis on one part of a sentence
• the intensity of facial expressions

For example: the type of a table, and the way people seat around it (side-by-side or facing) is a message about the type of relationships between persons

Meta-messages are often 'about' relationships within a group

Metamessages are necessary in order to interpret a message

SECTION 9.4 / MAP A

Key Points

The effectiveness of people to work as a group is dependent on their ability to communicate with one another.

Communication between the individual members of a group happens both verbally and non-verbally, and there are both verbal and non-verbal influences on the behavior of the group as a whole.

The basic process of communication involves the transmission of both messages, which carry the content of a communication, and 'meta-messages,' which are higher level messages about the content.

Meta messages are essential for the interpretation of a message; i.e., there is a difference between what a person 'says' and what he or she 'means' or intends.

Meta messages are typically about (a) the type or level of message being sent, (b) a person's state or (c) about the status or relationship between group members.

People also send meta messages about the messages that they have received.

The message received is not always the message that was intended or sent. And in practical reality, the meaning of a communication to another person is what that person received regardless of what was intended.

The geographical relationship between group members has both physical and symbolic implications.

Activities

Recall some examples of both effective and ineffective interactions you have had with people in a group or team. How much influence did non-verbal communication (such as voice tone, facial expression, physical proximity, etc.) have on the outcome of these interactions?

Think of some examples of how you have been misinterpreted because someone misread your non-verbal 'meta messages.'

Think of some examples of how you have misinterpreted someone else because you misread his or her non-verbal 'meta messages.'

Think of some examples in which you have consciously and purposefully used certain kinds of non-verbal meta messages to communicate something to someone else. What kinds of things are most easily and appropriately communicated non-verbally?

Think about the influence that your geographical relationship to other group members has on your participation in that group.

Think of some ways in which you consciously and purposefully use or change certain kinds of geographical or physical relationships with other people as you are communicating with them? What kinds of things do you communicate through your spatial relationships with others?

Section 9.5
Stimulating and
Enriching the Maps of Others

The Dreamer phase (or 'brainstorming' phase) of a group project is often the most crucial and challenging; especially in a situation involving complementary relationships. A key challenge in leading the Dreamer phase is how to direct creativity without limiting it. The role of the leader is to direct the 'why' and the 'how' more so than the 'what.' This can might be done both verbally and non-verbally.

In many ways, creativity is such a natural and spontaneous process that most of what a manager has to do is simply to not get in the way of it. Optimally, the manager can create a space in which creativity can simply flow naturally.

It is possible to structure a framework which would encourage, or maybe unintentionally inhibit, different kinds of creativity. For example, setting a particular timeframe might in and of itself bring out a Dreamer, Realist, a Critic response. For instance, if a team leader said "I want to know your best dream: you each have one minute!" This might be contradictory to the process he or she is actually trying to encourage. When you say, "OK everybody we have 5 more minutes," it is more likely to draw out the Realist than the Dreamer.

The creativity of a group is shaped by context, attitude, states, cognitive processes, communication channels and rules of interaction between group members. The whole reason for Disney's dreaming room was to set a context that encouraged the kind of process that was appropriate there. As the leader, Disney modeled the type of meta program he wanted people to use.

A manager can establish an environment or context that helps widen freedom in terms of expression. For instance, in Disney's dreaming room, there weren't any tables. And inspirational pictures were plastered all over the walls of the room. Thus, there are certain constraints rules of interaction that might favor the widest expression of ideas and perspectives. For instance, not having a defined time frame and not disqualifying even impossible sounding ideas. A manger can help take off the constraints of reality by encouraging exaggeration and "as if" thinking by saying, "Even if you can't imagine it, act as if you could." It is also helpful to encourage the use of metaphors and symbolic language as we have explored in earlier Sections.

There are different kinds of operations that help to interactively stimulate and manage the creative process of a group:

- Having people participate by stimulating more physical actions.
- Underlining what is common and what is different between different perspectives.
- Asking questions, expressing doubts and approval, and provoking new perspectives.
- Giving tools, instruments and resources.
- Giving feedback, making proposals, asking for the integration and synthesis of ideas.
- Switching communication channels by writing, using flip charts, blackboards, etc.

In a problem solving context, or when an impasse is reached in 'brainstorming,' there are a number of ways in which a leader can influence the cognitive maps of group members to open up more creativity including:

- Reframing the problem or goal from a different point of view.
- Reprioritizing criteria or values.
- Changing level of focus and finding limiting assumptions.
- Looking for 'missing links.'
- Chunking down to set sub goals, or dealing with partial areas of problem space.
- Changing perspectives or states (by using humor, for example).
- Switching representational channels and encouraging lateral thinking.
- Encouraging "as if" thinking.

Operations to facilitate the dreamer's position	A 'non-interference' space must be created

① **Don't set 'time' constraints**

② **There are no 'prohibited' 'themes' / ideas**

③ **There is no 'immediate' critcism in terms of:**
- 'call back to reality'
- expenditure constraints

④ **Select a physical environment that favors freedom of expression: there is a symbolic value in contexts**

⑤ **Make decisions to 'get dreams started':**
- start thinking 'As If'
- use metaphors

⑥ **Think of responses to problems when in the dreamer space**

SECTION 9.5 / MAP A

Key Points

The Dreamer phase (or 'brainstorming' phase) of a group project is often the most crucial and challenging; especially in a situation involving complementary relationships.

A key challenge in leading the Dreamer phase is how to direct creativity without limiting it.

The role of the leader is to direct the 'why' and the 'how' more so than the 'what.'

The creativity of a group is shaped by context, attitude, states, cognitive processes, communication channels and rules of interaction between group members.

Activities

Recall some examples of effective and ineffective 'brainstorming' sessions you have participated in.

What kinds of factors influenced the effectiveness or ineffectiveness of the group?

What influence did the contextual constraints have on the group?

What influence did the attitude of the group members or leader have on the group?

What influence did the state of the group members or leader have on the group?

What influence did the types of available communication channels have on the group?

What influence did the rules of interaction between the group members and the leader have on the group?

Recall some examples of effective and ineffective 'brainstorming' sessions in which you have been the leader. How did you set up the context, attitude, states, cognitive processes, communication channels and rules of interaction? On which factor(s) did you place the most emphasis? Which factors made the most difference between the effective and ineffective situations?

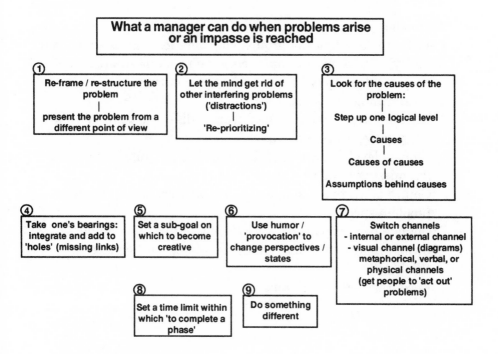

SECTION 9.5 / MAP B

Key Points

In a problem solving context, or when an impasse is reached in 'brainstorming,' there are a number of ways in which a leader can influence the cognitive maps of group members to open up more creativity including:

*Reframing the problem or goal from a different point of view.

*Reprioritizing criteria or values.

*Changing level of focus and finding limiting assumptions.

*Looking for 'missing links.'

*Chunking down to set sub goals, or dealing with partial areas of problem space.

*Changing perspectives or states (by using humor, for example).

*Switching representational channels and encouraging lateral thinking.

*Encouraging "as if" thinking.

Activities

Recall some examples of groups you were leading in which you
were trying to stimulate more creative thinking in order to
solve a problem or overcome an impasse during
'brainstorming.' How did you:

   *Reframe the problem or goal from a different point of view?

   *Reprioritize criteria or values?

   *Change level of focus and find limiting assumptions an look
   for 'missing links'?

   *Chunk down to set sub goals, or deal with partial areas of
   problem space?

   *Change perspectives or states? How did you use humor?

   *Switch representational channels and encourage lateral
   thinking?

   *Encourage "as if" thinking?

Section 9.6
Team Roles and
the Creative Cycle

The exercise for this Chapter involves a role play related to the establishment of a project team. The purpose of the role play is to explore in more detail the kinds of issues and operations that might be involved in coordinating dreamer, realist, critic around the establishment of a new idea or solving a problem. The exercise involves four role-players who will enact a situation in front of the rest of the group in a "fish bowl" format. The rest of the group will be assigned different kinds of patterns to watch and listen for. One group will look at physiology; another will be looking for the different levels of creativity and interaction; another will observer for kinds of meta programs and thinking styles.

This format is useful for integrating the learnings that have been accumulating throughout the book and deepening insight into the kinds micro skills that are useful for managing the creative process of a group. Role plays provide a way in which many of the skills, distinctions and principles of managing creativity and group process can be experientially demonstrated, evaluated and refined. Role playing is another form of acting "as if" which engages a high commitment of 'neurology' without having to get too involved in the content. Role plays often have a symbolic value that enhances other levels of learning.

In enacting the role play it is a good idea keep the product or problem simple so that the role players do not need any special technical knowledge. It should be something like a team whose purpose is to design a new kind of bicycle.

The roles include a team leader and people representing:

1. Engineering,

2. Marketing, and

3. Production.

The context of the role play will presuppose that these people have met before and they know in general what their project or problem is. The role play is a first meeting to discuss the type of problem, product or the product features.

Different thinking styles will be assigned to each of these different roles. In this particular role-play, engineering manager will be a dreamer; the marketing manager will be a realist; and the production manager will be in the attitude of a critic. The role players will be using the cluster of meta program listed below as a guide to enacting the appropriate attitude and thinking style.

	Dreamer	**Realist**	**Critic**
	What	*How*	*Why*
Representational			
Preference	Vision	Action	Logic
Approach	Toward	Toward	Away
Time Frame	Long Term	Short Term	Long/Short Term
Time Orientation	Future	Present	Past/Future
Reference	Internal - Self	External - Environment	External - Others
Mode of Comparison ..	Match	Match	Mismatch

The objective of the team leader for this 15 minutes is to try to coordinate the different thinking styles and stimulate all of the group to think creatively about the product or problem. NLP provides a number of different ways in which a leader may facilitate and coordinate innovative thinking within a group or team:

- Keeping track of and monitoring the sequence of activities in the group.
- Acknowledging and directing the phases of the creative cycle (Dreamer, Realist and Critic).
- Defining and monitoring the performance of individual and group T.O.T.E.s.
- Monitoring the overall T.O.T.E.s for task and relationship.
- Pacing and leading the:

    a. Physiology;

    b. Thinking styles, and

    c. Values of group members.

- Identifying and filling in holes or missing links with respect to:

    a. Meta programs,

    b. Levels of process, and

    c. Relevant perceptual positions.

- Using 'psychogeography' and behavioral cues to influence the interactive dynamics of the group.
- Sending and monitoring 'meta messages' to direct level of communication, state and status.
- To provide and clarify information related to the context or frame of the group's project to provide focus for the team members.

Generally, the role-play proceeds in 10-15 chunks with pauses for observations from the observers. The 10-15 minute time frame is to allow for a long enough interaction to get some examples of patterns on a micro-interactive level, but not to go so long that the observers become overwhelmed.

Exercise - 'Fish Bowl' Role Play Goal: to define the characteristics of a new product or solve a problem	Define the types of functions/organizational roles involved, and the Project Leader

4 groups of observers
(groups of 2/3) to
separately identify the
'types of cues'
in terms of :
• Physiology
• Thinking styles
• Logical levels
• Metaprograms
	Sequence:
	1. (15') Role playing
	   action. Task:
	   Exploring the
	   creativity space
	   (including values)
	2. (10') The Observers'
	   observations
	3. (10') Comments by
	   players in
	   metaposition about
	   their experience
	   ("What worked?")
	Based on observations
	and comments:
	"What to change/
	What to add?"
		Assign creativity
		positions and the
		metaprograms for
		each player (congruent
		with the type of roles)

Observe:
• Macroaspects of
  the creative process
  and
• The group's
  interactive/micro
  aspects
		Example:
		• Project Leader:
		  managing group
		  dynamics
		• R&D: Dreamer
		• Manufacturing:Critic
		• Marketing:Realist

		Context:
		• People who know
		  one another
		• First brain-storming
		  session

SECTION 9.6 / MAP A

Key Points

Role plays provide a way in which many of the skills, distinctions and principles of managing creativity and group process can be interactively enacted, evaluated and refined. Role playing is another form of acting "as if."

A role play engages a high commitment of 'neurology' without having to get too involved in the content.

Role plays often have a symbolic value that enhances other levels of learning.

Activities

Review some of the things that you have learned by role playing or observing role plays in the past.

What are the kinds of skills that can be learned most effectively through role playing?

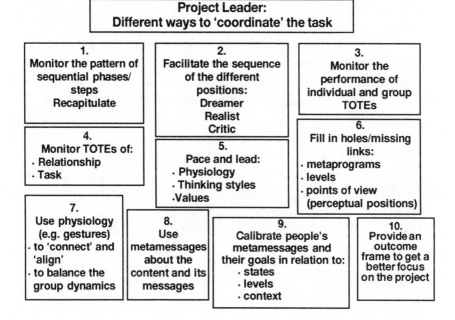

| Project Leader: Different ways to 'coordinate' the task |

| 1. Monitor the pattern of sequential phases/ steps Recapitulate | 2. Facilitate the sequence of the different positions: Dreamer Realist Critic | 3. Monitor the performance of individual and group TOTEs |

| 4. Monitor TOTEs of: · Relationship · Task | 5. Pace and lead: · Physiology · Thinking styles ·Values | 6. Fill in holes/missing links: · metaprograms · levels · points of view (perceptual positions) |

| 7. Use physiology (e.g. gestures) · to 'connect' and 'align' · to balance the group dynamics | 8. Use metamessages about the content and its messages | 9. Calibrate people's metamessages and their goals in relation to: · states · levels · context | 10. Provide an outcome frame to get a better focus on the project |

Section 9.6 / map B

Key Points

NLP provides a number of different ways in which a leader may facilitate and coordinate innovative thinking within a group or team:

*Keeping track of and monitoring the sequence of activities in the group.

*Acknowledging and directing the phases of the creative cycle (Dreamer, Realist and Critic).

*Defining and monitoring the performance of individual and group T.O.T.E.s.

*Monitoring the overall T.O.T.E.s for task and relationship.

*Pacing and leading the (a) physiology, (b) thinking styles and (c) values of group members.

*Identifying and filling in holes or missing links with respect to (a) meta programs, (b) levels of process and (c) relevant perceptual positions.

*Using 'psychogeography' and behavioral cues to influence the interactive dynamics of the group.

*Sending and monitoring 'meta messages' to direct the level of communication, state and status.

*To provide and clarify information related to the context or frame of the group's project to provide focus for the team members.

Activities

Review what you have learned so far in the book and your professional experience of leading groups and managing their creative process. Identify examples from your professional reality of what it is like to:

Keep track of and monitor the sequence of activities of a group.

Acknowledge and direct the phases of the creative cycle (Dreamer, Realist and Critic).

Define and monitor the performance of individual and group T.O.T.E.s.

Monitor the overall T.O.T.E.s for task and relationship.

Pace and lead the (a) physiology, (b) thinking styles and (c) values of group members.

Identify and fill in holes or missing links with respect to (a) meta programs, (b) levels of process and (c) relevant perceptual positions.

Use 'psychogeography' and behavioral cues to influence the interactive dynamics of the group.

Send and monitor 'meta messages' to direct the levels of communication, state and status.

Provide and clarify information related to the context or frame of the group's project to provide focus for the team members.

Section 9.7
Making Observations
in a Group

Observing dynamic patterns within groups involves a different focus than observing individuals. It is a crucial skill for managers. Observing patterns of the language and behavior of others is an important way to solidify what you have learned and assess what you know.

One group of observers will focus on patterns of physiology. There are two aspects of physiology to pay attention to, the micro aspects and the macro aspects. On a micro level, observers might notice kind of a meta message someone is giving in a particular moment about what that person is sending or receiving. Leaning toward, leaning away, gesturing, etc., are different types of behavioral cues that are meta messages. These will occur in some particular moment as some kind of feedback about the individual experience or response to what is happening. It can be very important to be able to track how someone's physiology changes in response to a particular stimulus. These observers will want to look not only for the kinds of clues individual role players express, but also how those clues change based upon interventions by the team leader. They should notice how the team leader either consciously or unconsciously uses physiology, such as posture or gestures, to trigger or shape the direction of the group process.

In addition to key behavioral cues given by individual members of the group, it is important to observe how cues change relative to the leader's interventions and to the responses of other group members. It is also important to observe how the team leader utilize these cues to 'calibrate' and lead the group. Observers should pay attention to how the project leader personally uses his or her physiology to either show neutrality to certain communications, or possibly to form an alliance with different people at different times through the process of mirroring or pacing and leading. For example, empathy toward a particular person or perspective might be shown through body, posture which then becomes a message to others in the group.

On a macro level, observers might notice patterns of physiology and movement between people. For example, the amount of activity as it travels back and forth between group members might be an indication of how much people are participating. Macro level behavioral patterns are an evidence about the group as opposed to a meta message about a particular individual.

A second group of observers is to pay attention to the cognitive patterns and the thinking styles expressed by the individuals. Which representational channels are being used by the different role players? What kinds of things are being represented verbally, logically? In addition to the kind of language that a person is using, somebody might draw something, using a visual channel, or switch to a more metaphorical mode of representation.

A third group of observers is to pay attention to meta program patterns. How do group members punctuate events in terms of their approach towards, away, generalities, details, past/future, long-term/short-term, etc.? In addition to noticing which meta program patterns are emphasized by different individuals, it is relevant to observe in what sequence they unfold and in what ways individuals shift or exaggerate meta programs in relation to the meta programs of others.

The fourth group of observers is to pay attention to how levels of process are expressed or addressed in terms of *where, when, what, how, why, who*. In particular they should watch and listen for how different role-players give inputs or responses on different levels. For instance, one individual might focus his or her words at the level of the *what*. Another might focus at the level of how or why. In addition to observing which specific individuals give cues about the different levels (*what, how, why, who*, etc.) it is useful to observe in what sequence issues relating to different levels are raised and addressed and in what order the team leader manages issues related to levels.

Notice how the team leader either consciously or unconsciously addresses or responds to the different levels of focus. In terms of managing the group, for example, does the leader focus first on why, who, what, etc.? In observing the dynamics of a group it is especially relevant to notice how different levels of process are managed. A key skill of a leader is to determine which levels are relevant to manage given a particular problem space and group of individuals. The thoroughness with which the different levels are covered often determines the degree of alignment of group members with respect to both task and relationship. Thoroughness of coverage is based on:

1. Which levels are covered;

2. How deeply each level is covered (i.e., self - others, long term - short term, what is being approached - what is being avoided, etc.);

3. How many group members are involved in defining each level.

The purpose of making observations in a group is not to judge the performance of the leader or role players but rather to contribute to the awareness of the group process for all group members (including other observers).

Individuals involved in a group process may also move into an observer position during or after a group process in order to develop meta cognition and expand his or her map of a problem or solution space.

Example: 'TransTech' Role Play

The following example is an illustration of a 'role play' enactment and the types of observations that may be made applying NLP distinctions to a group's creative process.

Background

TransTech is a young, innovative company which produces a revolutionary hand-held language translator. A user may speak English in one side of the translator and it will translate the words into another language and play out the translation to the listener. Likewise the listener may speak in his own language and the TransTech unit will translate it into English. Demand for the TransTech translator has grown tremendously. As sales have increased, however, quality problems have begun to arise. There are an increasing number of customer complaints relating to malfunctions in the translator unit and sales have begun to drop off. Competitors have begun to make imitations of the TransTech translator and there is a growing concern about losing market share.

The Vice President of the company has been given the task by the CEO to solve the quality problem. The Vice President will be interacting with three functional heads of the company: Marketing, Engineering and Production. The Marketing manager tends to be a fairly concrete thinker who focuses on the accomplishment of immediate and short term goals—a "realist." The Engineering manager is a very creative person who tends to focus on long term future goals—a "dreamer." Since the translator was introduced Engineering has primarily been concentrating on research and development for new products. The Production manager is under a lot of pressure and tends focus on finding and avoiding immediate and short term problems—a "critic."

Context

The Vice President has informed the functional heads of the problem and called a first meeting to define the scope of the problem and brainstorm some possible solutions. The members of the group know each other but have not worked together as a team before.

[Note: The picture below shows the starting physiologies and states of the team members.]

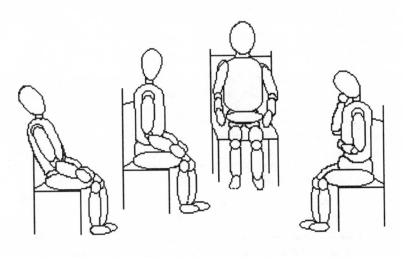

Engineering	Marketing	Leader	Production
'Dreamer'	*'Realist'*		*'Critic'*

Transcript	Comments
LEADER: *(leans back, crosses arms and touches hand to chin)*	

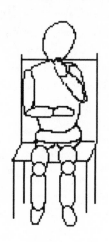

I think you all know why we're here today. Things are not going well. Our new language translator is a great product, but Customer Complaints are skyrocketing. Unit defects are at an all time high and sales are down.

The leader presupposes the 'why' of the meeting but does not define it explicitly. He immediately sets a 'problem frame,' focusing on the symptoms of the problem situation—'complaints' and 'defects' and their influence on sales and financing.

If we don't get to the bottom of this we're going to lose the next round of financing... and with that, maybe the company.

The leader emphasizes an 'away from' metaprogram—essentially taking the role of a 'critic.'

I would like to get some of your ideas of what we should do about it?

ENGINEERING: *(leans forward, head and eyes up)*

The leader attempts to set a 'we' frame and focuses the group to the level of the 'what.'

Well, there's a lot we've already been doing to improve the translator. We've rewritten the firmware for the new chips, and have already got the circuit board designed for version 4.2. I'm sure it will solve a lot of the current problems and it offers a lot more features for the users.

Engineering takes the role of the 'dreamer' on the 'what' level and focuses toward longer term future solutions.

Engineering orients to relatively 'big chunks' and matches to future positives.

Engineering has also presupposed that the solution will come from design changes even though the 'causes' of the symptoms have not been explicilty identified.

The 'we' that Engineering refers to is not the team, but the engineering department.

Transcript	**Comments**

MARKETING: *(leans back)*

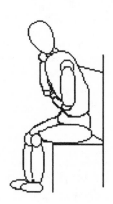

That's great, but it's all in the future. I think we've got to improve the quality of the existing product now. The market is becoming more competitive. And I am winding up spending half my time dealing with complaints from dealers about bad units!

Emphasizing a more 'realistic' stance, Marketing brings the orientation back to short term actions. However, Marketing also focuses on personally related problem areas to be avoided, moving more into a 'critic' attitude. Marketing has kept the focus to 'large chunks' and widened the problem space to include competition in the market.

PRODUCTION: *(hunching forward)*

Don't lay this on Production. Engineering made the thing too complicated to produce easily. We're doing everything we can. You've got to take the pressure of your quotas off me!

Production has followed the trend of shifting to an 'I' frame of reference, interpreting Marketing's comments as a personal criticism on a 'who' level. Responding as a 'critic' who has been criticized, production tries to shift the perceived 'blame' back to Engineering and Marketing.
Production has widened the problem space to include 'complicated design' and production 'pressures.'

MARKETING:
My quotas?!

Transcript	Comments
ENGINEERING: *(leaning back and looking away)*	*Engineering and Marketing respond to the perceived blame on a personal 'who' level.*

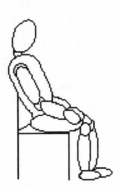

Look, everyone on the committee accepted the design months ago. If production can't handle it don't point the finger at me.

Engineering has shifted from being a 'dreamer' to mismatching Production. Engineering has also widened the problem space to include the actions of 'the committee.'

LEADER:
Okay. Enough. Enough. This isn't getting us anywhere. We're meeting with our bankers at the end quarter and we've got to have good news or else the expansion deal is off.

The Leader maintains a critic role but applies it to the overall process of the group.
It appears that sometimes the Leader uses the term 'we' to refer to the team itself, and other times to refer to the larger system of the company or to top management.
At this point the Leader has stimulated more of 'critic' metaprogram in all of the group members. This has to some degree widened the perception of the problem space, but has also created quite a bit of mismatching at the 'who' level in the group.

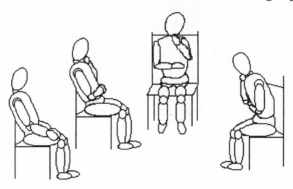

Engineering   Marketing   Leader   Production

{Current state of group's physiology.}

Transcript	Comments

LEADER: *(dropping hands and leaning forward)*

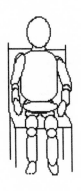

I'd like for this to be more of a brainstorming meeting. Let's shift the focus from the problem to some possible solutions.

(To Engineering) You know the translator better than anyone in the company, how do you think we could approach solving this problem right now?

The Leader attempts to change the metaprogram of the group from that of 'critic' to being more solution oriented (although it is not clear if the whole problem space has been defined yet).

The Leader has used the term 'brainstorming,' indicating a 'dreamer' mode, but has assumed more of a realist stance in terms of physiology and language (focusing on the 'how' level and on a short term time frame). The Leader is also attempting to be more directive by calling upon a specific group member and trying to reinstate a 'we' frame.

ENGINEERING: *(head and eyes move up)*

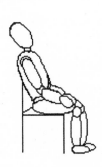

Like I was saying before, we can redesign the whole thing, tripling its current capabilities. This is something we are working on right now. We've got a long list of new features we want to see in the next version. We've got a new operating system in the works that I envision will open up the translator's potential.

Engineering does not follow the Leader's meta-messages about shifting to more of a realist mode and returns to the 'dreamer' metaprogram. Engineering does make reference to action being taken 'right now,' although they are conceptual and not operational.

Again, the 'we' referred to by Engineering is not the problem solving team, but rather the engineering group.

Consistent with a 'dreamer' metaprogram, Engineering is more visual than action oriented.

Transcript	**Comments**

MARKETING: *(remains sitting back with arms folded)*

But that is not going to help us with the problem as it stands now. I think we need to decrease customer complaints about the defects and increase sales by reducing those defects. Getting better quality materials to start with would probably help us a lot too.

Marketing orients to the immediate time frame, but retains an 'away from' meta program.
Marketing does shift to a 'we' frame that is more associated with the team and the company.
Marketing also widens the problem / solution space to include the quality of manufacturing materials.

ENGINEERING: *(leans back and folds arms)*

Look, you're the one who is worried

about competition. We can't just take a 'bandaid' approach and come up with a temporary solution. Other companies are going to be making new innovations that we are going to have to keep up with. We've got to prepare for the future and come up with fundamental solutions to these quality problems.

Engineering widens the problem space to include future innovations by competitors and indicates that the solutions proposed by Marketing are not wide enough to cover all of the problem space. Engineering also indicates that a longer term view is necessary to reach more fundamental and lasting solutions.
It is significant that, while both Marketing and Engineering are essentially in a 'critic' mode and in disagreement, they are focusing more on the problem space than on each other. They are pacing each other in a way.

Transcript	Comments
MARKETING: There won't be any future for us unless we get our next round of financing.	*Marketing widens the problem space to include the urgency of the short term financing issue.*
LEADER: *(To Production)* What is your map of how we could approach a solution?	*The Leader attempts to maintain balance with the group's contributions by calling upon Production. The meta message of the Leader's statement acknowledges that all of the team members have different maps.*

PRODUCTION: *(sits up, arms still folded)*

Hey, I'm trying to make this work too. Look, I'll put more pressure on the line until we're out of this crunch. I'll have someone double-check all incoming materials and add more inspectors to catch the defects. I don't like what's happening anymore than you do.

Production remains in a primarily 'critic' mode, but does begin to focus on short term actions.

Production also remains primarily in an 'I' frame but has made an important shift from the earlier attitude of shifting the blame by moving to a 'what' and 'how' level and aligning himself with the values and reactions of the other group members.

The Leader has made some progress, but has actually not accomplished much in relation to his stated outcome of 'brainstorming.' The group members have predictabley stayed primarily within the metaprogram consistent with their roles. This may be partly because their physiology has remained relatively unchanged. Also the representational channel of communication has been essentially verbal

As Einstein said, "You cannot solve the problem with the same thinking that is creating it." To achieve more innovative thinking, the Leader needs all of the team members to shift their perspectives in some fundamental way.

Transcript	Comments
LEADER: *(Stands up, walks over to flip chart and begins to write. Group adjusts physiology to be able to see what the Leader is writing.)*	*The Leader shifts physiology by standing and moving to the flip chart—taking a kind of 'meta position' to the group.*
OK. Let's summarize what we have so far. There is a problem that has both long term and short term dimensions and there are both long term and short term solutions.	*The Leader paces and acknowledges all of the contributions of the group members by framing them in terms of the definition of problem space and potential solutions related to different time frames.*
	By writing, the Leader has begun to shift the primary representational channel to a more visual one.

Engineering   **Marketing**   **Leader**   **Production**

{State of group's physiology}

Problem Space	Short Term	Long Term
defects complaints sales down financing problem competition complicated manufacturing better materails too much pressure	better materials pressure on the line double check materials add inspectors	rewrite firmware new circuit board new operating system new features

[Flip Chart Pages]

Transcript

LEADER: *(Pointing to writing on the flip charts.)*
If I understand well, there is a concern among us that either one of these types of solutions by themselves may not be an adequate answer.
Usually a 'quality problem' is not the result or 'fault' of a single person or cause. It involves the whole system. And often its solution requires the right communication and commitment between all of the principals involved.
I don't think that there is only one right solution. We may need a number of them. I also think we need to look at the whole system and take all of the perspectives that might be relevant.
For instance, Production, I'm not sure that more inspectors and pressure on the line is necessarily going to solve the problem. If pressure is already a part of the problem space, it may even make things worse.
Another thing is that there may be areas of possible 'solution space' that we haven't yet considered. That's what I would like to brainstorm about for a few moments.
Sit back and think for moment—start from scratch and check your assump-

Comments

The Leader has now fully assumed a 'meta position' role. The leader has externalized the problem space from the group and meta commented about the positive intentions of the different maps involved.
The Leader has introduced a perspective involving the 'whole system' and introduced key values (the 'why' level) of 'communication' and 'commitment'. The Leader sets the frame that there is no one 'right' map of the situation and emphasizes the need for the integration of different perspectives.
The Leader brings up the issue of 'ecology' and the potential problems from the systemic effects of implementing a particular solution.
The Leader introduces the notion of 'solution space' (as opposed to simply solutions) to the group and gives both a direction and a time frame to the brainstorming.
The Leader indicates that both short term and long term perspectives will be balanced eventually, aleviating the need for any one individual to push for a particular perspective.
The Leader reiterates the 'we' frame and gives instructions to the whole group about the kind of physiology,

Transcript	Comments
term. What else do you see that could possibly improve the situation? Open up your imagination. What might be something that is completely different from the way you have been thinking about this.	*state and cognitive processes to apply in order to brainstorm effectively.*

PRODUCTION:

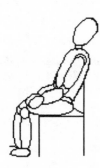

I don't know if this is actually feasible, but we could bring up a second assembly line and add another shift. We could probably do it in a week. That would actually take a little pressure off people for a while. If they had a little more time, maybe their work would improve.

Regardless of the viability of the suggestion, Production has shifted physiology and meta program and began to think in a framework that is more 'toward' than 'away from.' Production has also made the transition from an 'I' frame to thinking in terms of others.

LEADER:

We'll consider its feasibility later. Let's write it down for now and keep going. (To Engineering) What can Engineering do to help us (gestures to team) out in the short term?

The Leader puts aside any evaluation of the idea in order to postpone the influence of 'realist' or 'critic' thinking and to encourage brainstorming.
The Leader sends a non-verbal meta message with the hand gesture toward the team to clarify for Engineering the 'us' referred to is the problem solving team.

Transcript	Comments

ENGINEERING:

Let's see... we could redesign the LCD screen connector... and... create a better anti-static environment for the chip assembly. We can do those two things right away. That could help until the other revisions are ready and in place.

Engineering has begun to 'chunk smaller' and think in terms of more incremental changes.
Engineering has also successfully made the transition to proposing actions that may be accomplished in a shorter term frame of reference.

LEADER:

Let's step back a bit further and look at the big picture. Really widen your perspective of the total situation and be open to any possibilities. Are there any other solution areas that we haven't even considered yet?

The Leader becomes even more cognitively directive, encouraging the visual thinking structure and 'as if' attitude of the 'dreamer.'

MARKETING: *(leans back and looks up)*
Well... It just occurred to me that there might be the possibility for some kind of 'seconds' market.

Marketing also makes the transition to a more 'toward' meta program and has dropped the constraint of immediate results.

ENGINEERING:
'Seconds' market?

Transcript	**Comments**

MARKETING:

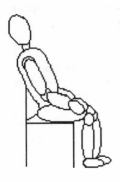 Yeh. Products that aren't good enough for a primary market are often sold at a discount to another market that has a different use for the goods and doesn't need the same degree of quality. It's standard practice in some industries to optimize their production speed around the percentage of 'seconds' they can sell to this other market. I had just never thought that it would apply to a product as technical or sophisticated as ours.

More so than Production or Engineering, Marketing has succeeded in widening the perception of the possible solution space to include a dimension of the larger system that has been unexplored in relation to the problem space.

Marketing acknowledges an unconscious assumption that has prevented the exploration of this potential solution area.

LEADER:
Well this is brainstorming. Let's see if we can dream such a market up for our product.

The Leader continues to maintain the brainstorming frame by deflecting constraints and even overtly uses the term 'dream.'

PRODUCTION: *(leans forward)*
Ummm...This is probably just a crazy idea.

LEADER: *(leans forward)*
That's OK, this is kind of a crazy situation. *(laughter)*

The Leader uses humor which helps to encourage freer thinking and to send the meta message the even though the situation is serious it should be kept in perspective.

Transcript	**Comments**

PRODUCTION:

Well, I was talking to a person who manufactures toys at this conference I went to a couple of weeks ago. He was really interested in our product. He was talking about how he had a need for something like what we were making, but less expensive. I was just thinking that maybe some of the units that aren't good enough for our purposes might work for his company.

Production is no longer thinking just in terms of the formal role of production in the company and has begun to make contributions based on personal experience from a context outside of that related to a formal role.

LEADER:
Well it's a possibility. As long as we're brainstorming, let's consider it. What do you think Marketing?

The Leader again reaffirms the brainstorming frame, then encourages a feedback loop between Production and Marketing.

MARKETING:
Sure, it could be workable. Of course,

it depends on what his needs are and whether the kind of defects we are having to deal with will be a problem for his application. If you give me his name, I'll follow up on it. It might be interesting.

Marketing shifts to more of a 'realist' stance, but is matching and 'moving toward' instead of the more critical attitude that was taken earlier.

Marketing makes a commitment to pursue Production's lead, sending a meta message about willingness to cooperate as a team member.

Transcript	Comments
LEADER: Engineering, would you be available to talk to Marketing if there are technical questions?	*The Leader encourages a completion of the feedback loop by involving Engineering on a 'how' level.*
ENGINEERING: Sure.	
LEADER: Great. Let's see if we can brainstorm some other possible 'seconds' markets for a moment, and then see if there any areas of long term 'solution space' that we haven't thought of...	*The Leader has been successful in encouraging the group to brainstorm and, perhaps more importantly, to begin to operate as a team.*
	Most people in an organization have developed their own way of looking at things, and in order to see the whole, and contribute to it, they need to widen their point of view. *The key to helping them do that is to get them to see their role and responsibilities from a different position. Given a chance, most people will then contribute their best.*

The influence of the leader's style in a group

The leader's beliefs and assumptions influence the way he/she operates in the group	1. For example: Beliefs about the relationship of creativity to 'odd/wild ideas'	2. 'Assessment of the function' (whether positive or negative) of the 'critic' position

3. Width of expectations about the 'realist' position e.g., only as an 'economist'	4. Orientation of a leader's major contributions: - as the 'facilitator' of the relationship - as the 'focalizer' of the task	
5. Conscious use of meta messages (e.g., on the group's relationship/thinking styles)		The leader's beliefs and styles influence his/her selection of evidence: what is important for him/her to 'observe' in the various stages of the group's creative process

SECTION 9.7 / MAP A

Key Points

There is no one right way to manage the creativity in a group. Different styles of leadership encourage different dynamics between members of the group.

Sometimes group members have to become familiar with a particular leadership style in order for it to be effective.

In general a leader serves as (1) a facilitator of the relationship and (2) the focal point of the task.

Shared experiences and observations help to enrich and add to natural perceptual abilities and interactive skills by helping to widening the collective perceptual space of group members.

A leader's beliefs and assumptions influence the way he or she manages the group.

Leaders will have different degrees of conscious awareness of behavioral cues, meta messages, group dynamics, etc.

A person's beliefs and assumptions will influence what he or she sorts for as evidence in various stages of the creative process and how he or she interprets behavioral cues, meta messages, group dynamics, etc.

People often have many unconscious competences of which they are not aware.

Activities

Recall some situations in which you were leading the creative process of a group.

In what ways did you facilitate the relationship between group members?

In what ways did you help focus the group on the task?

What are some of your beliefs and assumptions about managing the creative process of a group.

What kinds of behavioral cues, meta messages, group dynamics, etc., do you pay most attention to when you are leading the creative process of a group?

Which aspects of your own behavior in a group are you least aware of? Most aware of?

The observers' tasks		
Physiology cues	**Logic level cues**	**Metaprogram cues**

· What cues are given by each member?
  -microcues
  -macrocues (physical movements)
· How do they change relative to the leader's interventions?
· How does the team leader use these and other cues to stimulate/ lead the group?
	· Who gives cues about the what, how, why?
	· What is the sequence of levels necessary to cover the overall space?
	· How does the leader 'manage' the levels (which ones first, which ones later?)
		· What metaprograms are 'used' by each member
		· What patterns of interaction are there?
		· What metaprograms occur in a sequence?
		· How do metaprograms shift in response to others?

SECTION 9.7 / MAP B

Key Points

Observing patterns of the language and behavior of others is an important way to learn and assess what you know. It is also a crucial skill for managers.

Observing dynamic patterns within groups involves a different focus than observing individuals:

In addition to key micro and macro behavioral cues given by individual members of the group it is important to observe how they change relative to the leader's interventions and to the responses of other group members. It is also important to observe how the team leader utilizes these cues to 'calibrate' and lead the group.

In addition to observing which specific individuals give cues about the different levels (*what, how, why, who*, etc.) it is useful to observe in what sequence issues relating to different levels are raised and addressed and in what order the team leader manages issues related to levels.

In addition to noticing which meta program patterns are emphasized by different individuals, it is relevant to observe in what sequence they unfold and in what ways individuals shift or exaggerate meta programs in relation to the meta programs of others.

Activities

Review some of the previous exercises in the book in which you have observed patterns of behavior or language.

Think of how you observe the dynamic patterns of groups in your own professional reality. What do you typically observe for?

What areas of observational skill would you like to expand in order to improve your effectiveness as a manger?

Logical levels of experience:
Relevant aspects

Width of coverage of levels:
which levels are covered in a
group's interactions?
(Vertical dimension of levels)

Depth of coverage of
levels:
which perceptual posi-
tions/points of view are
covered?
E.g., the 'why' with re-
spect to self and others
in the organization

Horizontal dimensions
of levels:
How many people/func-
tions are involved at
each level?

The dreamer is often at
the level of 'what', the
realist at 'how' and the
critic at 'why'

Avoid the risk of
having and unbal-
anced/non-aligned
situation among the
group's members

Given a problem space and a system (the
relevant people in the propblem/relation-
ship), test what is appropriate to 'manage'
in terms of which levels

SECTION 9.7 / MAP C

Key Points

In observing the dynamics of a group it is especially relevant
to notice how different levels of process are managed. The
thoroughness with which the different levels are covered often
determines the degree of alignment of group members with
respect to both task and relationship.

Thoroughness of coverage is based on (a) which levels are
covered, (b) how deeply each level is covered (i.e., self - others,
long term - short term, what is being approached - what is
being avoided, etc.) and (c) how many group members are
involved in defining each level.

A key skill of a leader is to determine which levels are
relevant to manage given a particular problem space and
group of individuals.

Activities

Review what you have learned in this book about different levels of experience and managing different levels of experience. What issues relating to levels do you think are most important for a leader to monitor and influence during a group's creative process?

What kinds of problems and interferences do you think arises in groups when the relevant levels have not been covered thoroughly?

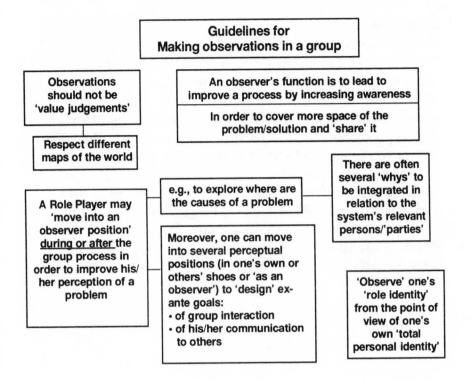

SECTION 9.7 / MAP D

Key Points

The purpose of making observations in a group is not to judge the performance of the leader or role players but rather to contribute to the awareness of the group process for all group members (including other observers).

Individuals involved in a group process may also move into an observer position during or after a group process in order to develop meta cognition and expand his or her map of a problem or solution space.

Activities

Think of some examples of situations in which you influenced the process of a group by simply making them aware of something that was happening in the group.

Think of situations in which you have been able to move between both a participant role and an observer position with respect to yourself or your participation in a group. How does it help you to more effectively perceive and manage the process you are involved in?

Think of situations in which you have been able to be an impartial observer. What kinds of benefits and contributions are you able to make in that position?

Think of situations in which you have been observed by someone who is impartial. What kinds of benefits were you able to derive?

Chapter 10

Summary
and
Conclusions

At the beginning of this book we established four general objectives:

1. Defining the creative process on an individual, group and organizational level within the terms and scope of NLP;

2. To create a vocabulary, a set of words, language, and distinctions that could support and enhance the creative process;

3. To provide some specific ways people could more effectively work, enhance and direct creativity, in individuals and groups; and

4. To determine some ways of identifying different types of creative people.

The desired effects of reaching these objectives were (a) to stimulate personal creativity, by enhancing your own flexibility and creativity on a day-to-day level, (b) to manage group creativity, stimulating innovation within the dynamic patterns of a group working team; and (c) to promote entrepreneurial attitudes and beliefs.

419

In Part One we explored the process of personal creativity. We started by distinguishing between the process and products of creativity and establishing the basic presupposition of NLP that 'the map is not the territory.' Within this frame, creativity springs out of changes or enrichments to our maps.

We established the belief that creativity was an ongoing process, a process of continually adding to our flexibility and widening the maps we lived by. According to the *law of requisite variety*, creativity is necessary because within the environment in which we interact and operate there are uncertainties, variations, and changes. The process of continual creativity is even more necessary as change and uncertainties of the systems around us increase or intensify.

We explored the structure of the creative process in terms of the basic feedback loop defined by the T.O.T.E. Model. What kind of goals, evidences and operations make up an individual's creative process? How does that individual respond to problems? This lead us to the notion of thinking strategies and thinking styles. We acknowledged that the process of establishing and representing goals, assessing evidences, and taking actions—at least on a personal level—arise from the human nervous system in the form of 'neuro-linguistic programs.' These 'programs' have a cognitive structure that can be defined in terms of representational channels and thinking styles related to the five senses. The structure of a creative process can be cast in terms of the R.O.L.E. Model distinctions: The modality of representation, the orientation of that modality. The linking between modalities, and the effect a representation has with respect to the larger process.

We then investigated some of the physiological influences on personal creativity in terms of the distinctions provided by the B.A.G.E.L. Model. We explored how mental processes are facilitated or directed by physiological processes that are on both a micro and macro level. We demonstrated how very subtle micro physiology might in some particular moment support or inhibit creativity on a personal level. We acknowledged that there are also macro aspects of physiology in terms of the kinds of general activities or states that prepare you to be creative.

We also acknowledged that there are many levels of influence on creativity: environmental, behavioral, cognitive, influences related to beliefs, values and assumptions, and finally influences related to a sense of personal and professional identity.

We concluded that there was no one right way to be creative but that all creativity shares some basic principles. There are different variations for different people, situations and stages of creativity. Different kinds of tasks require different types of creativity (innovation, discovery and invention). Applying NLP models and distinctions we formed and 'installed' a strategy modeled from the creative process of Walt Disney which established a general cycle of cognitive processes characterized by the functions of Dreamer, Realist and Critic.

In Part Two we explored the process of co-creativity and the applications of creativity to problem solving. We established that creativity in problem solving involves comprehensively representing the problem space via the S.C.O.R.E Model and then enriching the map in order to find a solution space of other choices and alternatives.

Operating from the underlying principle of creative problem solving that 'you can't solve a problem with the same type of thinking that is creating it,' we acknowledged that the cognitive and behavioral patterns of a strategy that is effectively creative in one context may be identified and transferred to other contexts. We explored the co-creative process of coaching another person in transferring a T.O.T.E. from a positive reference context to a situation requiring more creative ability. The goal of the process was to transfer process elements from an effective context in order to widen the map, the perceptual space that was being brought into solving a problem, or in representing the elements that might be the symptoms, causes, outcomes or effects of a particular problem situation. We reaffirmed that the essential function of creativity was to widen perceptual space.

One of the discoveries that emerged from the T.O.T.E. transfer exercise is that often there are assumptions and beliefs that we have which can filter or block aspects of creative ability that we in fact already possess. Identifying and challenging or reframing some of these assumptions can, metaphorically speaking, "let the rabbit out of the cage."

We explored how multiple perspectives and different modes of representation and lateral thinking processes are effective ways to widen perception of a problem space, identify and challenge limiting assumptions and seek new solution space. We presented the 'intervision' process, utilizing a visual channel of representation and lateral thinking, as a way of being able to widen perspectives, and elicit multiple representations of a problem space.

In Part Three we explored Group Creativity and the applications of creativity to organizational problems and goals. We established that managing the creative process of a group essentially involves the coordination of different thinking styles, the balance of the phases of the creative cycle and the alignment of different levels of group process (*what, how, why, who*) along a path of transition states leading to a desired state (SOAR).

We explored strategies for managing situations in which people have different models of the world and different strengths and weaknesses with respect to creativity. This lead us to the exploration of 'meta program' patterns as a way to direct personal processes of creativity at a more general level of timeframe, chunk size, emphasis on task versus relationship, etc. This brought up issues related to the management of the cycle of Dreamer, Realist and Critic in a group, and how a manager goes about supporting and balancing these kinds of thinking processes both sequentially and simultaneously in a group.

We raised a number of group issues relating to the influence of the *who* on the creative process of the group:, the *who* with respect to the organization, the team, and the group leader. We established the significance of relationship with respect to group creativity and confronted issues of consensus and ownership in relation to complementary versus peer relations in a group.

We defined how different tools such as representational channels, meta messages, psychogeography, rules of interaction and other cognitive and behavioral patterns may be observed and utilized to pace and lead the process of a group. We then synthesized some of these distinctions and operations into communication strategies that would allow us to explore new perspectives and create shared understanding.

Our final exercise explored the synthesis and significance of all the different NLP distinctions, skills and models in relation to managing the creative process within a group's interaction through a role-play, observing for the influence of physiology, levels, meta programs, and thinking styles.

We may conclude by casting all of the various methods of managing creativity in NLP—micro and macro, on a personal or group level—into the framework of the three basic principles of creativity:

1. The notion of *outcome frame*—that even avoiding something needs to be done in a larger framework of seeking some outcome;

2. The notion of *a feedback* versus *a failure frame*—that lack of success is not a sign of failure. In fact it's an indication of what to change in order reach the outcome;

3. The *flexibility frame*—the basic principle that if what you're doing isn't working almost anything is a better choice. If what you're doing isn't working do something different; do anything different.

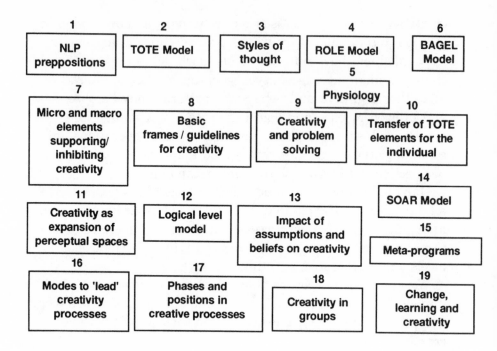

1	2	3	4	6
NLP preppositions	TOTE Model	Styles of thought	ROLE Model	BAGEL Model

5
Physiology

7	8	9	10
Micro and macro elements supporting/ inhibiting creativity	Basic frames / guidelines for creativity	Creativity and problem solving	Transfer of TOTE elements for the individual

14
SOAR Model

11	12	13	15
Creativity as expansion of perceptual spaces	Logical level model	Impact of assumptions and beliefs on creativity	Meta-programs

16	17	18	19
Modes to 'lead' creativity processes	Phases and positions in creative processes	Creativity in groups	Change, learning and creativity

SECTION 10 / MAP A

Key Points

NLP focuses on the process of creativity as opposed to its content or products.

NLP emphasizes generalizable strategies and principles and 'transcontextual skills' as opposed to limited behavioral techniques.

A core presuppositions of NLP is that the *map is not the territory* and that creativity is essentially the process of widening and enriching our maps in order to be more effective and find more opportunities in the 'territory.'

Creativity is essential for success and survival because we must constantly update and enhance our maps to deal with the increasing rate of change and uncertainty in the systems of which we are a part.

Creativity is a process that is organized around the structure defined by the T.O.T.E. Its effectiveness is governed by the types of goals, evidences, operations and response to problems which define the "neuro-linguistic program" through which it is being enacted.

Creativity is a multi-level process that is influenced by both micro (R.O.L.E. and B.A.G.E.L.) and macro level (meta programs, states and assumptions) factors.

Cognitive and behavioral patterns of a strategy that is effectively creative in one context may be identified and transferred to other contexts.

There are three basic types of creativity (innovation, discovery and invention) which correspond to a general cycle of the creative process characterized by the functions of Dreamer, Realist and Critic.

Creativity in problem solving involves comprehensively representing the problem space and then enriching the map in order find a solution space of other choices and alternatives (S.C.O.R.E.).

Multiple perspectives and different modes of representation and lateral thinking processes are effective ways to widen perception of a problem space and seek new solution space. You cannot solve a problem with the same thinking that is creating it.

Managing the creative process of a group essentially involves the coordination of different thinking styles, the balance of the phases of the creative cycle and the alignment of different levels of group process (*what, how, why, who*) along a path of transition states leading to a desired state (SOAR).

Different tools such as representational channels, meta messages, psychogeography, rules of interaction and other cognitive and behavioral patterns may be observed and utilized to pace and lead the process of a group.

All of the various methods of managing creativity in NLP—
micro and macro, on a personal or group level—revolve around
three fundamental principles:

Outcome Frame: While the stimulus for creativity may either
be to achieve or to avoid, the creative process always occurs in
seeking a positive outcome or a solution space.

Feedback versus *Failure Frame*: Within the frame of creativity
there are no failures. Rather, lack of success is perceived as
either (a) a solution to a different problem, or (b) feedback
providing information about what needs to be adjusted or how
it needs to be adjusted.

Flexibility Frame: Creativity is deeply related to choices.
Having several options before starting something is important.
Having a choice is always better than not having one. If what
you are doing is not working, then do something different.

Activities

Review what you did and learned throughout this book.
Which new cognitive learnings and understandings stand out
the most to you?
Which reference experiences stand out the most to you?
What conscious competences did you develop?
What unconscious competences did you discover?
What is the basic lesson you learned with respect to your own
personal creativity?
What is the basic lesson you learned with respect to the
process of co-creativity?
What is the basic lesson you learned with respect to managing
group creativity?
What were the most valuable lessons from the seminar for
you personally?
Which models, distinctions or skills do you think will be most
useful or applicable with your professional reality?
What lessons have you learned that extend beyond the specific
scope of creativity?

Appendix A

The Communication Matrix

The Communication Matrix summarizes some of the key dimensions involved in communication.

1. *People*: **Transmitter —> Receiver(s)**
    a. **Physical Dimensions**

One - Self	Few - Self	Many - Self
One - One	Few - One	Many - One
One - Few	Few - Few	Many - Few
One - Many	Few - Many	Many - Many

    b. **Relationship Dimensions—'Status'**

    Complementary (CEO=>Functional Manager)

    Symmetrical (Marketing<=>Marketing)

    Reciprocal (Marketing<=> Research and
    Development)

    Meta-Complementary (Financial=>Marketing—
    "some peers are more peers than others")

c. State
1. Attitude   2. Meta Program

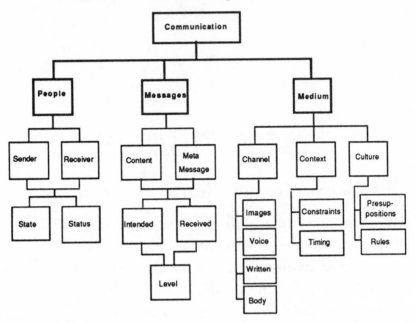

Figure 9.1   Communication Matrix

2. *Messages* (Intended vs. Received)

a. Message Dimensions

Micro   Macro   Para-Message (same level)

b. Meta-Message: higher level message about:

1. The type of message being sent.

2. The state/status of the Messenger.

3. The state/status of the receiver.

4. The context in which the message is being sent.

c. Types/Levels of Messages

1. Identity	*Who*	Mission
2. Beliefs/Values	*Why*	Permission/ Motivation
3. Capabilities	*How*	Direction
4. Behavior	*What*	Actions
5. Environment	*Where / When*	Boundaries/ Constraints

3. *Medium*

a. Context (Micro and Macro)

1. **Physical Dimensions** (external constraints, "psycho-geography," audience, etc.)

2. **Non-Physical Dimensions** (Objective, Role, Timing, etc.)

b. Culture

1. Presuppositions

2. Rules

c. Communication Channels (amount of redundancy and feedback)

1. Images

2. Voice

3. Written

4. Body

Bibliography

Tools for Dreamers: Strategies for Creativity and the Structure of Invention, Dilts, R. B., Epstein, T., Dilts, R. W., Meta Publications, Cupertino, CA, 1991.

Albert Einstein: Neuro-Linguistic Analysis of a Genius, Dilts, R., Dynamic Learning Publications, Ben Lomond, CA, 1990.

The Ascent of Man; J. Bronowski, Little, Brown and Co., Boston, MA, 1973.

Neuro-Linguistic Programming: The Study of the Structure of Subjective Experience, Volume I, Dilts, R., Grinder, J., Bandler, R., DeLozier, J., Meta Publications, Cupertino, CA, 1980.

Principles of Psychology, William James, *Britannica Great Books*, Encyclopedia Britannica Inc., Chicago IL, 1979.

On the Soul, Aristotle, *Britannica Great Books*, Encyclopedia Britannica Inc., Chicago IL, 1979.

Plans and the Structure of Behavior, Miller, G., Galanter, E., Pribram, K., Henry Holt and Co., Inc., 1960.

Language and Mind, Chomsky, N., Harcourt Brace Jovanovich, Inc., New York, NY, 1968.

Introduction to Cybernetics, Ashby, W. Ross, Chapman and Hall, Ltd., London, England, 1956.

Design for a Brain, Ashby, W. Ross, Chapman and Hall, Ltd., London, England, 1960.

Steps to an Ecology of Mind, Bateson, Gregory, Ballantine Books, New York, NY, 1972.

The Fifth Discipline: The Art and Practice of the Learning Organization, Senge, P., Doubleday, New York, NY, 1990.

Walt Disney; The Dreamer, The Realist and The Critic, Dilts, R., Dynamic Learning Publications, Ben Lomond, CA, 1990.

The Art of Walt Disney, Finch, C., Harry N. Abrahms Inc., New York, NY, 1973.

Disney Animation; The Illusion of Life, Thomas, F., Johnson, O., Abbeyville Press, New York, NY, 1981.

Growing Pains, Walt Disney (1941) Reprinted in SMPTE Journal, July 1991.

Toward a Unifying Theory of Cognition, Waldrop M., *Science*, Vol. 241, July 1988.

SOAR: An Architecture for General Intelligence, Laird, J. E., Rosenbloom, P., Newell, A., *Artificial Intelligence*, 33:1-64, 1987.

Metaphors We Live By; Lakeoff, G., Johnson, M., University of Chicago Press, Chicago, IL, 1980.

Pragmatics of Human Communication, Watzlawick, Bevelas, Jackson, W. W. Norton Company, New York, NY, 1967.

Turtles All the Way Down: Prerequisites to Personal Genius, DeLozier J., Grinder J., Grinder DeLozier and Associates, Santa Cruz, CA, 1987.

The Structure of Magic Vol. I & II, Grinder, J., Bandler, R., Science and Behavior Books, Palo Alto, CA, 1975, 1976.

Using Your Brain, Bandler, R., Real People Press, Moab, UT, 1984.

Frogs into Princes, Bandler, R., Grinder, J., Real People Press, Moab, UT, 1979.

Applications of Neuro-Linguistic Programming: A practical guide to communication, learning and change, Dilts, R., Meta Publications, Cupertino, CA, 1983.

Changing Belief Systems with NLP, Dilts, R., Meta Publications, Cupertino, CA, 1990.

"Let NLP Work for You," Dilts, R., 1982, *Real Estate Today*, February, 1982, Vol. 15, Nov. 2.

"Wolfgang Amadeus Mozart: Songs from the Spirit, Dilts, R., Dynamic Learning Publications, Ben Lomond, CA, 1992.

"Overcoming Resistance to Persuasion with NLP," Dilts, R., Yeager J., Dynamic Learning Publications, Ben Lomond, CA, 1990.

"The Parable of the Porpoise: A New Paradigm for Learning and Management," Dilts, R., Dynamic Learning Publications, Ben Lomond, CA, 1990.

"NLP In Training Groups," Dilts, R., Epstein, T., Dynamic Learning Publications, Ben Lomond, CA, 1989.